The Scarecrow Author Bibliographies

1. John Steinbeck (Tetsumaro Hayashi). 1973.
2. Joseph Conrad (Theodore G. Ehrsam). 1969.
3. Arthur Miller (Tetsumaro Hayashi). 2d ed. 1976.
4. Katherine Anne Porter (Waldrip & Bauer). 1969.
5. Philip Freneau (Philip M. Marsh). 1970.
6. Robert Greene (Tetsumaro Hayashi). 1971.
7. Benjamin Disraeli (R.W. Stewart). 1972.
8. John Berryman (Richard W. Kelly). 1972.
9. William Dean Howells (Vito J. Brenni). 1973.
10. Jean Anouilh (Kathleen W. Kelly). 1973.
11. E.M. Forster (Alfred Borrello). 1973.
12. The Marquis de Sade (E. Pierre Chanover). 1973.
13. Alain Robbe-Grillet (Dale W. Frazier). 1973.
14. Northrop Frye (Robert D. Denham). 1974.
15. Federico García Lorca (Laurenti & Siracusa). 1974.
16. Ben Jonson (Brock & Welsh). 1974.
17. Four French Dramatists: Eugène Brieux, François de Curel, Emile Fabre, Paul Hervieu (Edmund F. Santa Vicca). 1974.
18. Ralph Waldo Ellison (Jacqueline Covo). 1974.
19. Philip Roth (Bernard F. Rodgers, Jr.). 1974.
20. Norman Mailer (Laura Adams). 1974.
21. Sir John Betjeman (Margaret Stapleton). 1974.
22. Elie Wiesel (Molly Abramowitz). 1974.
23. Paul Laurence Dunbar (Eugene W. Metcalf, Jr.). 1975.
24. Henry James (Beatrice Ricks). 1975.
25. Robert Frost (Lentricchia & Lentricchia). 1976.
26. Sherwood Anderson (Douglas G. Rogers). 1976.
27. Iris Murdoch and Muriel Spark (Tominaga & Schneidermeyer). 1976.
28. John Ruskin (Kirk H. Beetz). 1976.
29. Georges Simenon (Trudee Young). 1976.
30. George Gordon, Lord Byron (Oscar José Santucho). 1976.
31. John Barth (Richard Vine). 1977.
32. John Hawkes (Carol A. Hryciw). 1977.
33. William Everson (Bartlett & Campo). 1977.
34. May Sarton (Lenora Blouin). 1978.
35. Wilkie Collins (Kirk H. Beetz). 1978.
36. Sylvia Plath (Lane & Stevens). 1978.
37. E.B. White (A.J. Anderson). 1978.
38. Henry Miller (Lawrence J. Shifreen). 1979.
39. Ralph Waldo Emerson (Jeanetta Boswell). 1979.
40. James Dickey (Jim Elledge). 1979.
41. Henry Fielding (H. George Hahn). 1979.
42. Paul Goodman (Tom Nicely). 1979.

RALPH WALDO EMERSON AND THE CRITICS

A Checklist of Criticism,
1900-1977

by

Jeanetta Boswell

The Scarecrow Author Bibliographies, No. 39

The Scarecrow Press, Inc.
Metuchen, N.J. & London
1979

PS
1638
B64

Library of Congress Cataloging in Publication Data

Boswell, Jeanetta, 1922-
   Ralph Waldo Emerson and the critics.

   (The Scarecrow author bibliographies ; no. 40)
   Includes indexes.
   1. Emerson, Ralph Waldo, 1803-1882--Criticism and
interpretation--Bibliography. I. Title.
Z8265.B64 [PS1638] 016.814'3   79-4670
ISBN 0-8108-1211-8

Copyright © 1979 by Jeanetta Boswell

Manufactured in the United States of America

To the memory
of my husband
Fred P. Boswell

CONTENTS

Mottoes	vii
Prefatory Remarks	ix
A Note on Using This Book	xi
The Checklist	1
Index of Coauthors, Editors, Translators	185
Subject Index	187

MOTTOES

"In literature, quotation is good only when the writer whom I follow goes my way, and, being better mounted than I, gives me a cast, as we say; but if I like the gay equipage so well as to go out of my road, I had better have gone afoot. " --"Quotation and Originality" (1868), Works, VIII, 189.

"Next to the originator of a good sentence is the first quoter of it. Many will read the book before one thinks of quoting a passage. As soon as he has done this, that line will be quoted east and west. " --"Quotation and Originality" (1868), Works, VIII, 191.

"After a few more turnings of the globe in its orbit, manhood, age & life itself will have passed, and as I advance, that which I have left behind will continually grow less & less. As I reach & pass successively the several epochs of existence the things of former pursuit will degenerate in my esteem. All, all will be unremembered as if they had never been. " --Journal, 1823. Journals & Miscellaneous Notebooks, II, 82.

"I know a song which is more hurtful than strychnine or the kiss of the asp. It blasts those who hear it, changes their colour and shape, and dissipates their substance. It is called Time. " --Journal, 1856. Journals, IX, 32.

"I am a bard least of bards. I cannot, like them, make lofty arguments in stately, continuous verse, constraining the rocks, trees, animals, and the periodic stars to say my thoughts, --for that is the gift of great poets; but I am a bard because I stand near them, and apprehend all they utter, and with pure joy hear that which I also would say.... " --Journal, 1862. Journals, IX, 472.

"Among fossil remains, the willow and the pine appear with the ferns. They bend all day to every wind; the cart-wheel in the road may crush them; every passenger may strike off a twig with his cane; every boy cuts them for a whistle; the cow, the rabbit, the insect, bite the sweet and tender bark; yet, in spite of accident and enemy, their gentle persistency lives when the oak is shattered by storm, and grows in the night, and snow and cold. When I see in these brave plants this vigor and immortality in weakness, I find a sudden relief and pleasure in observing the mighty law of vegetation." --"Resources," (1875), Works, VIII, 152-153.

PREFATORY REMARKS

Of the quotations used as "mottoes" for this work, I am particularly impressed with the last passage. It is almost prophetic, it seems, in that Emerson's life and work have been subjected to almost every conceivable point of view, and are still alive and well, growing, one might say "in the night, and snow and cold." In compiling this work, however, I have naturally read hundreds of pieces of criticism, and have come out of the experience feeling that Emerson has had his share of really good critics. Unlike some authors, Melville for example, Emerson rarely attracts what we sometimes call "the lunatic fringe," and hence those who have commented on his works have been for the most part men and women of good common sense and right judgment. A good many very useful compilations of Emerson criticism have been made, but these do not reveal, I think, the real variety which exists within the field. In the near future I hope to edit a collection of significantly unusual Emerson criticism; and I have already begun a large collection labeled Emerson in Public and Political Affairs.

The objective of this work is quite simple: to list in one alphabetical order all the books and articles which have been written about Ralph Waldo Emerson and his works since around 1900. No attempt has been made to be selective--the good and the bad are equally represented, and the students who use this bibliography will have to make these distinctions for themselves. Although this work is concerned with criticism since 1900, there are a few exceptions to this rule. Nineteenth-century criticism is listed if it has been reprinted recently, or if the author's life and career ran significantly into the twentieth century, or if it relates to Emerson's poetry. The best guide to Emerson criticism in the nineteenth century is, of course, by George Willis Cooke (Boston, 1908), and it would be pointless to duplicate all the listings in that work. I have listed all the studies of Emerson's poetry on the grounds that this area of study is of somewhat current interest to Emerson students, and will be a convenience to have under one cover.

This work lists mainly criticism written in English and published in American journals and books, although here there are a few exceptions also: works in other languages are listed if they have recently appeared in footnotes and bibliographies of American scholars. The whole question of Emerson criticism in other languages is immense, and might be undertaken by at least two or three doctoral candidates.

This work has been prepared largely for the use of my students in American literature courses, and I owe them many thanks for their contributions. On the subject of thanks, my debts are almost endless: to Miss Sarah Crouch as my research assistant for three years; to the library staff of the University of Texas at Arlington and to neighboring Metroplex libraries; to members of the English faculty at Arlington who occasionally contributed suggestions, but always contributed good wishes and moral support; and to members of my family who have maintained good order and discipline in their affairs so that I could work. Most of all I owe a debt of gratitude to my husband, my own best critic, who did not see the completion of this manuscript. On this score I have no comfort, except what Emerson himself said, "What is excellent, As God lives, is permanent."

Jeanetta Boswell

English Department
University of Texas at Arlington
Arlington, Texas

April 1, 1978.

A NOTE ON USING THIS BOOK

The first 32 numbered entries are of anonymous authorship and are listed chronologically.

Subarrangements under authors' names are chronological.

Abbreviations

Three abbreviations are used throughout:

<dl>
ESQ — Emerson Society Quarterly (After 1972, ESQ is cited with volume numbers; prior to that, under Cameron's editorship, issue number is cited.)

DA — Dissertation Abstracts

PMLA — Publications of the Modern Language Association
</dl>

In addition ATQ is used for American Transcendental Quarterly in a lengthy list of Cameron citations.

THE CHECKLIST

1. "A Half-Made Poet." London Quarterly, 73 (October, 1883), 25-35.

2. "American Poets." Quarterly Review, 163 (October, 1886), 363-394.

3. "Emerson's Correspondence with Herman Grimm." Atlantic Monthly, 91 (April, 1903), 467-479.

4. "Emerson the Citizen." Nation, 76 (May 28, 1903), 428.

5. "Ralph Waldo Emerson." Blackwood's Magazine, 173 (May, 1903), 714-719.

6. "Ralph Waldo Emerson." Macmillan's Magazine, 88 (May, 1903), 37-45.

7. "Letters of Thoreau and Emerson, 1843-1847." Magazine of History, 21 (August, 1915), 117-122.

8. "Reminiscence of Emerson." Journal of Education, 83 (March 30, 1916), 349.

9. "Emerson." London Times Literary Supplement, January 25, 1917, pp. 37-38.

10. "Emerson." Living Age, 292 (March 17, 1917), 674-679.

11. "When Mark Twain Petrified the 'Brahmans.'" Literary Digest, 62 (July 12, 1919), 28-29.

12. "Belaboring the 'Brahmans' Again." Literary Digest, 63 (October 4, 1919), 31.

13. "Emerson in French." Living Age, 314 (September 16, 1922), 739-740.

14 "Emerson Publishes His First Book Anonymously." Literary Digest, 84 (March 21, 1925), 52.

15 "The Milk of Emerson." Saturday Review of Literature, 3 (December 4, 1926), 355-364.

16 "Emerson and Humanism." London Times Literary Supplement, April 5, 1934, pp. 233-234.

17 "French Estimate of Emerson in 1846." New England Quarterly, 10 (September, 1937), 447-463. [See Howard, Besse D.]

18 "The Friendship of Emerson and Carlyle." Hibbert Journal, 38 (October, 1939), 102-114.

19 "Shelley, Emerson, and Sir William Osler," by W. R. Notes & Queries, 190 (March 23, 1946), 120-121.

20 "Emerson in Indianapolis." Indiana History Bulletin, 30 (July, 1953), 115-116.

21 "Arise, Ye Silent Class of '57." Life, June 17, 1957. Editorial page: "You've Nothing to Lose but Your Conformity."

22 "Emerson in Modern Germany." ESQ, 12 (1958), 50-51.

23 "Emerson, Poet and Philosopher." Indian Review, 60 (April, 1959), 404-405.

24 "The Writing on the Wall." London Times Literary Supplement, April 13, 1962, p. 248.

25 "Emerson, Ralph Waldo--Photographs of Literary Concord, Emerson, and His Family." ESQ, 32 (1963), 1-43. 41 photographs. See also item 414.

26 "Emerson's Farewell Letter to the Second Church: Pamphlet and Broadside." Reprint in ESQ, 35 (1964), 95-99.

27 "American Books Published in Great Britain before 1848." ESQ, 51 (1968), 129-136.

28 "Review of 'Nature.'" Democratic Review, 1 (February, 1838), 319-321. Reprinted in Sealts and Ferguson,

eds., Emerson's Nature (1969), pp. 90-97.

29 "Emerson and Robert Frost." ESQ, 58 (1970), 157-159.

30 "Emerson and Emily Dickinson." ESQ, 58 (1970), 111.

31 "A Sheaf of Emerson Pictures." American Transcendental Quarterly, 9 (1971), 71-85.

32 "Emerson's 'The Poet I,' lines 1-6." Explicator, 33 (March, 1975), item 54. By the "Seventeenth Century Poetry Group."

33 AARON, Daniel. "Emerson and the Progressive Tradition," in Men of Good Hope. New York: Oxford University Press, 1951. Pp. 3-20.

34 ABBOTT, John P. "Ralph Waldo Emerson and the Conduct of Life: The Early Years." Ph.D. diss., Iowa, 1939.

35 ABBOTT, L. F. "A Transcendental Humorist." Outlook, 136 (February 20, 1924), 299-300.

36 ──────. "Two Literary Sportsmen." Outlook, 147 (October 12, 1927), 177.

37 ABEL, Darrel. "Strangers in Nature: Arnold and Emerson." University of Kansas City Review, 15 (September, 1949), 205-215.

38 ──────. "The American Renaissance and the Civil War: Concentric Circles." ESQ, 44 (1966), 86-91.

39 ──────, ed. Critical Theory in the American Renaissance: A Symposium. Hartford: Transcendental Books, 1969.

40 ABRAMS, M. H. "The Correspondent Breeze: A Romantic Metaphor." Kenyon Review, 19 (1957), 113-130. The aeolian harp in Romantic poetry.

41 ──────. Natural Supernaturalism: Tradition and Revolution in Romantic Literature. New York: W. W. Norton, 1971.

42 ADAMS, J. Donald. "Speaking of Books." New York Times Book Review, April 12, 1959, p. 2. Robert Frost and Emerson.

43 ———. "Speaking of Books." New York Times Book Review, November 1, 1959, p. 2. Robert Frost and Emerson, continued.

44 ———, ed. Poems by Emerson. New York: Thomas Y. Crowell, 1976. (Poets Series, illustrated.)

45 ADAMS, James Truslow. "Emerson Re-Read." Atlantic Monthly, 146 (October, 1930), 484-492.

46 ———. The Epic of America. Boston: Little, Brown, 1932. Emerson, pp. 196-199 and passim.

47 ADAMS, John M. "The Philosophical Historian: Ralph Waldo Emerson's Concept of History." Ph.D. diss., Kansas, 1960. DA, 21 (1961), 2708-2709.

48 ADAMS, Raymond. "Emerson's Brother and the Mousetrap." Modern Language Notes, 42 (November, 1927), 483-486.

49 ———. "Emerson's House at Walden." Thoreau Society Bulletin, no. 24 (July, 1948), 3-8.

50 ADAMS, Richard P. "Romanticism and the American Renaissance." American Literature, 23 (January, 1952), 419-432.

51 ———. "Emerson and the Organic Metaphor." PMLA, 69 (March, 1954), 117-130. Reprinted in Browne, Ray B., and Martin Light, eds., Critical Approaches to American Literature, 2 vols. (New York: Thomas Y. Crowell, 1965), vol. I, pp. 149-163.

52 ———. "How to Read Emerson in Class." ESQ, 10 (1958), 1-2.

53 ———. "American Renaissance: An Epistemological Problem." ESQ, 35 (1964), 2-7.

54 ———. "The Basic Contradiction in Emerson." ESQ, 55 (1969), 106-110.

55 _____. "Permutations of American Romanticism." Studies in Romanticism, 9 (1970), 249-268.

56 ADKINS, Nelson F. "Emerson's 'Days' and Edward Young." Modern Language Notes, 63 (April, 1948), 269-271.

57 _____. "Emerson and the Bardic Tradition." PMLA, 63 (June, 1948), 662-677.

58 _____. "My Classroom Experiences with Emerson." ESQ, 10 (1958), 2-4.

59 ADLER, Felix. An Ethical Philosophy of Life. New York and London: D. Appleton, 1918. Emerson, pp. 27-29.

59a AGGERTT, Otis. "The Public Speaking of Ralph Waldo Emerson." M.A. thesis, University of Illinois, 1947.

60 ALBEE, John. Remembrances of Emerson, rev. ed. New York: Robert Grier Cooke, 1901. Original ed., 1901.

61 _____. "Tribute to Emerson." Independent, 55 (May, 1921), 1178-1182.

62 ALBONESE, Catherine. "The Kinetic Revolution: Transformation in the Language of the Transcendentalists." New England Quarterly, 48 (1975), 319-340.

63 ALBRECHT, Robert C. "The Theological Response of the Transcendentalists to the Civil War." New England Quarterly, 38 (March, 1965), 21-34. Reprinted in Barbour, American Transcendentalism (1973), pp. 211-221.

64 ALCOTT, Amos Bronson, ed. Conversations with Children on Gospels (Boston, 1836-1837). Reprinted New York: Arno Press, 1976.

65 _____. Ralph Waldo Emerson: An Estimate of His Character and Genius. Boston: A. Williams, 1882 Reprinted New York: Haskell House, 1968. In prose and verse, 81 pp.

66 _____. Ralph Waldo Emerson: Philosopher and Seer.

Boston: Cupples, Hurd, 1888.

67 _____. Journals of Bronson Alcott, (1837-1882) ed. Odell Shepard. Boston: Houghton, Mifflin, 1938. Emerson, pp. 77-78 and passim.

68 ALEXANDER, Colin C. "Emerson and the Concord Lyceum." The Stratford Journal, 5 (October-December, 1919), 206-216.

69 ALEXANDER, James Waddel, Albert Dod, and Charles Hodge. "Transcendentalism of the Germans and of Cousin and Its Influence on Opinion in This Country." The Biblical Repertory and Princeton Review, 2 articles, January, 1839. Comments on "The Divinity School Address." Reprinted in part in Konvitz, ed., Recognition (1972), pp. 13-15.

70 ALLEN, Gay Wilson. American Prosody. New York: American Book, 1935. Emerson, pp. 91-121.

71 _____. Walt Whitman Handbook. Chicago: Packard, 1946. Emerson, pp. 75-78.

72 _____. The Solitary Singer. New York: Macmillan, 1955. Reprinted New York: New York University Press, 1967. Emerson, p. 152 and passim.

73 _____, et al., eds. American Poetry. New York: Harper & Row, 1965. Emerson poems, pp. 101-148; notes, pp. 1113-1120.

74 _____. A Reader's Guide to Walt Whitman. New York: Farrar, Straus & Giroux, 1970. Emerson, pp. 57-58 and passim.

75 _____. "Emerson and the Unconscious." American Transcendental Quarterly, 19 (1973), 26-30.

76 _____. "Emerson and the Establishment." University of Windsor Review, 9 (1973), 5-27.

77 _____. "A New Look at Emerson and Science," in Robert P. Falk, ed., Literature and Ideas in America (1975), pp. 58-78.

78 ALTERTON, Margaret, and Hardin Craig, eds. Edgar Allan Poe: Representative Selections. New York: American Book, 1935. (American Writers series.) Emerson, p. xiv and passim.

79 AMACHER, Richard E. "The Literary Reputation of Ralph Waldo Emerson." Ph.D. diss., Pittsburgh, 1947.

80 ———. "The Bohemian Hymn." Explicator, 5 (June, 1947), item 55.

81 ———. "Emerson's Divinity School Address." Explicator, 7 (June, 1949), item 59.

82 ———. "Emerson's English Traits, Chapter X." Explicator, 11 (March, 1953), item 33.

83 ANDERSON, Charles R., ed. American Literary Masters. 2 vols. New York: Holt, Rinehart & Winston, 1965. Emerson, vol. I, pp. 459-622.

84 ANDERSON, David. "Lincoln and Emerson." Lincoln Herald, 60 (Winter, 1958), 123-128.

85 ———. "A Comparison of the Poetic Theories of Emerson." Personalist, 41 (August, 1960), 471-483.

86 ANDERSON, John Q. "Ralph Waldo Emerson's Concept of the Poet." Ph.D. diss., North Carolina, 1952.

87 ———. "Emerson and the Language of the Folk," in Mody C. Boatright, et al., eds., Folk Travelers, Ballads, Tales, and Talk. Dallas: Southern Methodist University Press, 1953. (Texas Folklore Publication, no. 25.) Pp. 152-159.

88 ———. "Emerson and California." California Historical Society Quarterly, 33 (Summer, 1954), 241-248.

89 ———. "Emerson and 'Manifest Destiny.'" Boston Public Library Quarterly, 7 (January, 1955), 23-33.

90 ———. "Emerson's 'Horses of Thought.'" ESQ, 5 (1956), 1-2.

91 _____. "Emerson and the Ballad of George Nidever: 'Staring Down' a Grizzly Bear." Western Folklore, 15 (January, 1956), 40-45.

92 _____. "Emerson and Prince Achille Murat." Boston Public Library Quarterly, 10 (January, 1958), 27-35.

93 _____. "Emerson on Texas and the Mexican War." Western Humanities Review, 13 (September, 1959), 191-199.

94 _____. "Emerson and the 'Moral Sentiment.'" ESQ, 19 (1960), 13-15.

95 _____. The Liberating Gods: Emerson on Poets and Poetry. Coral Gables, Fl.: University of Miami Press, 1971.

96 _____. "Emerson's 'Young American' as Democratic Nobleman." American Transcendental Quarterly, 9 (1971), 16-20. Also in Carlson, Eric W., and J. Lasley Dameron, eds., Emerson's Relevance Today: A Symposium (1971), pp. 16-20.

97 _____. "Emerson's 'Eternal Pan': The Re-Creation of a Myth," in Strauch, Carl F., ed., Characteristics of Emerson, Transcendental Poet: A Symposium (1975), pp. 2-6.

98 ANDERSON, Paul Russell, and Max Harold Fisch, eds. Philosophy in America from the Puritans to James. New York: D. Appleton-Century, 1939. (A Book of Readings with comments.) Emerson, pp. 329-349. Contains bibliography.

99 ANDERSON, Quentin. The Imperial Self: An Essay in American Literary and Cultural History. New York: Knopf, 1971. Emerson in "The Failure of the Fathers," pp. 3-58, and "Coming Out of Culture," pp. 201-244.

100 ANDLER, C. Nietzsche: Sa Vie et sa pensée. 2 vols. Paris, 1920. Emerson, vol. I, pp. 340-371.

101 ANDREWS, W. P., ed. Poems, Original and Translated by Charles T. Brooks (Boston, 1885). Re-

printed New York: Arno Press, 1975.

102 ANG, Gertrude R. "Ralph Waldo Emerson and Shakespeare." Ph.D. diss., New York University, 1961. DA, 23 (1962), 625.

103 ANZILOTTI, Ronaldo. "Emerson in Italia." Rivista di Letterature Moderne e Comparate (Firenze), 11 (March, 1958), 3-14.

104 ARMS, George. "Concord Hymn." Explicator, 1 (December, 1942), item 23.

105 _____. "Emerson's 'Days.'" Explicator, 4 (November, 1945), item 8.

106 _____. "Emerson's 'Ode Inscribed to W. H. Channing.'" College English, 22 (March, 1961), 407-409.

107 _____. "The Dramatic Movement of Emerson's 'Each and All.'" English Language Notes, 1 (March, 1964), 207-211.

108 ARNOLD, Matthew. Discourses in America. London: Macmillan, 1885. Emerson, pp. 138-207.

109 ARVIN, Newton. "The House of Pain: Emerson and the Tragic Sense." Hudson Review, 12 (Spring, 1959), 37-53. Reprinted in Konvitz, Milton R., and Stephen E. Whicher, eds., Emerson: A Collection (1962), pp. 46-59.

110 ATKINS, J. W. H. Literary Criticism in Antiquity. 2 vols. Cambridge, England: Cambridge University Press, 1934. Emerson, passim.

111 ATKINSON, Brooks, ed. Complete Essays and Other Writings of Ralph Waldo Emerson. New York: Random House, 1950. (Modern Library edition.)

112 AUSSINGER, Gloria Roth. "The Romantic Concept of the Self Applied to the Works of Emerson, Whitman, Hawthorne, and Melville." Ph.D. diss., Lehigh University, 1973. DA, 34 (1974), 5963A.

113 AXELROD, Steven G. "Teaching Emerson's 'The

Rhodora.'" College English Association, 36 (1974), 34-35.

114 BABBITT, Irving. Masters of Modern French Criticism. Boston: Houghton Mifflin, 1912. "Emerson as a Critical Standard," pp. 352-362.

115 BADGER, Kingsbury, ed. American Literature for Colleges. 2 vols. Harrisburg, Pa.: Stackpole, 1954. Emerson, vol. II, pp. 32-80.

116 BAILEY, Elmer James. Religious Thought in the Greater American Poets (1922). Reprinted Freeport, N. Y.: Books for Libraries, 1968. Emerson, pp. 47-69.

117 BAIM, Joseph. "The Vision of the Child and the Romantic Dilemma: A Note on the Child-Motif in Emerson." Thoth (Syracuse University), 7 (1966), 22-30.

118 BAKER, Carlos. "Emerson and Jones Very." New England Quarterly, 7 (March, 1934), 90-99.

119 _____. "The Road to Concord: Another Milestone in the Whitman-Emerson Friendship." Princeton University Library Chronicle, 7 (1946), 100-117.

120 BAKER, Joseph E. "Carlyle and Emerson on Great Men." Ph.D. diss., University of Iowa, 1940.

121 BALDWIN, Marilyn. "Emerson's 'Brahma.'" Explicator 20 (December, 1961), item 29.

122 BALDWIN, Richard Eugene. "The Influence of Emerson on the Fiction of Henry James." Ph.D. diss., University of California, Berkeley, 1967. DA, 28 (1968), 4162A.

123 BALSIERO, J. A. "Emerson y Whitman." Atlántico, 2 (1956), 49-71. In Spanish.

124 BANTA, Martha. "The Man of History and the Mythy Man in Melville." American Transcendental Quar-

terly, 10 (1971), 3-11. Ben Franklin and Emerson in Israel Potter and The Confidence Man.

125 _____. "Gymnasts of Faith, Fate, and Hazard." American Transcendental Quarterly, 21 (1974), 6-20.

126 BARBOUR, Brian M., ed. American Transcendentalism: An Anthology of Criticism. Notre Dame, Ind.: University of Notre Dame Press, 1973. "The Central Man: Emerson," Part IV, pp. 225-288.

127 _____. "Emerson's Poetic Prose." Modern Language Quarterly, 35 (1974), 157-172.

128 BARITZ, Loren. City on a Hill: A History of Ideas and Myths in America. New York: Wiley, 1965. "Transcendence: Ralph Waldo Emerson," pp. 205-269.

129 BARKER, Charles Albro. American Convictions: Cycles of Public Thought, 1600-1850. Philadelphia: Lippincott, 1970. "Individualism Made Philosophical: Self-assertion of Ralph Waldo Emerson," pp. 514-522, and "Transcendentalism in Society: Emerson, Thoreau, and Others," pp. 522-529.

130 BARNES, D. R. "Emerson, Transcendentalism, and the Methodist Ladies." ESQ, 47 (1967), 62-65.

131 BARNETT, Peter Herbert. "Retreat from Idealism: Emersonian Themes in American Religious Philosophy." Ph.D. diss., Columbia University, Philosophy, 1970. DA, 32 (1971), 481A-482A.

132 BARRUS, Paul W. "Ralph Waldo Emerson and Quakerism." Ph.D. diss., University of Iowa, 1949.

133 BARTLETT, William I. "Early Years of Jones Very--Emerson's 'Brave Saint.'" Essex Institute Historical Collection, 73 (1937), 1-23.

133a _____. Jones Very: Emerson's 'Brave Saint.' Durham, N.C.: Duke University Press, 1942.

134 BARTOL, Cyrus A. "Emerson's Religion," in Sanborn,

Franklin B., ed., The Genius and Character of Emerson (1885; reprinted 1970), pp. 109-145.

135 ———. Discourses on the Christian Spirit and Life (1850). Reprinted New York: Arno Press, 1976.

136 BARTON, William B. "Emerson's Method as a Philosopher." American Transcendental Quarterly, 9 (1971), 20-28. Also in Carlson and Dameron, eds., Emerson's Relevance Today: A Symposium (1971), pp. 20-28.

137 BAUGH, Hansell. "Emerson and the Elder Henry James." Bookman, 68 (November, 1928), 320-322.

138 BAUMGARTEN, Edourd. Der Pragmatismus: R. W. Emerson, William James, John Dewey. Frankfurt am Main, 1938. Emerson, pp. 3-96. In German.

139 BAUMGARTNER, Alex M. "The Mind of Ralph Waldo Emerson: 1817-1832." Ph.D. diss., University of Pennsylvania, c. 1960.

140 ———. "'The Lyceum Is My Pulpit': Homiletics in Emerson's Early Lectures." American Literature, 34 (January, 1963), 477-486.

141 BAYLEY, Jonathan. "Review of 'Nature.'" Intellectual Repository and New Jerusalem Magazine (London), 1 (April, 1840), 188-191. Reprinted in Sealts and Ferguson, Emerson's Nature (1969), 106-107.

142 BAYM, Max I. "Emma Lazarus and Emerson." Publications of American Jewish Historical Society, 38 (June, 1949), 261-287.

143 ———. A History of Literary Aesthetics in America. New York: Ungar, 1973. Emerson, pp. 54-59.

144 BAYM, Nina. "From Metaphysics to Metaphor: The Image of Water in Emerson and Thoreau." Studies in Romanticism, 5 (1966), 231-243.

145 BAZALGETTE, Leon. Henry Thoreau: Bachelor of Nature, trans. from the French by Van Wyck Brooks (1924). Reprinted Port Washington, N.Y.: Kennikat Press, 1976.

146 BEACH, Joseph Warren. The Outlook for American Prose. Chicago: University of Chicago Press, 1926.

147 _____. "Emerson and Evolution." University of Toronto Quarterly, 3 (July, 1934), 474-497.

148 _____. The Concept of Nature in 19th Century English Poetry. New York: Pageant, 1936. "Coleridge, Emerson, and Naturalism," and "Emerson's Nature Poetry," pp. 318-369.

149 BEALS, Carleton. Our Yankee Heritage: New England's Contribution to American Civilization. New York: David McKay, 1955. Emerson in "New England's Golden Harvest," pp. 277-307.

150 BECK, Ronald. "Emerson's Organic Structures." ESQ, 50 Supplement (1968), 76-77.

151 BEERS, Henry Augustin. Initial Studies in American Letters. New York: Chautauque Press, 1891.

152 _____. "Emerson and His Journals." Yale Review 5 (1916), 568-583.

153 _____. Four Americans: Roosevelt, Hawthorne, Emerson, Whitman. New Haven, Conn.: Yale University Press, 1919. Emerson in "Pilgrim in Concord," pp. 59-83. Printed earlier in Yale Review, 3 (1914), 673-688.

154 BELL, George E. "Emerson and Baltimore: A Biographical Study." Maryland History Magazine, 65 (1970), 331-368.

155 BELL, Millicent. "Review of Nathaniel Hawthorne: Transcendental Symbolist, by Marjorie J. Elder." American Literature, 43 (1971), 287-289.

156 BELTZ, Lynda. "Emerson's Lectures in Indianapolis." Indiana Magazine of History, 60 (1964), 269-280.

157 BENOIT, Raymond. "Emerson on Plato: The Fire's Center." American Literature, 34 (January, 1963), 487-498.

158 _____. Single Nature's Double Name. Atlantic Highlands, N.J.: Humanities Press, 1973. "Emerson on Plato," pp. 57-67.

159 BENSON, Nelson P. "Ralph Waldo Emerson as a Critic of Literature." Ph.D. diss., New York University, 1919.

160 BENTON, Joel E. Emerson as a Poet. New York: Mansfield and Wessels, 1883.

161 _____. "Emerson's Optimism." Outlook, 69 (June 15, 1901), 407-410.

162 BERCOVITCH, Sacvan. "Emerson's 'The American Scholar,' Paragraph 6." Explicator 25 (1966), item 9.

163 _____. "The Philosophical Background to the Fable of Emerson's 'The American Scholar.'" Journal of History of Ideas, 28 (January-March, 1967), 123-128.

164 _____. "The Image of America: From Hermeneutics to Symbolism." Bucknell Review, 20 (1973), 3-12.

165 _____. "Emerson the Prophet: Romanticism, Puritanism, and Auto-American Biography," in Levin, David, ed., Emerson: Prophecy, Metamorphosis, and Influence (English Institute Essays, 1975), pp. 1-27.

166 _____. The Puritan Origins of the American Self. New Haven, Conn.: Yale University Press, 1975. Emerson, pp. 163-186. Earlier version in Levin (1975), pp. 1-27.

167 BERGER, Harold L. "Emerson and Carlyle--Stylists at Odds." ESQ, 33 (1963), 61-65.

168 _____. "Emerson and Carlyle--The Dissenting Believers." ESQ, 38 (1965), 87-90.

169 BERGER, Patrick Frederick. "Margaret Fuller: Critical Realist as Seen in Her Works." Ph.D. diss., St. Louis University, 1972. DA, 34 (1974), 5157A.

170 BERNARD, Kenneth. "Emerson and Slavery--And the Other Man." Lincoln Herald, 57 (Winter, 1956), 3-10.

171 BERNSTEIN, Melvin H. "Emerson's Sea-Shells." American Quarterly, 12 (Summer, 1960), 231-236; also in ESQ, 20 (1960), 2-4.

172 BERRY, Edmund G. Emerson's Plutarch. Cambridge, Mass.: Harvard University Press, 1961.

173 BERRYMAN, Charles. "The Artist-Prophet: Emerson and Thoreau." ESQ, 43 (1966), 81-86.

174 BERTHOFF, Warren, ed. Nature by Ralph Waldo Emerson (1836). San Francisco: Chandler, 1968. Facsimile ed.

175 _____. "'Building Discourse': The Genesis of Emerson's Nature," in Fiction and Events. New York: E. P. Dutton, 1971. Pp. 182-218.

176 BESTERMAN, Theodore. A World Bibliography of Bibliographies. Totowa, N. J.: Rowman & Littlefield, 1971. Emerson, vol. II, pp. 228-229.

177 BESTOR, A. E., Jr. "Emerson's Adaptation of a Line from Spenser." Modern Language Notes, 49 (April, 1934), 265-267.

178 BEWLEY, Marius. Masks and Mirrors. New York: Atheneum Press, 1970. "Wallace Stevens and Emerson," pp. 271-280.

179 BHATTACHER, M. M. "Ralph Waldo Emerson as a Thinker." Visva-Bharati Quarterly (West Bengal, India), 21 (Spring, 1956), 400-415.

180 BIER, Jesse. "Weberism, Franklin, and the Transcendental Style." New England Quarterly, 43 (1970), 179-192.

181 _____. "The Romantic Co-ordinates of American Literature." Bucknell Review, 18 (1970), 16-33.

182 BIGELOW, C. C., ed. Emerson's Uncollected Writings: Essays, Addresses, Poems, Reviews,

and Letters. New York: Lamb Publishers, 1912. Reprinted Port Washington, N. Y.: Kennikat Press, 1976. Consists of papers from The Dial not included in Collected Works (1903).

183 BIKLE, C. B., Jr. "Kitamura Tokoku's Search for Salvation." Thought, 48 (1973), 286-304.

184 BINNEY, James. "Emerson Revisited." Mid-West Quarterly, 12 (1970), 109-122. Denies that Emerson was an incurable optimist.

185 BIRDSALL, R. D. "Emerson and the Church of Rome." American Literature, 31 (November, 1959), 273-281.

186 BIRRELL, Augustine. "Prophets on the Wave." Nation and Athenaeum (London), 40 (March 12, 1927), 793-794.

187 BIRSS, John H. "Emerson and Poe: A Similitude." Notes & Queries, 166 (April 21, 1934), 279.

188 BISHOP, Jonathan. Emerson on the Soul. Cambridge, Mass.: Harvard University Press, 1964.

189 BIXBY, J. T. "Emerson as Writer and Man." Arena, 39 (May, 1908), 538-543.

190 ———. "Emerson's Message." Arena, 39 (June, 1908), 665-673.

191 BLAIR, Walter, et al., eds. Literature of the United States, 3d ed. 2 vols. New York: Scott, Foresman, 1966. Emerson, vol. I, pp. 1037-1162.

192 ———, and Clarence Faust. "Emeron's Literary Method." Modern Philology, 42 (November, 1944), 79-95. Discusses essays and poems.

193 BLAKE, W. B. "Emerson: A Mystic Who Lives Again in His Journals." Forum, 52 (October, 1914), 612-620.

194 BLAKENEY, Richard J. "Emerson and the Berkeleian Idealism." ESQ, 58 (1970), 90-97.

195 BLAKEWELL, Charles M., ed. Poems by Emerson. New York: E. P. Dutton, 1914. (Everyman's Library Edition.)

196 BLANCK, Jacob. Bibliography of American Literature. 6 vols. New Haven, Conn.: Yale University Press, 1955-1963. Emerson, vol. III (1959), pp. 16-70. Lists primary source material.

197 BLANSETT, Barbara R. Nieweg. "Melville and Emersonian Transcendentalism." Ph.D. diss., University of Texas, Austin, 1963. DA, 24 (1964), 2904.

198 BLAU, J. L. Men and Movements in American Philosophy. Englewood Cliffs, N. J.: Prentice-Hall, 1952. Emerson, pp. 121-131.

199 BLINDERMAN, Abraham. American Writers on Education before 1865. Boston: Twayne, 1975. Emerson, pp. 133-151, 166-167.

200 BLIVIN, Bruce. "Emerson's Vital Message for Today." Readers' Digest, 77 (August, 1960), 96-102.

201 BLOOM, Harold. "The Central Man: Emerson, Whitman, Wallace Stevens." Massachusetts Review, 7 (Winter, 1966), 23-42.

202 _____. The Ringers in the Tower: Studies in Romantic Tradition. Chicago: University of Chicago Press, 1971.

203 _____. "Bacchus and Merlin: The Dialectic of Romantic Poetry in America." Southern Review, 7 (1971), 140-175.

204 _____. "Emerson: The Glory and Sorrows of American Romanticism," in Thorburn, D., and G. H. Hartman, eds., Romanticism (1973), pp. 155-173.

205 _____. "New Transcendentalism: The Visionary Strain in Merwin, Ashberry, and Ammans." Chicago Review, 24 (1973-1974), 25-43.

206 _____. "The Freshness of Transformation:

Emerson's Dialectics of Influence." American Transcendental Quarterly, 21 (1974), 57-63. Reprinted in Levin, ed., Emerson: Prophecy, Metamorphosis, and Influence (English Institute Essays, 1975), pp. 129-148.

207 _____. A Map of Misreading. New York: Oxford University Press, 1975. Emerson, pp. 160-192. Same material as listed in item 206.

208 _____. Kabbalah and Criticism. New York: Seabury, 1975.

209 _____. "Emerson and Whitman: The American Sublime," in Poetry and Repression. New Haven, Conn.: Yale University Press, 1976. Pp. 235-266.

210 BLOOM, Robert. "Irving Babbitt's Emerson." New England Quarterly, 30 (December, 1957), 448-473.

211 BLUESTEIN, E. Gene. "Emerson's Epiphanies." New England Quarterly, 39 (December, 1966), 447-460.

212 _____. The Voice of the Folk: Folklore and American Literary Theory. Amherst: University of Massachusetts Press, 1972. "The Emerson-Whitman Tradition," pp. 17-36.

213 BLUM, I. D. "The Parallel Philosophy of Emerson's Nature and Faulkner's The Bear." ESQ, 13 (1958), 22-25.

214 BOAS, George. Romanticism in America (1940). Reprinted New York: Russell & Russell, 1961. Emerson, pp. 191-202.

215 BODE, Carl. The American Lyceum: Town Meeting of the Mind. New York: Oxford University Press, 1956. Emerson, pp. 221-223 and passim.

216 _____. "Emerson, to Be Taught." ESQ, 10 (1958), 4-6.

217 _____, ed. Ralph Waldo Emerson: A Profile. New York: Hill & Wang, 1968. A collection of critical essays.

218 BOGART, Herbert. "Ralph Waldo Emerson: Self and Society, 1850-1870." Ph.D. diss., New York University, 1963. DA, 28 (1967), 1428A.

219 BOLGERI, M. L. "Riflessioni su Emerson." Humanities, 6 (June, 1958), 467-472. In Italian.

220 BOLLER, Paul F., Jr. American Transcendentalism: 1830-1860. New York: G. P. Putnam's Sons, 1974. Emerson, passim. Contains a good bibliography.

221 BOLTON, Sara Knowles. Ralph Waldo Emerson. New York: Thomas Y. Crowell, 1889, 1904.

222 BOND, Brian C. "Emerson's 'Spiritual Laws': The Subtle Logic of Form." ESQ, 69 (1972), 222-226.

223 BOOTH, Edward Townsend. God Made the Country. New York: Knopf, 1946. "Concord Alluvial: Emerson, Thoreau, Alcott," pp. 186-201.

224 BOOTH, R. A., and Roland Stromberg, eds. "Bibliography of Ralph Waldo Emerson, 1908-1920." Bulletin of Bibliography, 19 (1948), 180-183.

225 BOTTORF, William K. "'Whatever Inly Rejoices Me': The Paradox of 'Self-Reliance.'" ESQ, 69 (1972), 207-217.

226 _____. "Emerson's 'Power.'" Explicator, 31 (1973), item 45.

227 BOWEN, Edwin W. Makers of American Literature. New York: Neale, 1908. Emerson, pp. 193-212.

228 BOWEN, Francis. "Review of Nature." Christian Examiner, 21 (January, 1837), 371-385. Reprinted in Sealts and Ferguson, eds., Emerson's Nature (1969), 81-88.

229 _____. "Nine New Poets." North American Review, 44 (April, 1847), 402-434. Has not been reprinted.

230 BOYNTON, H. W. "Impressions of Emerson." Reader, 5 (January, 1905), 250-253.

231 BOYNTON, Percy H. "Democracy in Emerson's Journals." New Republic, 1 (November 28, 1914), 25-26.

232 _____. "Emerson's Feeling Toward Reform." New Republic, 2 (January 30, 1915), 16-18.

233 _____. "Emerson's Solitude." New Republic, 3 (May 22, 1915), 68-70.

234 _____. A History of American Literature. Boston: Ginn, 1919. Emerson, pp. 199-220.

235 _____. "Emerson, a Rediscovered Modern." Independent, 119 (September 24, 1927), 294-296.

236 _____. "Emerson in His Period." International Journal of Ethics, 39 (January, 1929), 177-189.

237 BRADLEY, Sculley. "Lowell, Emerson, and The Pioneer." American Literature, 19 (November, 1947), 231-244.

238 _____, et al., eds. The American Tradition in Literature. 2 vols. New York: W. W. Norton, 1967. Emerson, vol. I, pp. 1061-1235.

239 _____, et al., eds. The American Tradition in Literature. 1 vols. New York: W. W. Norton, 1967. Emerson, pp. 569-687.

240 BRAHAM, Lionel. "Emerson and Boehme: A Comparative Study in Mystical Ideas." Modern Language Quarterly, 20 (March, 1959), 31-35.

241 BRANN, Henry A. "Hegel and His New England Echo." Catholic World, 41 (1885), 56.

242 BRASWELL, William. "Melville as a Critic of Emerson." American Literature, 9 (November, 1937), 317-334.

243 BRAUN, Frederick A. Margaret Fuller and Goethe. New York: Henry Holt, 1910. Emerson, pp. 71-147.

243a _____. "Goethe as Viewed by Emerson." Journal

of English and Germanic Philology, 15 (1916), 23-24.

244 BRAWNER, J. P. "Emerson's Debt to Italian Art." West Virginia University Philological Papers, 8 (October, 1951), 49-58.

244a BRENNER, Rica. Twelve American Poets Before 1900. New York: Harcourt, Brace, 1933. Reprinted Freeport, N. Y.: Books for Libraries, 1968. "Emerson," pp. 48-79.

245 BRIDGES, William E. "Transcendentalism and Psychotherapy: Another Look at Emerson." American Literature, 41 (1969), 157-177.

246 _____, ed. Spokesmen for the Self: Emerson, Thoreau, and Whitman. Scranton, Pa.: Chandler, 1971. Emerson, pp. 25-81. Book of quotations on the Self.

247 BRIDGMAN, Richard. "The Meaning of Emerson's Title 'Hamatreya.'" ESQ, 27 (1962), 16.

248 BRIEN, Dolores. "Robert Duncan: A Poet in the Emerson-Whitman Tradition." Centennial Review, 19 (1975), 308-316.

249 BRIGANCE, W. N., ed. A History and Criticism of American Public Address. 2 vols. New York: McGraw-Hill, 1943. "Emerson," by Herbert A. Wichelus, vol. II, pp. 501-525.

250 BRITTIN, N. A. "Emerson and the Metaphysical Poets." American Literature, 8 (March, 1936), 1-15.

251 BRODERICK, John C. "An Emerson-Ruskin Parallel." Notes & Queries, n.s. 1 (1954), 314

252 _____. "The Concord Club." Notes & Queries, 2 (1955), 83.

253 _____. "American Reviews of Thoreau's Posthumous Books, 1863-1866: Checklist and Analysis." Texas Studies in English, 34 (1955), 125-139. Accounts for some of Emerson's influence.

254 _____. "Thoreau's Proposals for Legislation." American Quarterly, 7 (Fall, 1955), 285-290.

255 _____. "The Date and Source of Emerson's 'Grace.'" Modern Language Notes, 73 (February, 1958), 91-95.

256 _____. "Emerson, Alcott, and the American Institute of Instruction." ESQ, 13 (1958), 27-29.

257 _____. "Emerson's 1841 Lecture." Bulletin of New York Public Library, 66 (June, 1962), 347.

258 _____. "Emerson, Not Yet Clarified." ESQ, 27 (1962), 24.

259 _____. "Emerson and Moorfield Storey: A Lost Journal Found." American Literature, 38 (May, 1966), 177-186.

260 BRODWIN, Stanley. "Emerson's Version of Plotinus: The Flight to Beauty." Journal of History of Ideas, 35 (July, 1974), 465-483.

261 BROMWICH, David. "Suburbs and Extremities." Prose, 8 (1974), 25-38. Emerson, Whitman, Wallace Stevens, and the American sublime.

262 BRONSON, Walter Cochrane. A Short History of American Literature. Boston: D. C. Heath, 1901. Rev. ed., 1919. Emerson, pp. 195-209.

263 BROOKS, Cleanth, R. W. B. Lewis, and Robert Penn Warren, eds. American Literature: The Makers and the Making. New York: St. Martin's Press, 1973.

264 BROOKS, Van Wyck. America's Coming of Age. New York: Huebsch, 1915. Emerson, pp. 70-85.

265 _____. "Emerson and the Reformers." Harper's Magazine, 54 (December, 1926), 114-119.

266 _____. Emerson and Others. London: J. Cape, 1927. Six episodes of Emerson's life in Concord.

267 _____. The Life of Emerson. New York: E. P. Dutton, 1932.

268 _____. The Flowering of New England: 1815-1865. New York: E. P. Dutton, 1937.

269 _____. "Emerson in His Time." New Republic, 100 (August 23, 1939), 78-80.

270 BROWN, Clarence A., and John T. Flanagan, eds. American Literature: A College Survey. New York: McGraw-Hill, 1961. Good introduction to Emerson's poetry, pp. 196-197.

271 BROWN, E. B. "The Modern Emerson." Critic, 42 (May, 1903), 440-444.

272 BROWN, Maurice F. "Santayana on Emerson: An Unpublished Essay." ESQ, 37 (1964), 60-70.

273 BROWN, P. W. "Emerson's Philosophy of Aesthetics." Journal of Aesthetics and Art Criticism, 15 (March, 1957), 350-354.

274 BROWN, Stuart G. "Emerson's Platonism." New England Quarterly, 18 (September, 1945), 325-345.

275 _____. "Emerson." University of Kansas City Review, 15 (August, 1948), 27-37.

276 _____. "John Jay Chapman and the Emersonian Gospel." New England Quarterly, 25 (June, 1952), 147-180.

277 _____. "Emerson: 1803-1953." Ethics, 64 (April, 1954), 217-225.

278 BROWN, Theodore M. "Greenough, Paine, Emerson, and the Organic Aesthetic." Journal of Aesthetics and Art Criticism, 14 (March, 1956), 304-317.

279 BROWNELL, William C. "Emerson." Scribner's Magazine, 46 (November, 1909), 608-624.

280 _____. American Prose Masters. New York: Scribner's, 1909. Emerson, pp. 133-204.

281 BROWNSON, Orestes A. "On the Divinity School Address." Boston Quarterly Review, October, 1838. Reprinted in Konvitz, Recognition (1972), pp. 10-12.

282 _____. "Ralph Waldo Emerson's Poems." Boston Quarterly Review, April, 1847. Has not been reprinted.

283 _____. Essays and Reviews: Chiefly on Theology, Politics, and Socialism (New York, 1852). Reprinted New York: Arno Press, 1976.

284 BRUEL, André. "Ralph Waldo Emerson et Thoreau." Ph.D. diss., Paris, 1929. In French.

285 BRUMM, Ursula. "Jonathan Edwards and Ralph Waldo Emerson," in American Thought and Religious Typology, translated by John Hoaglund. New Brunswick, N.J.: Rutgers University Press, 1970. Pp. 86-108.

286 BRYER, Jackson R. Sixteen Modern American Authors. Durham, N.C.: Duke University Press, 1969. Reprinted New York: W.W. Norton, 1973. Emerson, passim. Contains many references to but not a section on Emerson.

287 _____, and Robert A. Rees, eds. A Checklist of Emerson Criticism: 1951-1961. Hartford: Transcendental Books, 1964. Also printed in ESQ, 37 (1964). 450 items, annotated with index.

288 BUELL, Lawrence J. "Emerson: From Preacher to Poet." Ph.D. diss., Cornell University, 1966. DA, 28 (1967), 189A.

289 _____. "Transcendentalist Catalogue Rhetoric: Vision versus Form." American Literature, 40 (1968), 325-339.

290 _____. "Unitarian Aesthetics and Emerson's Poet-Priest." American Quarterly, 20 (1968), 3-20.

291 _____. "First Person Superlative: The Speaker in Emerson's Essays," in Carlson and Dameron, eds., Emerson's Relevance Today: A Symposium (1971), pp. 28-35.

292 _____. "Reading Emerson for the Structures: The Coherence of the Essays." Quarterly Journal of Speech, 58 (1972), 58-69.

293 _____. Literary Transcendentalism: Style and Vision in the American Renaissance. Ithaca, N. Y.: Cornell University Press, 1973.

294 _____. "Emerson and the Idea of Microcosmic Form," in Buell, Literary Transcendentalism (1973), pp. 145-165.

295 _____. "Emerson and Thoreau: Soul versus Self," in Buell, Literary Transcendentalism (1973), pp. 284-311.

296 BUFANO, Randolph J. "Emerson's Apprenticeship to Carlyle, 1827-1848." American Transcendental Quarterly 13 (1972), 17-25.

297 BURBICK, Joan Susan. "The Art of Days: Perspectives on The Journal of Henry Thoreau." Ph. D. diss., Brandeis University, 1974. DA, 35 (1974), 3672A.

298 BURKE, Kenneth. "Acceptance and Rejection." The Southern Review, 2 (Winter, 1937), 600-632.

299 _____. "I, Eye, Aye--Emerson's Early Essay 'Nature': Thoughts on the Machinery of Transcendence," in Simon and Parson, eds., Transcendentalism and Its Legacy (1966), pp. 3-24. Reprinted in Sealts and Ferguson, Emerson's Nature (1969), pp. 150-163. Also in Kenneth Burke, The Philosophy of Literary Form: Studies in Symbolic Action. Baton Rouge, La.: Louisiana State University Press, 1967.

300 BURKE, Phyllis Brown. "Emerson's Prose Style: His Created World." Ph. D. diss., University of Washington, 1969. DA, 30 (1970), 4937A.

301 BURKE, W. J., and Will D. Howe. American Authors and Books. New York: Crown, 1962. Emerson, p. 225. Biographical sketch.

302 BURNS, Harry H. "Ralph Waldo Emerson's Judgments on English Literature, and the Principles Which Underlay Them." Ph. D. diss., University of Washington, 1936.

303 BURRESS, Lee A., Jr. "The Relationship of Christian Theology to the Idea Content of Ralph Waldo Emer-

son's Poetry." Ph.D. diss., Boston University, 1955.

304 BURROUGHS, John. Birds and Poets with Other Papers. New York: Hurd & Houghton, 1877. "Emerson," pp. 185-210. Also in Works of John Burroughs. Boston: Houghton, Mifflin, 1904. Vol. III, pp. 179-205.

305 ———. "Matthew Arnold on Emerson and Carlyle." The Century, 27 (April, 1884), 925-932.

306 ———. Indoor Studies. Boston: Houghton, Mifflin, 1889. "Arnold's View of Emerson and Carlyle," pp. 129-162. Also in Works of John Burroughs (Boston: Houghton, Mifflin, 1904), vol. VIII, pp. 141-176.

307 ———. "Science and the Poets," in Works of John Burroughs. Boston: Houghton, Mifflin, 1904. Vol. VIII, pp. 75-87.

308 ———. "A Glance into Emerson's Journals." Art World, 3 (November, 1917), 105-108.

309 ———. The Last Harvest. Boston: Houghton, Mifflin, 1922. "Emerson and His Journals," pp. 1-85 and "Flies in Amber," pp. 86-102.

310 BURTON, Richard. Literary Leaders of America. New York: Scribner's, 1904, 1909. "Life and Literary Genius of Emerson," pp. 139-163.

311 BUTCHER, Philip. "Emerson and the South." Phylon, 17 (1956), 279-285.

312 CABOT, James Elliot. "A Glimpse of Emerson's Boyhood." Atlantic Monthly, 59 (May, 1887), 650-667.

313 ———. A Memoir of Ralph Waldo Emerson. 2 vols. Boston: Houghton, Mifflin, 1887. Reviewed by Henry James, Jr., in Macmillan's Magazine (1887), and reprinted in Partial Portraits (1888).

314 CADY, Edwin Harrison. The Gentleman in America. Syracuse, N. Y.: Syracuse University Press, 1949. "God's Democratic Gentleman: Ralph Waldo Emerson," pp. 160-183. See also Ph.D. diss., University of Wisconsin, 1943, pp. 368-429.

315 CAIRNS, William B. A History of American Literature. New York and London: Oxford University Press, 1912. Emerson, pp. 225-238.

316/7 CALL, A. D. "Leading Light of American Letters." Education, 29 (June, 1909), 660-662.

318 CAMERON, Kenneth Walter, ed. ESQ, 1955-1972. "Recent and/or Current Emerson Bibliography" throughout years of editorship.

319 _____, ed. [Emerson's] Nature with Intro., Index, Concordance, and Bibliography, with Appendices. New York: Scholar's Facsimiles and Reprints, 1940.

320 _____. Ralph Waldo Emerson's Reading, rev. ed. Hartford: Transcendental Books, 1962. Original ed., Raleigh, N. C.: Thistle Press, 1941.

321 _____. Emerson the Essayist: An Outline of His Philosophical Development Through 1836, 3d and enlarged ed. 2 vols. Hartford: Transcendental Books, 1971. Earlier ed., Raleigh, N. C.: Thistle Press, 1945.

322 _____. "An Early Prose Work of Emerson." American Literature, 22 (November, 1950), 332-338.

323 _____. "Coleridge and the Genesis of Emerson's 'Uriel.'" Philological Quarterly, 30 (April, 1951), 212-217.

324 _____. "Emerson's Early Reading List (1819-1824)." Bulletin of New York Public Library, 55 (July, 1951), 315-324.

325 _____. "Emerson, Thoreau, and the Society of Natural History." American Literature, 24 (March, 1952), 21-30.

326 _____. "The Potent Song in Emerson's Merlin Poems." Philological Quarterly, 32 (January, 1953), 22-28.

327 _____. "A Sheaf of Emerson Letters." American Literature, 24 (January, 1953), 476-480.

328 _____. "Thoreau Discovers Emerson: A College Reading Record." Bulletin of New York Public Library, 57 (June, 1953), 319-334.

329 _____. "Emerson's Early Review of Shattuck's History." ESQ, 1 (1955), 2.

330 _____. "The Rev. Ralph Waldo Emerson and Aunt Mary's Books." ESQ, 1 (1955), 6-7.

331 _____. "Surviving Emerson Checks for the Late Period." ESQ, 1 (1955), 9-10.

332 _____. "Emerson, Thoreau, and the Poet Henry Sutton." ESQ, 1 (1955), 10-16.

333 _____. "The Significance of Emerson's Second Merlin Song." ESQ, 2 (1956), 2-7.

334 _____. "Thoreau's Harvard Friends Discuss Emerson's Nature." ESQ, 2 (1956), 8.

335 _____. "Emerson's 'Capital Print' of Coleridge." ESQ, 2 (1956), 8-9.

336 _____. "Emerson Recommends Dr. Simon Hewett." ESQ, 2 (1956), 10-12.

337 _____. "Emerson Transmits News from Germany, 1824." ESQ, 2 (1956), 12-13.

338 _____. "Young Emerson, Bardism, and Circle Imagery." ESQ, 2 (1956), 17-18.

339 _____. "Emerson in the Lyceum Records of Littleton, Massachusetts." ESQ, 2 (1956), 25.

340 _____. "Some Emerson Letters: Ungathered and Migrant." ESQ, 3 (1956), 4-6.

341 _____. "Emerson's Early Use of the Encyclopedia Britannica." ESQ, 3 (1956), 6-10.

342 _____. "Emerson at the Boston Athenaeum: New Evidence." ESQ, 3 (1956), 12-13.

343 _____. "Emerson's Receipts Among the Papers of the Second Church." ESQ, 3 (1956), 13-14.

344 _____. "Emerson's Recommendations of Whitman in 1863: The Remainder of the Evidence." ESQ, 3 (1956), 14-20.

345 _____. "Some Collections of Emerson Manuscripts." ESQ, 3 (1956), 20-21.

346 _____. "Some Collections of Emerson Manuscripts, Part II." ESQ, 6 (1957), 21-23, 26-27.

347 _____. "Transcendental Hell in Emerson and Marlowe." ESQ, 6 (1957), 9-10.

348 _____. "A Further Note on Emerson's Second Merlin Song." ESQ, 6 (1957), 10-11.

349 _____. "Emerson and the Warsaw Ghetto." ESQ, 6 (1957), 13-15. Evidence that Emerson was read in the Warsaw Ghetto in World War II.

350 _____. "Emerson, Thoreau, Parson Frost, and 'The Problem.'" ESQ, 6 (1957), 16.

351 _____. "Emerson on His Father and Step-Grandfather." ESQ, 6 (1957), 16-19.

352 _____. "Ellen Tucker Emerson to John Page Hopps on Emerson's Poetry." ESQ, 6 (1957), 21.

353 _____. "William Allingham and Emerson: Some New Evidences." ESQ, 6 (1957), 23-26.

354 _____. "Emerson, Thoreau, Elegant Extracts, and Proverb Lore." ESQ, 6 (1957), 26-39.

355 _____. "Emerson and His Cousin, Hannah Upham (Haskins) Parsons." ESQ, 6 (1957), 27-28.

356 _____. "Thoreau, Parker, and Emerson's 'Mousetrap,'" in The Monitor." ESQ, 7 (1957), 42-46.

357 _____. "Emerson, Thoreau, and the Town and Country Club." ESQ, 8 (1957), 2-17.

358 _____. "History and Biography in Emerson's Unpublished Sermons." Proceedings of the American Antiquarian Society, 66 (1957), 103-118. Also in ESQ, 12 (1958), 2-9.

359 _____. Transcendental Workbook, rev. ed. Hartford: Transcendental Books, 1957.

360 _____. "Thoreau Witnesses Emerson Purchase Land at Walden." ESQ, 10 (1958), 15-16.

361 _____. "Emerson and Swedenborgism." ESQ, 10 (1958), 14-21. Study outline and analysis.

362 _____. "Introducing Emerson's Transcendentalism to Undergraduates." ESQ, 10 (1958), 22-24.

363 _____. "A Garland of Emerson Letters." ESQ, 10 (1958), 32-41.

364 _____. "Jones Very and the Emersons in Harvard's Official Records." ESQ, 10 (1958), 46-47.

365 _____. "Charles Chauncy Emerson's Library." ESQ, 10 (1958), 48-49.

366 _____. "Emerson at Wesleyan University, Middletown, Connecticut." ESQ, 11 (1958), 56-62.

367 _____. "Emerson's Anecdote from Goethe of St. Philip Neri and the Nun." ESQ, 11 (1958), 62-63.

368 _____. "Emerson in the Diaries of S. K. Lathrop and E. E. Hale." ESQ, 11 (1958), 63.

369 _____. "Emerson's Ideal Clergyman: Hercy Bradford Goodwin." ESQ, 12 (1958), 39-44.

370 _____. "Emerson and the Motif That 'Spirits Associate.'" ESQ, 12 (1958), 45-46.

371 _____. "Articles of Possible Interest to Emerson and Thoreau in Concord Newspapers." ESQ, 12 (1958), 48-49.

372 _____. "Emerson Among the Literati of the Massachusetts Historical Society." ESQ, 13 (1958), 3.

373 _____. "Emerson's Father to Samuel Lawrence on Private and Public Matters." ESQ, 13 (1958), 19.

374 _____. "The Emersons in Early Newspapers." ESQ, 13 (1958), 47-50.

375 _____. "Emerson's 'Second Merlin Song' and Economist H. C. Carey." ESQ, 13 (1958), 65-83.

376 _____. "List of Emerson's Favorite Stories." ESQ, 13 (1958), 83-85. Some 100 items from a list by Emerson.

377 _____. "Emerson's Address at the Concord Centennial, April 19, 1875." ESQ, 13 (1958), 85-87.

378 _____. "Emerson's Arabian Proverbs." ESQ, 13 (1958), 50.

379 _____. "New Emerson Letters in Special Collections." ESQ, 13 (1958), 96-97.

380 _____. The Transcendentalists and Minerva: Cultural Background of the American Renaissance with Fresh Discoveries in the Intellectual Climate of Emerson, Alcott, and Thoreau. 3 vols. Hartford: Transcendental Books, 1958.

381 _____. An Emerson Index. Hartford: Transcendental Books, 1958. Based on selected notebooks.

382 _____. Emerson, Thoreau, and Concord in Early Newspapers: Biographical and Historical Lore for the Scholar and General Reader. Hartford: Transcendental Books, 1958.

383 _____. "Emerson, Thomas Campbell, and Bacon's Definition of Poetry." ESQ, 14 (1959), 48-56.

384 _____. "Thoreau and Emerson in Channing's

Letters to the Watsons." ESQ, 14 (1959), 77-85.

385 _____. "Emerson and the Emersons." ESQ, 14 (1959), 93-96.

386 _____. "Geological Speculation at Emerson's Harvard in 1825." ESQ, 16 (1959), 30-43. Reproduces two 1825 Bowdoin Prize papers on geology.

387 _____. "Emerson and Thoreau in the Index to The Dial." ESQ, 18 (1960), 44-49.

388 _____. "Emerson and Bronson Alcott, Conversationalist." ESQ, 18 (1960), 50-51.

389 _____. "Emerson's Influence on Friedrich Nietzsche." ESQ, 18 (1960), 51. Review of a book in German.

390 _____. "Emerson's Tribute to Mrs. Hanna Joy." ESQ, 18 (1960), 51. Obituary notice April 2, 1842.

391 _____. "John Shepard Keyes' Reminiscences of Emerson." ESQ, 19 (1960), 15-16.

392 _____. "Memorabilia of Ruth Emerson." ESQ, 19 (1960), 49-51.

393 _____. "Emerson's Lecture Schedule in Danbury, Connecticut." ESQ, 19 (1960), 81-85.

394 _____. "Emerson and Melville Lecture in New Haven, 1856-1857." ESQ, 19 (1960), 85-96.

395 _____. "Emerson's Early Lectures: A Review of Vol. I, ed. Robert Spiller and Stephen E. Whicher." ESQ, 20 (1960), 6-8.

396 _____. "The Challenge of Emerson's Early Lectures." ESQ, 20 (1960), 8-10.

397 _____. "A New Source for Emerson's Lectures." ESQ, 20 (1960), 10-25.

398 _____. "Notes on the Early Lectures." ESQ, 20 (1960), 25-123.

399 _____. "Emerson, Thoreau, and Concord in Early Newspapers." ESQ, 21 (1960), 1-57.

400 _____. "Emerson's Walden Woodlots and the Fitchburg Railroad." ESQ, 22 (1961), 67-68.

401 _____. "More Notes on Orientalism in Emerson's Harvard." ESQ, 22 (1961), 81-90.

402 _____. "Emerson's Fight for His Walden Woodlots." ESQ, 22 (1961), 90-95.

403 _____. "A Bundle of Emerson Letters." ESQ, 22 (1961), 95-97.

404 _____. "The First Appearance of Emerson's 'Boston Hymn.'" ESQ, 22 (1961), 97-101.

405 _____. "Emerson in the New American Cyclopedia." ESQ, 23 (1961), 16-18.

406 _____. Commentary on Emerson's Early Lectures, 1833-1836, with Index and Concordance. Hartford: Transcendental Books, 1962.

407 _____. "Emerson, Thoreau, and the Atlantic Cable." ESQ, 26 (1962), 45-87.

408 _____. "Homiletical Background for Emerson's 'Gnothi Seauton.'" ESQ, 26 (1962), 87-111. Early poem, 1831. See JMN, III.

409 _____. "A New Japanese Translation of Emerson's Works: A Review." ESQ, 27 (1962), 19-23.

410 _____. "Early Background for Emerson's 'The Problem.'" ESQ, 27 (1962), 37-46.

411 _____. "Redpath Writes Whitman on the Transcendentalists." ESQ, 29 (1962), 21-26.

412 _____. "Emerson's Nature and British Swedenborgism, 1840-1841." ESQ, 30 (1963), 11-15.

413 _____. "Emerson's College Poem Indian Superstition." ESQ, 30 (1963). Also printed Hartford: Transcendental Books, 1954.

414 _____. "Photographs of Concord and the Emerson Family." ESQ, 32 (1963), 1-43.

415 _____. "Publication of the Index-Concordance to Emerson's Sermons." ESQ, 33 (1963), 2-7. Announcement and preview.

416 _____. Index-Concordance to Emerson's Sermons with Homiletical Papers. 2 vols. Hartford: Transcendental Books, 1963. Based on 150 unpublished sermons.

417 _____. "'Indian Superstition' and Orientalism in Emerson's Harvard." ESQ, 33 (1963), 7-15.

418 _____. Transcendental Climate: New Resources for the Study of Emerson, Thoreau, and their Contemporaries. Hartford: Transcendental Books, 1963. 3 vols.

419 _____. "Emerson's Right Hand of Fellowship," in Index-Concordance (1963), p. 663.

420 _____. "History and Biography in Emerson's Unpublished Sermons," in Index-Concordance (1963), pp. 654-661. Previously published in ESQ, 12 (1958), 2-9.

421 _____. "Outline of Three Emerson Sermons," in Index-Concordance (1963), 664-667.

422 _____. "Emerson's Preaching Record, 1826-1838," in Index-Concordance (1963), 695-703.

423 _____. "The Wider Emerson Family." ESQ, 37 (1964), 76-87.

424 _____. Emerson's Workshop: Reading in Periodicals Through 1836. Hartford: Transcendental Books, 1965.

425 _____. Transcendental Reading Patterns. Hartford: Transcendental Books, 1965.

426 _____. Transcendental Epilogue. Hartford: Transcendental Books, 1965. 3 vols.

427 _____. "Emerson's 'Bacchus' and Beethoven." ESQ, 43 (1966), 34-38.

428 _____. "Emerson Manuscripts: Ungathered and Migrant." ESQ, 43 (1966), 141-144; and ESQ, 47 (1967), 125-126.

429 _____. "Presentation Copies from Emerson." ESQ, 47 (1967), 106-108.

430 _____. "Anticipations of Emerson on Native American Art: S. F. Jarvis to Lydia Sigourney in 1832." ESQ, 47 (1967), 110-112.

431 _____. "More Background for Emerson's 'Indian Superstition,' Parish Circulation Libraries." ESQ, 47 (1967), 130-138.

432 _____. "A Glimpse of Young Emerson at Divinity School." ESQ, 48 (1967), 89-91.

433 _____. "Samuel and Ezra Ripley at Emerson's Ordination." ESQ, 48 (1967), 92-93.

434 _____. "Emerson and Hydrostatics: 'The Siphars.'" ESQ, 48 (1967), 93-98.

435 _____. Emerson Among His Contemporaries. Hartford: Transcendental Books, 1967. 499 pages, comments about Emerson.

436 _____. "Emerson, Alcott, and the Cogswell Estate." ESQ, 51 (1968), 9-10.

437 _____. "Beriah Green and Emerson's Phi Beta Kappa Address of 1867." ESQ, 51 (1968), 26-32.

438 _____. "Emerson and Charles Edward Rawlins, Jr." ESQ, 51 (1968), 33-37.

439 _____. "Notes on Emerson in Japan." ESQ, 51 (1968), 102-107.

440 _____. "Emerson and the Phonographic Reporter, Walter Bachelor." ESQ, 51 (1968), 143-146.

441 _____. "Frank Bellew and Emerson in Concord in 1855." ESQ, 52 (1968), 82-85.

442 _____. Contemporary Dimension: Notebook of the American Renaissance Newspaper Clippings. Hartford: Transcendental Books, 1970.

443 _____. Young Emerson's Transcendental Vision. Hartford: Transcendental Books, 1971. Abridgement of Emerson the Essayist (1945).

444 _____. Emerson and Thoreau as Readers. Hartford: Transcendental Books, 1972.

445 _____. Emerson and Thoreau Speak. Hartford: Transcendental Books, 1972. Lyceum platforms of Concord and Lincoln.

446 _____. Massachusetts Lyceum During the American Renaissance. Hartford: Transcendental Books, 1972.

447 _____. "Bunyan and the Writers of the American Renaissance." ATQ [American Transcendental Quarterly], 13 (1972), Supplement, Part I, pp. 1-47.

448 _____. "Death and Beyond in the American Renaissance." ATQ, 13 (1972), Supplement, Part 2, pp. 1-27.

449 _____. "The Rowse Drawings of the Emersons." ATQ, 13 (1972), 49-52.

450 _____. "Henry Ware's 'Divinity School Address,' --a Reply to Emerson's." ATQ, 13 (1972), 84-91.

451 _____. "Emerson and Thoreau Lecture at Lynn." ATQ, 14 (1972), 158-164.

452 _____. "Some Alcott Conversations in 1863." ATQ, 17 (1973), 3-9.

453 _____. "The Ending of Emerson's 'Thoreau.'" ATQ, 17 (1973), 24.

454 _____. "Reports of Emerson's Lectures in 1864." ATQ, 17 (1973), 41-45.

455 _____. "Emerson and Thoreau as Readers: Selected Chapters from The Transcendentalists and Minerva." New edition, ATQ, 18 (1973), 1-133.

456 _____. "Literary News in American Renaissance Newspapers." ATQ, 20 (1973), 13-36.

457 _____. "Emerson, Transcendentalism, and Literary Notes in the Stearns Wheeler Papers." ATQ, 20 (1973), 69-98.

458 _____. "Emerson Manuscripts: Ungathered and Migrant." ATQ, 20 (1973), 122-126.

459 _____. Transcendental Log. Hartford: Transcendental Books, 1973. Later published in ATQ, 28 (1975), 1-345.

460 _____. A Study of Emerson's Major Poems by Charles Malloy. Hartford: Transcendental Books, 1973. Later published in ATQ, 23 (1974), 1-123.

461 _____. Emerson's Apprenticeship. Hartford: Transcendental Books, 1974.

462 _____. Response to Transcendentalism in Concord: The Last Decades of the Era of Emerson, Thoreau, and the Concord School as Recorded in Newspapers. Hartford: Transcendental Books, 1974.

462a CAMPBELL, Harry Modean. "Emerson and Whitehead." PMLA, 75 (December, 1960), 577-582.

463 CANBY, Henry Seidel. Classic Americans: A Study of Eminent American Writers from Irving to Whitman. New York: Harcourt, Brace, 1931. Emerson, pp. 143-183.

464 _____. Thoreau. Boston: Houghton, Mifflin, 1939. Emerson, pp. 88-92, 166-171, 303-306 and passim.

465 CANNON, Charles W. "The Influences Determining Ralph Waldo Emerson's Conception of Jesus." Ph.D. diss., University of Iowa, 1937.

466 CAPONIGRI, A. Robert. "Brownson and Emerson: Nature and History." New England Quarterly, 18 (September, 1945), 368-390. Reprinted in Barbour, American Transcendentalism (1973), pp. 239-254.

467 CAPPS, Jack L. Emily Dickinson's Reading, 1836-1886.

Cambridge, Mass.: Harvard University Press, 1966. Emerson, pp. 111-118 and passim.

468 CARLEY, Peter King. "The Early Life and Thought of Frederick Henry Hedge, 1805-1850." Ph.D. diss., Syracuse University, 1973. DA, 34 (1974), 6558A.

469 CARLSON, Eric W. "Emerson's 'The Bohemian Hymn.'" ESQ, 6 (1957), 6-7.

470 _____. "Lecture Outlines for Teaching Emerson." ESQ, 22 (1961), 38-42.

471 _____. "Emerson's Modernism--New Insights." American Transcendental Quarterly, 9 (1971), 3-6.

472 _____, and J. Lasley Dameron, eds. Emerson's Relevance Today: A Symposium. Hartford: Transcendental Books, 1971.

473 CARMAN, Bliss. The Poetry of Life. Boston: L. C. Page, 1905. Emerson, pp. 151-158.

474 CARPENTER, Edward. Days with Walt Whitman. New York: Macmillan, 1906. "Whitman and Emerson," pp. 153-187.

475 CARPENTER, Frederic I. "Ralph Waldo Emerson's Use of Translations from the Oriental." Ph.D. diss., University of Chicago, 1929.

476 _____. "Points of Comparison between Emerson and William James." New England Quarterly, 2 (July, 1929), 458-474.

477 _____. "Immortality from India." American Literature, 1 (November, 1929), 233-242.

478 _____. Emerson and Asia. Cambridge, Mass.: Harvard University Press, 1930.

479 _____. "Thoreau et Emerson." Revue Anglo-Américaine, 7 (February, 1930), 215-230. In French.

480 _____, ed. Ralph Waldo Emerson: Representative

Selections. New York: American Book Co., 1934. (American Writers Series.)

481 _____. "Tristram, the Transcendent." New England Quarterly, 11 (September, 1938), 501-523.

482 _____. "William James and Emerson." American Literature, 11 (March, 1939), 39-57.

483 _____. "The Values of Robinson Jeffers." American Literature, 11 (January, 1940), 353-366.

484 _____. "Bronson Alcott: Genteel Transcendentalist." New England Quarterly, 13 (March, 1940), 34-48.

485 _____. "The Philosophical Joads." College English, 2 (January, 1941), 315-325.

486 _____. "C. S. Peirce: Pragmatic Transcendentalist." New England Quarterly, 14 (March, 1941), 34-48.

487 _____. "The Genteel Tradition: A Re-interpretation." New England Quarterly, 15 (March, 1942), 427-443.

488 _____. "Scarlet A--Minus." College English 5 (January, 1944), 173-180.

489 _____. "Thomas Wolfe: The Autobiography of an Idea." University of Kansas City Review, 12 (Spring, 1946), 179-ff.

490 _____. Emerson Handbook. New York: Hendricks House, 1953.

491 _____. American Literature and the Dream. New York: Philosophical Library, 1956. Emerson, pp. 19-29.

492 _____. "American Transcendentalism in India: 1961." ESQ, 31 (1963), 59-62.

493 CARPENTER, Hazen C. "Emerson's Views Concerning Education and the Scholar." Ph.D. diss., University of Wisconsin, 1938.

494 _____. "Emerson at West Point." Education, 71 (September, 1950), 57-61.

495 _____. "Emerson, Elliot, and the Elective System." New England Quarterly, 24 (March, 1951), 13-34.

496 _____. "Emerson and Christopher Pearse Cranch." New England Quarterly, 36 (March, 1964), 18-42.

497 CARSON, Barbara H. "Orpheus in New England: Alcott, Emerson, and Thoreau." Ph.D. diss., Johns Hopkins University, 1968. DA, 29 (1968), 1533A.

498 CARTER, George E. "Democrat in Heaven--Whig on Earth: The Politics of Ralph Waldo Emerson." Historical New Hampshire, 27 (1972), 123-140.

499 CARTER, R. C. "Margaret Fuller and the Two Sages." Colby Library Quarterly, 6 (March, 1963), 198-201.

500 CARUTHERS, J. Wade. "Who Was Octavius Brooks Frothingham?" New England Quarterly, 43 (1970), 631-637.

501 CARY, Elizabeth Luther. "Hawthorne and Emerson." Critic, 45 (July, 1904), 25-27.

502 _____. "Ralph Waldo Emerson." Dial, 37 (December 1, 1904), 366-367.

503 _____. Emerson, Poet and Thinker. New York: G. P. Putnam's, 1904.

504 CASALE, Ottavio M. "Poe on Transcendentalism." ESQ, 50 Supplement (1968), 85-97.

505 CASS, Richard Welke. "The Implications of Ralph Waldo Emerson's Statements on Knowing for Revising Curriculum Concepts." Ph.D. diss., Wisconsin University at Milwaukee, Education, 1971. DA, 33 (1972), 3251A.

506 CASSERES, Benjamin de. "Emerson: Sceptic and Pessimist." Critic, 42 (May, 1903), 437-440.

507 _____. "Emerson, the Individualist." Bookman, 17 (May, 1903), 300-302.

508 CAWELTI, John G. The Apostles of the Self-Made Man.

Chicago: University of Chicago Press, 1965. "Self-Improvement and Self-Culture: Ralph Waldo Emerson," pp. 77-98.

509 CELIERES, André. The Prose Style of Emerson. Ph. D. diss., Paris, 1936. Published in English.

510 Centenary of the Birth of Ralph Waldo Emerson. Concord, May 25, 1903. Cambridge, Mass.: Riverside Press, 1903. 137 pages by the following: William Lorenzo Eaton, LeBaron Russell Briggs, Samuel Hoar, Charles Eliot Norton, Thomas Wentworth Higginson, William James, George Frisbie Hoar, Caroline Hazard, Moorfield Storey, Hugo Munsterberg, and Edward Waldo Emerson.

511 CESTRÉ, Charles. "Emerson." Revue Anglo-Américaine (1929). In French.

512 ———. "Thoreau et Emerson." Revue Anglo-Américaine (1930). In French.

513 ———. "Emerson poète." Etudes Anglaises, 4 (June, 1940). In French.

514 CHANDRASEKHARAN, K. R. "Emerson's 'Brahma': An Indian Interpretation." New England Quarterly, 33 (December, 1960), 506-512.

515 CHANNING, William Ellery (the younger). Poems: The Major Phase (Boston, 1843). Reprinted New York: Arno Press, 1976.

516 ———. Poems or Sixty-Five Years, ed. Frank B. Sanborn (Philadelphia & Concord, 1902). Reprinted New York: Arno Press, 1975.

517 CHAPIN, Edward W. Evenings with Shakespeare and Other Essays. Cambridge, Mass.: Riverside Press, 1911. "Ralph Waldo Emerson," pp. 156-178.

518 CHAPMAN, John Jay. "Emerson, Sixty Years Later." The Atlantic Monthly, 79 (January-February, 1897), 27-41, 222-240. Also in Emerson and Other Essays (New York: Scribner's, 1898; reprinted, 1909), pp. 3-108. Reprinted in Wilson, Edmund, ed., The Shock of Recognition (1943), pp. 595-658.

519 CHARVAT, Charles C. "Ralph Waldo Emerson and Catholicism." Ph.D. diss., University of Iowa, 1940.

520 CHARVAT, William. The Origins of American Critical Thought, 1810-1835. Philadelphia: University of Pennsylvania Press, 1936. Emerson, passim.

521 _____. "American Romanticism and the Depression of 1837." Science and Society, 2 (Winter, 1937), 67-82.

522 _____. "A Chronological List of Emerson's American Lecture Engagements." Bulletin of New York Public Library, 64 (September, October, November, December, 1960), 492-507, 551-559, 606-610, 657, 663. Part II, 65 (January, 1961), 40-46. Later collected and published as a separate booklet.

523 CHAWNER, M. G. "Nature in Emerson's Essays." New England Magazine, 32 (April, 1905), 215-219.

524 CHAZIN, Maurice. "Quinet, an Early Discoverer of Emerson." PMLA, 48 (March, 1933), 147-163.

525 _____. "Emerson's Disciple in Belgium: Marie Mali." Romanic Review, 24 (1933), 2-24.

525a CHEVIGNY, Bell Gale. The Woman and the Myth: Margaret Fuller's Life and Writings. Old Westbury, N. Y.: Feminist Press, 1976. Review by Vivian Gornick in New York Times Book Review, January 9, 1977.

526 CHITTICK, V. L. O. "Emerson's 'Frolic Health.'" New England Quarterly, 30 (June, 1957), 209-234.

527 CHOATE, Joseph H. "Emerson." Critic, 43 (September, 1903), 212-216.

528 _____. Abraham Lincoln and Other Addresses in England. New York: Century, 1910. Emerson, pp. 141-154.

529 CHRISTADLER, Martin. "Ralph Waldo Emerson in Modern Germany." ESQ, 38 (1965), 112-130.

530 CHRISTY, Arthur E. "Emerson's Debt to the Orient." Monist, 38 (January, 1928), 38-64.

531 _____. The Orient in American Transcendentalism. New York: Columbia University Press, 1932. Emerson, pp. 63-183.

532 CICARDO, Barbara Ann. "The Mystery of the American Eve: Alienation of the Feminine as a Tragic Theme in American Literature." Ph.D. diss., St. Louis University, 1971. Emerson, passim.

533 CLAPP, E. R. "Emerson Revisited: The American Scholar, New Style." Western Humanities Review, 16 (August, 1962), 339-348.

534 CLARK, Harry Hayden. "Emerson and Science." Philological Quarterly, 10 (July, 1931), 225-260.

535 _____. Major American Poets. New York: American Book, 1936. Emerson, pp. 191-241.

536 _____. Transitions in American Literary History. Durham, N. C.: Duke University Press, 1953. "The Rise of Transcendentalism, 1815-1860," Chapter V, pp. 245-314.

537 _____. "Changing Attitudes in Early American Literary Criticism," in Stovall, Floyd, ed., Development of American Literary Criticism (1955), pp. 15-73.

538 _____. "Conservative and Mediatory Emphases in Emerson's Thought," in Simon, Myron, and Thornton H. Parsons, eds., Transcendentalism and Its Legacy (1966), pp. 25-62.

539 _____, and Gay Wilson Allen, eds. Literary Criticism: Pope to Croce. Detroit: Wayne State University Press, 1962. Emerson, Notes and "The Poet," pp. 369-393.

540 CLARK, J. Scott. A Study of English and American Poets: A Laboratory Method. New York: Scribner's, 1900. Emerson, pp. 497-529.

541 CLARK, T. H. "An Emerson Reminiscence." South

Atlantic Quarterly, 4 (July, 1905), 284-286.

542 CLARKE, James Freeman. "The Religious Philosophy of Ralph Waldo Emerson." American Transcendental Quarterly, 17 (1973), 38-40. Reprint.

543 CLAUDEL, Alice M. "Emerson: Man Alive!" Discourse, 11 (1968), 382-385.

544 CLEBSCH, William. American Religious Thought: A History. Chicago: University of Chicago Press, 1973. Emerson, pp. 69-111.

545 CLENDENNING, John. "Ralph Waldo Emerson's Response to Skepticism." Ph.D. diss., Iowa University, 1962.

546 _____. "Emerson and Bayle." Philological Quarterly, 43 (January, 1964), 76-86.

547 _____. "Time, Doubt, and Vision: Notes on Emerson and T. S. Eliot." American Scholar, 36 (Winter, 1967), 125-132.

548 _____. "Emerson's 'Days': A Psychoanalytic Study," in Strauch, Carl, ed., Characteristics of Emerson, Transcendental Poet: A Symposium (1975), pp. 6-11.

549 CLEVELAND, Eunice J., ed. Emerson's Essays on Manners, Self-Reliance, Compensation, Nature, Friendship. New York: Longmans Green, 1915. Contains notes and introduction.

550 CLOER, Roberta Kay. "Emerson's Philosophy of Rhetoric." Ph.D. diss., in speech, University of Southern California, 1969. DA, 31 (1970), 848A.

551 COAD, O. S. "An Unpublished Lecture by Emerson." American Literature, 14 (January, 1943), 421-426.

552 COBB, Robert P. "Society versus Solitude: Studies in Ralph Waldo Emerson, Thoreau, Hawthorne, and Whitman." Ph.D. diss., University of Michigan, 1955.

553 COHEN, Aaron G. "Emerson--Time's Clearer Image."

Rosicrucian Digest, 39 (May, 1961), 195-196.

554 COHEN, B. B. "'Threnody': Emerson's Struggle with Grief." Indiana University Folio, 14 (October, 1948), 13-15.

555 _____. "Emerson's 'The Young American' and Hawthorne's 'The Intelligence Office.'" American Literature, 26 (March, 1954), 32-43.

556 _____. "Emerson's Poem 'Pan.'" Modern Language Notes, 70 (January, 1955), 32-33.

557 _____. "A Penny Paper's Review of Emerson's Essays: 1841." New England Quarterly, 29 (December, 1956), 516-521.

558 _____. "Emerson and Hawthorne on England." Boston Public Library Quarterly, 9 (April, 1957), 73-85.

559 COLACURIO, Michael J. "A Better Mode of Evidence: The Transcendental Problem of Faith and Spirit," in Cook, Reginald L., ed., Themes, Tones, and Motifs in the American Renaissance: A Symposium (1968), 12-22.

560 COLE, P. B. "Emerson, England, and Fate," in Levin, David, ed., Emerson: Prophecy, Metamorphosis, and Influence (1975), pp. 83-105.

561 COLEMAN, R. A. "Two Meetings with Emerson." Modern Language Notes, 65 (November, 1950), 482-484. About John T. Trowbridge.

562 COLLINS, Christopher. "The Uses of Observation: A Study of Correspondential Vision in the Writings of Emerson, Thoreau, and Whitman." Ph.D. diss., Columbia University, 1964. DA, 26 (1965), 352.

563 COLLINS, John C. The Posthumous Essays of John C. Collins, ed. L. C. Collins. New York: E. P. Dutton, 1912. "The Writings of Emerson," pp. 127-170.

564 COLLINS, Robert E., ed. Theodore Parker, American Transcendentalist: A Critical Study and a Collection

of His Writings. Metuchen, N. J.: Scarecrow Press, 1973.

565 COLTON, Delia M. "Ralph Waldo Emerson." The Continental Monthly, 1 (1862), 49-62. Reprinted in Sealts and Ferguson, eds., Emerson's Nature (1969), pp. 111-112.

566 COMMAGER, Henry Steele. "The Dilemma of Theodore Parker." New England Quarterly, 6 (June, 1933), 257-277.

567 _____. "Tempest in a Boston Tea Cup." New England Quarterly, 6 (December, 1933), 651-675.

568 _____. Theodore Parker: Yankee Reformer. Boston: Little, Brown, 1936. Emerson, passim.

569 CONGDON, Charles T. Reminiscences of a Journalist. Boston: Osgood, 1880. Emerson, pp. 33, 116.

570 CONKIN, Paul K. Puritans and Pragmatists: Eight Eminent American Thinkers. New York: Dodd, Mead, 1968.

571 CONNER, Frederick William. Cosmic Optimism: A Study of the Interpretation of Evolution by American Poets from Emerson to Robinson. Gainsville: University of Florida Press, 1949. "Emerson: The Beginnings," pp. 37-66. Contains an extensive bibliography on philosophy and science.

572 CONNOR, M. H. "Emerson's Interest in Contemporary Practical Affairs." English Journal, 38 (October, 1949), 428-432.

573 CONROY, Stephen S. "Emerson and Phrenology." American Quarterly, 16 (Summer, 1964), 215-217.

574 CONWAY, Adaline M. The Essay in American Literature. New York: New York University Press, 1914. (Ph.D. diss., New York University, 1914.) "Emerson as Essayist," pp. 63-68.

575 CONWAY, Moncure Daniel. Emerson at Home and Abroad. Boston: Osgood, 1882. Reprinted New York: Haskell House, 1968.

576 _____. "The Ministry of Emerson." Open Court, 17 (1903), 257-264.

577 _____. "Emerson, the Teacher and the Man." Critic, 42 (May, 1903), 404-411.

578 _____. "Emerson, Thoreau, and the Transcendentalists in 1864-1866." American Transcendental Quarterly, 16 (1972), 62-81. Reprint of 1904 article.

579 COOK, Reginald L. "Teaching Emerson at Middlebury." ESQ, 10 (1958), 6-7.

580 _____. "Emerson and Frost: A Parallel of Seers." New England Quarterly, 31 (June, 1958), 209-217.

581 _____, ed. Ralph Waldo Emerson: Selected Prose and Poetry. New York: Holt, Rinehart, & Winston, 1950, 1969. (Rinehart Edition.)

582 _____, ed. Themes, Tones, and Motifs in the American Renaissance: A Symposium. Hartford: Transcendental Books, 1968.

583 _____. "Emerson and the American Joke," in Cook, ed., Themes, Tones, and Motifs ... (1968), pp. 22-27.

584 _____. "Emerson and the Third America." American Transcendental Quarterly, 9 (1971), 7-11.

585 COOKE, George Willis. Ralph Waldo Emerson: His Life, Writings, and Philosophy. Boston: Osgood, 1881. Enlarged ed., Boston: Houghton, Mifflin, 1882.

586 _____. Unitarianism in America. Boston: American Unitarian Association, 1902. Emerson, passim.

587 _____. An Historical and Biographical Introduction to Accompany "The Dial." Reprinted in numbers for the Rowfant Club. 2 vols. Cleveland: Rowfant Club, 1902. Reprinted in American Transcendental Quarterly, 27 (1975), 1-122.

588 _____, ed. The Poets of Transcendentalism: An Anthology. Boston: Houghton, Mifflin, 1903.

Emerson, pp. 3-29. Reprinted Hartford: Transcendental Books, 1971. Also reprinted in American Transcendental Quarterly, 16 (1972), Pts. 3 and 4.

589 ———. "The Emerson Centennial." New England Magazine, 27 (May, 1903), 255-264.

590 ———. "Emerson and Transcendentalism." New England Magazine, 27 (May, 1903), 264-280.

591 ———. Bibliography of Emerson. Boston: Houghton, Mifflin, 1908.

592 CORNWELL, Charmles Landrum. "Emerson: The Organic Theory of Art." Ph.D. diss., University of Virginia, 1963.

593 CORY, A. M. "Humor in Emerson's Journals." University of Texas Studies in English, 34 (1955), 114-124.

594 COSMAN, Max. "Emerson's English Traits and the English." Mark Twain Quarterly, 8 (Summer-Fall, 1948), 7-9.

595 COWAN, Michael H. "Emerson's 'Give All to Love.'" Explicator, 18 (May, 1960), item 49.

596 ———. "Ralph Waldo Emerson and the City: A Case Study in the Urban Tradition in American Literature." Ph.D. diss., Yale, 1964.

597 ———. City of the West: Emerson, America, and the Urban Metaphor. New Haven, Conn.: Yale University Press, 1967.

598 ———. "The Many Structures of Emerson's Essays." Paper read at MLA, December 29, 1971. Abstract in Annual Report of the American Literature Section, January, 1972, p. 12.

599 ———. "The Loving Proteus: Metamorphosis in Emerson's Poetry," in Strauch, Carl, ed., Characteristics of Emerson: Transcendental Poet (1975), pp. 11-22.

600 COWAN, S. A. "In Praise of Self-Reliance: The Role

of Bulkington in Moby-Dick." American Literature, 38 (January, 1967), 547-556.

601 COWIE, Alexander. "Still a Good Light to Guide By." New York Times Book Review, September 1, 1963, pp. 1 and 16.

602 _____. "Emerson in an Existential Age." ESQ, 35 (1964), 92-94.

603 COWLEY, Malcolm. "Conrad Aiken: From Savannah to Emerson." Southern Review, 11 (April, 1975), 245-259.

604 COX, James M. "Ralph Waldo Emerson: The Circles of the Eye," in Levin, David, ed., Emerson: Prophecy, Metamorphosis, and Influence (English Institute Essays, 1975), pp. 57-81.

605 COX, James W. "Emerson and Hawthorne: Trust and Doubt." Virginia Quarterly Review, 45 (1969), 88-107.

606 COYLE, William. "Emerson and Luther." Hamma Digest, 54 (May, 1957), 16-19.

607 CRANCH, Christopher Pearse. The Bird and the Bell, with Other Poems. Boston: Osgood, 1875. Reprinted New York: Arno Press, 1976.

608 CRONIN, Morton. "Some Notes on Emerson's Prose Diction." American Speech, 29 (May, 1954), 105-113.

609 CRONKHITE, G. F. "The Transcendental Railroad." New England Quarterly, 24 (Summer, 1951), 306-328.

610 CROTHERS, Samuel McCord. Ralph Waldo Emerson: How to Know Him. Indianapolis: Bobbs-Merrill, 1921. Reprinted Port Washington, N. Y.: Kennikat Press, 1975.

611 CROW, Charles R., Jr. "The Rhythmic Organization of Ralph Waldo Emerson's Four-Stress Verse." Ph.D. diss., Pittsburgh, 1949.

612 CROWE, Charles. George Ripley: Transcendentalist and Utopian Socialist. Athens: University of Georgia Press, 1967. Emerson, passim.

613 CROZIER, J. B. "Emerson, Cicero, the Stoics, and Myself." Contemporary Review, 112 (September, 1917), 293-299.

614 _____. "Emerson as a Thinker and Man of Letters." Fortnightly Review, 116 (August, 1921), 229-242.

615 _____. "Key to Emerson." Fortnightly Review, 116 (September, 1921), 383-395.

616 CUMMINS, Roger W. "Three Unpublished Emerson Letters to Louise Prang and Whittier." American Literature, 43 (1971), 257-259.

617 CUNLIFFE, Marcus. The Literature of the United States. Penguin Books, 1954. Emerson, pp. 82-89 and passim.

618 CURRAN, J. W. "Emerson's Phi Beta Kappa Oration." American Book Collector, 6 (May, 1956), 10.

619 CURTI, Merle. "The Great Mr. Locke: 'America's' Philosopher, 1783-1861." Huntington Library Bulletin, 11 (1937), 107-155.

620 CURTIS, G. W. "Emerson Lecturing," in From the Easy Chair: First Series. New York: Harpers, 1893. Pp. 21-26.

621 CURTIUS, E. R. "Emerson," in Curtius, E. R., ed., Essays on European Literature, translated by Michael Kowal. Princeton, N. J.: Princeton University Press, 1973. Pp. 211-227.

622 CUSTARD, Harry Lewis, and Edith May. The Essence of Emerson: A Guide to the Unity of Life, Nature, and Knowledge. Arlington, Va.: Unity of Knowledge Press, 1955.

623 CUTLER, D. B. "An Unpublished Letter of Emerson." Yale University Library Gazeteer, 4 (July, 1929), 15-17.

624 DAHL, Curtis. "A Parallel to Emerson's 'Conscious Stone.'" ESQ, 19 (1960), 18-19.

625 DALL, Caroline, ed. Margaret Fuller and Her Friends: Ten Conversations in 1841 (Boston, 1895). Reprinted New York: Arno Press, 1976

626 DAMERON, J. Lasley. "Emerson and the Edinburgh Review of Coleridge's Statesman's Manual." ESQ, 8 (1957), 31.

627 DANA, William Franklin. The Optimism of Ralph Waldo Emerson. Boston: Cupples, Upham, 1886.

628 DANIEL, Stephen Lewis. "From Letter to Spirit: A Four-fold Hermeneutic and Its Application to Selected American Poems." Ph.D. diss., Emory University, 1973. DA, 35 (1974), 2935A-36A. Studies in Edward Taylor, Emerson, William Carlos Williams.

629 DARNELL, F. M. "Two Disciples of Transcendentalism: Emerson and Tennyson." Modern Language Notes, 29 (December, 1914), 239-242.

630 DARROW, F. S. "The Transcendental and Theosophy." New Outlook, 11 (March, 1958), 9-18.

631 DAS, S. P. "Emerson's Concept of Man." Literary Criterion (India), 8 (1967), 13-20.

632 DAUGHERTY, James, ed. and illus. Sound of Trumpets: Essays by Ralph Waldo Emerson. New York: Viking Press, 1976.

633 D'AVANZO, Mario L. "The Emersonian Context of Dickinson's 'The Reticent Volcano.'" American Transcendental Quarterly, 14 (1971), 11-13.

634 _____. "'Unto the White Creator': The Snow of Dickinson and Emerson." New England Quarterly, 45 (1972), 278-280.

635 _____. "Emersonian Revelation in 'The Way I Read a Letter's--This.'" American Transcendental Quarterly, 17 (1973), 14-15.

636 _____. "Seeing and Hearing in 'Each and All.'" ESQ, 73 (1973), 231-235.

637 DAVIDSON, Ellen C. "Emerson's Rhetorical Theories."
Ph. D. diss., University of Chicago, 1942.

638 DAVIDSON, Frank, ed. with Intro. Napoleon: or, The
Man of the World, by Ralph Waldo Emerson.
Bloomington: Indiana University, 1947. (Humanities
Series, no. 16.)

639 _____. "Emerson and the Double Consciousness."
Earlham Review, 3 (April, 1960), 1-15.

640 _____. "Notes for Emerson's Commemoration Day
Speech (1865)." ESQ, 22 (1961), 49-54.

641 _____. "'This Consciousness': Emerson and Emily
Dickinson." ESQ, 44 (1966), 2-7.

642 DAVIES, George R. "Emerson as a Social Philosopher."
University of North Dakota Quarterly Journal, 7
(July, 1917), 339-350.

643 DAVIS, Ada E. "Emerson's Thought on Education."
Education, 45 (February, 1925), 253-272.

644 DAVIS, Joe Lee. "Santayana as a Critic of Transcendentalism," in Simon, Myron, and Thornton H.
Parsons, eds., Transcendentalism and Its Legacy
(1966), pp. 150-184.

645 DAVIS, Merrell R. "Emerson's 'Reason' and the
Scottish Philosophers." New England Quarterly, 17
(June, 1944), 209-228.

646 DAVIS, N. C. "Emerson and Ohio: A New Emerson
Letter." Ohio State Archives and History Quarterly,
58 (January, 1949), 101-102.

647 DAVIS, R. B. "An Introduction to Emerson: Teaching
'Each and All.'" Exercise Exchange, 7 (February,
1960), 3-5.

648 DEATON, M. B. "Order and Organization in Emerson's
'Self-Reliance.'" Exercise Exchange, 3 (December,
1955), 4-5.

649 DEDMOND, F. B. "A New Note on Ralph Waldo
Emerson, Public Official." Notes & Queries, 195
(June, 1950), 278-279.

650 _____. "Emerson and the Concord Libraries." Boston Public Library Quarterly, 2 (October, 1951), 318-319.

651 _____. "A Further Note on Emerson's Interest in Concord Libraries." Notes & Queries, 197 (August, 1952), 367-368.

652 DEISS, Joseph J. "Men, Women, and Margaret Fuller." American Heritage, 23 (1972), 43-47, 94-97.

653 DE JONG, John A. "American Attitudes toward Evolution Before Darwin." Ph.D. diss., University of Iowa, 1962.

654 DE JONG, Mary Cynthia. "Structure in the Poetry of Ralph Waldo Emerson, Emily Dickinson, and Robert Frost." Ph.D. diss., University of Michigan, 1968. DA, 29 (1968), 867A.

655 DE MAJO, M. T. "La fortuna di Ralph Waldo Emerson in Italia." Studi Americani, 12 (1966), 45-87. In Italian.

656 DE MILLE, George E. Literary Criticism in America: A Preliminary Survey. New York: Russell & Russell, 1931. "Emerson and Margaret Fuller," pp. 118-132.

657 DE MOTT, Robert J., and Sanford E. Marovitz, eds. Artful Thunder: Versions of the Romantic Tradition in American Literature in Honor of Howard P. Vincent. Kent: Kent State University Press, 1975.

658 DENDINGER, Lloyd N. "Emerson's Influence on Frost Through Howells," in Tharpe, Jac, ed., Frost: Centennial Essays. Jackson: University Press of Mississippi, 1973. Pp. 265-274.

659 DENNIS, Carl Edward. "The Poetry of Mind and Nature: A Study of the Idea of Nature in American Transcendental Poetry." Ph.D. diss., University of California, Berkeley, 1966. DA, 27 (1967), 2496A.

660 _____. "Emerson's Poetry of Mind and Matter." ESQ, 58 (1970), 139-153.

661 _____. "Emerson's Poetics of Inspiration," in Strauch, Carl, ed., Characteristics of Emerson: Transcendental Poet (1975), pp. 22-28.

662 DENNY, Margaret, and William H. Gilman, eds. The American Writer and the European Tradition. Minneapolis: University of Minnesota Press, 1952. "Emerson," by Willard Thorp, pp. 90-105.

663 DENTON, Charles Richard. "American Unitarians, 1830-1865: A Study of Religious Opinion on War, Slavery, and the Union." Ph.D. diss., Michigan State University, 1969. DA, 30 (1970), 5373A-74A, History.

664 DERLETH, August. Emerson, Our Contemporary. London: Crowell-Collier Press, 1970. Juvenilia.

665 DETWEILER, Robert. "Emerson and Zen." American Quarterly, 14 (Fall, 1962), 422-438.

666 _____. "The Over-Rated Over-Soul." American Literature, 36 (March, 1964), 65-68.

667 _____. "Ralph Waldo Emerson's Concept of God." Ph.D. diss., University of Florida, 1962. DA, 29 (1968), 868A.

668 DEUTSCH, Leonard. "Ralph Waldo Ellison and Ralph Waldo Emerson: A Shared Moral Vision." College Language Association Journal, 16 (1972), 159-178.

669 DEWEY, John. "The Philosopher of Democracy." International Journal of Ethics, 13 (July, 1903), 405-413.

670 _____. "Ralph Waldo Emerson," in Characters and Events. New York: Henry Holt, 1929. Vol. I, pp. 69-77. Also in The Philosophy of John Dewey (1973 reprint), pp. 24-31.

671 _____. "Charles Sanders Peirce." The New Republic, 89 (February 3, 1937).

672 DE ZURKO, Robert. "Greenough's Theory of Beauty in Architecture." Rice Institute Pamphlet, 39 (October, 1952), 96-119.

673 DIGGINS, John P. "Thoreau, Marx, and the 'Riddle of Alienation.'" Social Research, 39 (Winter, 1972), 571-598.

674 DILLAWAY, Newton. Prophet of America: Emerson and the Problems of Today. Boston: Houghton, Mifflin, 1936.

675 ———. "Emerson's Remarkable Face." Christian Science Monitor, 38 (January 3, 1946), 8.

676 DI MAGGIO, Richard. "A Note on Sons and Lovers and Emerson's 'Experience.'" D. H. Lawrence Review, 6 (1973), 214-216.

677 DOHERTY, J. F. "Emerson and the Loneliness of the Gods." Texas Studies in Literature and Language, 16 (1974), 65-75.

678 DOUGHTY, Oswald. Dante Gabriel Rossetti. New Haven, Conn.: Yale University Press, 1949. Emerson, p. 450 and passim.

679 DOW, B. H. "A New Emphasis in American Thought." Catholic World, 145 (October, 1927), 65-71.

680 DOWNS, A. J. "The Legendary Visit of Emerson to Tallahassee." Florida Historical Quarterly, 34 (April, 1956), 334-338.

681 DOWNS, L. H. "Emerson and Dr. Channing: Two Men from Boston." New England Quarterly, 20 (December, 1947), 516-534. Derived from Ph.D. diss., University of Iowa, 1940.

682 DRESSER, H. W. "Emerson at College." Outlook, 94 (January 22, 1910), 146-149.

683 ———. "Emerson in the Making." Outlook, 96 (December 17, 1910), 852-854.

684 ———. "Emerson as Critic." New-Church Review, 21 (July, 1914), 338-341.

685 ———. "Emerson." Living Age, 292 (May 17, 1917), 674-679.

686 DRUMMOND, C. Q. "Nature: Meek Ass or White Whale." Sage (University of Wyoming), 1 (Spring, 1966), 71-84.

687 DUFFY, Charles. "Material Relating to Ralph Waldo Emerson in the Grimm Nachlass." American Literature, 30 (January, 1959), 523-528. Bibliography of the Grimm collection in University Library at Tübingen, Germany.

688 DUGANNE, Augustine J. H. Parnassus in Pillary: A Satire (1851). Reprint Port Washington, N. Y.: Kennikat Press, 1976.

689 DUGARD, Marie. Ralph Waldo Emerson: Sa vie et son oeuvre. Paris: Libraire Armand Colin, 1907. In French.

690 DUGGAN, Francis X. "Paul Elmer More and the New England Tradition." American Literature, 34 (January, 1963), 542-561.

691 DUHAMEL, P. Albert. "Humpty Dumpty, Li'l Abner, and Ralph Waldo Emerson." Delta Epsilon Sigma Bulletin (Alton, Ill.), 7 (1962), 39-44.

692 DUNCAN, Jeffrey L. "Power and Form: The Theme of Dualism in Ralph Waldo Emerson's Work." Ph.D. diss., University of Virginia, 1965.

693 _____. The Power and Form of Emerson's Thought. Charlottsville: University Press of Virginia, 1973. Review by John Lydenberg, American Literature, 47 (March, 1975).

694 DUSSINGER, Gloria R. "The Romantic Concept of the Self, Applied to the Works of Emerson, Whitman, Hawthorne, and Melville." Ph.D. diss., Lehigh University, 1973. DA, 34 (1974), 5963A.

695 DUTTON, J. F. "Emerson's Optimism." Unitarian Review, 35 (1891), 127.

696 DYKEMA, K. W. "Why Did Lydia Jackson Become Lidian Emerson?" American Speech, 17 (December, 1942), 285-286.

697 EARLE, P. G. "Emerson and Unamuno: Notes on a Congeniality." Symposium, 10 (Fall, 1956), 189-203.

698 EATON, Richard J. "Thoreau's Herbarium." Man and Nature (December, 1972), 2-5.

699 EATON, Wyatt. "Pencil Sketch of Ralph Waldo Emerson in July, 1878." ESQ, 31 (1963), 80.

700 EBERHART, Richard. "Emerson and Wallace Stevens." Literary Review, 7 (August, 1963), 51-71.

701 EDEL, Leon. "Walden: The Myth and the Mystery." The American Scholar, 44 (Spring, 1975), 272-281. Contains remarks on Emerson.

702 EDGELEY, W. Todd. "Philosophical Ideas at Harvard College, 1817-1837." New England Quarterly, 16 (March, 1943), 64.

703 EDGELL, David P. "A Note on Channing's Transcendentalism." New England Quarterly, 22 (September, 1949), 394-397.

704 ———. "A Note on a Transcendental Friendship." New England Quarterly, 24 (December, 1951), 528-532. Emerson and E. Channing.

705 EDMAN, Irwin. "Anniversary Speech." New Republic, February 15, 1943.

706 ———, ed. Essays: First and Second Series (Complete). New York: Thomas Y. Crowell, 1976. (Apollo edition.)

707 EDMUNDS, A. J. "Emerson's Misquotation from Boehme." Notes & Queries, 175 (July 23, 1938), 63.

708 EDRICH, Mary W. "Ralph Waldo Emerson's Apostasy." Ph.D. diss., Wisconsin, 1965. DA, 25 (1965), 7242-43.

709 ———. "The Rhetoric of Apostasy." Texas Studies in Literature and Language, 8 (1967), 547-560.

710 EIDSON, John Olin. Tennyson in America: His Reputation and Influence from 1827-1858. Athens: University of Georgia Press, 1943. Emerson, passim.

711 _____. Charles Stearns Wheeler: Friend of Emerson. Athens: University of Georgia Press, 1951.

712 _____. "Charles Stearns Wheeler: Emerson's 'Good Grecian.'" New England Quarterly, 27 (December, 1954), 472-483.

713 _____. "Two Unpublished Letters of Emerson." American Literature, 21 (November, 1949), 335-338.

714 EISINGER, Chadwick E. "Ralph Waldo Emerson's Nature--Gospel of Transcendentalism," in Hendrick, George, ed., American Renaissance (1961), pp. 39-51.

715 EKHTIAR, Mansur A. "Ralph Waldo Emerson's Poetic Language: A Linguistic and Literary Investigation." Ph. D. diss., Indiana, 1960.

716 ELIOT, Charles W., ed. Essays and English Traits. New York: P. F. Collier, 1909. (Harvard Classics, vol. V.)

717 _____. "Emerson as Seer." Atlantic Monthly, 91 (1903), 844.

718 _____. Four American Leaders. Boston: American Unitarian Association, 1906. "Emerson," pp. 73-126.

719 ELIOT, T. S. "Tradition and the Individual Talent" (1919), in Selected Prose by T. S. Eliot, ed. Frank Kermode. New York: Farrar, Straus & Giroux, 1975. Pp. 37-45. Contains remarks on Emerson.

720 ELLIOTT, George Roy. "Some Remarks on Emerson's 'Grace' and 'Self-Reliance.'" New England Quarterly, 2 (January, 1929), 93-104. Also in Humanism and Imagination (Chapel Hill: University of North Carolina Press, 1938), pp. 148-168.

721 _____. "Emerson as Diarist." University of

Toronto Quarterly, 6 (April, 1937), 299-308.

722 ELLIS, C. R. "John Jay Chapman and Emersonian Individualism." Studies on the Left, 2 (November 3, 1962), 35-42.

723 ELLIS, Charles Mayo. An Essay on Transcendentalism (1842). Reprinted, Walter Harding, ed., Gainsville: University of Florida Press, 1954.

724 EMANUEL, J. A. "Emersonian Virtue: A Definition." American Speech, 36 (May, 1961), 117-132.

725 EMERSON, B. K. The Ipswitch Emersons. Boston: Houghton, Mifflin, 1900.

726 EMERSON, Edward W. Emerson in Concord. Boston: Houghton, Mifflin, 1889.

727 _____. "Ralph Waldo Emerson." Bookman, 24 (June, 1903), 92-96.

728 _____. "Emerson and Scholars." Harvard Graduate Magazine, 14 (March, 1906), 383-391.

729 _____. "Sketch of Ralph Waldo Emerson," in Early Years of the Saturday Club, 1855-1870. Boston: Houghton, Mifflin, 1918. Pp. 53-62.

730 _____, ed. A Correspondence Between John Sterling and Ralph Waldo Emerson. Boston: Houghton, Mifflin, 1897. Reprinted Port Washington, N. Y.: Kennikat Press, 1975.

731 _____, ed. Complete Works of Ralph Waldo Emerson, 12 vols. with Notes and Index. Boston: Houghton, Mifflin, 1903-04. Reprinted New York: AMS Press, 1968.

732 _____, and Waldo Emerson Forbes, eds. The Journals of Ralph Waldo Emerson, 10 vols. Boston: Houghton, Mifflin, 1909-1914.

733 EMERSON, Ralph Waldo, ed. Parnassas: A Book of Poems. Boston: Osgood, 1874. Reprinted Haverton, Pa.: Richard West, 1976.

734 _____. "Address at the Concord Centennial" (April 19, 1875). Reprinted ESQ, 13 (1958), 85-87.

735 _____. "Three Letters from Ralph Waldo Emerson." Proceedings of the Massachusetts Historical Society, 60 (December, 1926), 83-85.

736 _____, William Henry Channing, and James Freeman Clarke, eds. Memoirs of Margaret Fuller Ossoli. Boston: Osgood, 1852.

737 EMERSON, William [father of Ralph Waldo]. "Letter to Rebecca Emerson, 1793." Printed in ESQ, 12 (1958), 47.

738 _____. "Sermon on the Death of Mr. Charles Austin." Printed in American Transcendental Quarterly, 13 (1972), 91-97.

739 EMLEY, Edward. "Emerson's Literary Criticisms as Seen in His Journals and Letters." Ph.D. diss., New York University, 1948.

740 ENGEL, Mary M. I Remember the Emersons. Los Angeles: Times-Mirror Publisher, 1941.

741 ENGLEKIRK, J. E. "Notes on Emerson in Latin America." PMLA, 74 (June, 1961), 227-232.

742 ERSKINE, John. "Emerson's 'The American Scholar.'" The American Scholar, 1 (Winter, 1932), 5-15.

743 EULERT, D. D. "Matter and Method: Emerson and the Way of Zen." East-West Review (Japan), 3 (Winter, 1966-1967), 48-65.

744 EVANS, T. C. "Early English Criticism of Emerson." Lamp, 26 (July, 1903), 470-473.

745 EVERETT, Charles Carroll. The Poems of Emerson. Boston: Houghton, Mifflin, 1887. Pamphlet reprinted from Andover Review, 7 (March, 1887), 229-248.

746 EVERSON, J. G. "William J. Stillman: Emerson's 'Gallant Artist.'" New England Quarterly, 31 (March, 1958), 32-46.

747 FAIRBANKS, Henry G. "From Theocracy to Transcendentalism in America." ESQ, 44 (1966), 45-59.

748 FALK, Robert P. "Emerson and Shakespeare." PMLA, 56 (March, 1941), 532-543.

749 _____, ed. Literature and Ideas in America: Essays in Memory of Harry Haydn Clark. Columbus: Ohio University Press, 1975. "A New Look at Emerson and Science," by Gay Wilson Allen, pp. 58-78.

750 FAUST, Clarence. "The Background of the Unitarian Opposition to Transcendentalism." Modern Philology, 35 (February, 1938), 297-324.

751 FEIDELSON, Charles N., Jr. "The Idea of Symbolism in American Writing, with Particular Reference to Ralph Waldo Emerson and Herman Melville." Ph.D. diss., Yale, 1948.

752 _____. Symbolism and American Literature. Chicago: University of Chicago Press, 1953.

753 _____. "Toward Melville: Some Versions of Emerson," in Symbolism and American Literature (1953). Reprinted in Konvitz and Whicher, eds., Emerson: A Collection (1962), pp. 136-157.

754 FELTENSTEIN, Rosalie. "Mary Moody Emerson: The Gadfly of Concord." American Quarterly, 5 (Fall, 1953), 231-246.

755 FELTON, C. C. "A Review of Essays: First Series" (1841) in Rountree, Thomas J., ed., Critics on Emerson (1973). Reprinted in part, pp. 28-31.

756 FERGUSON, Alfred R. The Merrill Checklist of Ralph Waldo Emerson. Columbus, Ohio: Charles E. Merrill, 1970. 44 pp.

757 _____, and Robert Spiller, eds. Collected Works of Ralph Waldo Emerson. Cambridge, Mass.: Harvard University Press, 1972. Vol. I, Nature, Addresses, & Lectures. (CEAA edition.)

758 FERGUSON, John D. American Literature in Spain. New York: Columbia University Press, 1916. Emerson, pp. 157-170; bibliography, pp. 213-215.

759 FEUER, Lewis S. "James Marsh and the Conservative Transcendental Philosophy: A Political Interpretation." New England Quarterly, 31 (March, 1958), 3-31.

760 ———. "Ralph Waldo Emerson's Reference to Karl Marx." New England Quarterly, 33 (Summer, 1960), 378-379.

761 FIECHTER, F. C., Jr. "The Preparation of an American Aristocrat." New England Quarterly, 6 (March, 1933), 3-28.

762 FIEDLER, Leslie. Waiting for the End. New York: Stein & Day, 1944. Emerson, pp. 196-215. Influence on Frost and Robinson.

763 FIELDS, Annie. "Mr. Emerson in the Lecture Room." Atlantic Monthly, 51 (June, 1883), 818-832.

764 FINNIGAN, David F. "The Man Himself: Emerson's Prose Style." ESQ, 39 (1965), 13-15.

765 FIRKINS, Oscar W. Ralph Waldo Emerson. Boston: Houghton, Mifflin, 1914, 1915. Early study of Emerson's thought.

766 ———. "Has Emerson a Future?" in Selected Essays. Minneapolis: University of Minnesota Press, 1933. Pp. 79-93.

767 FISH, H. M. "Five Emerson Letters." American Literature, 27 (March, 1955), 25-30.

768 ———. "The Influence of Thomas Carlyle upon Ralph Waldo Emerson." Ph.D. diss., Edinburgh, 1957-1958.

769 FISHER, Marvin. "The Iconology of Industrialism, 1830-1860." American Quarterly, 13 (Fall, 1961), 347-364.

770 FISHER, Mary. A General Survey of American

Literature. Chicago: McClurg, 1899. "Emerson, pp. 143-175.

771 FITCH, George H. "Emerson, the Literary Pioneer," in Great Spiritual Writers of America. San Francisco: P. Elder, 1916. Pp. 3-11.

772 FLANAGAN, John T. "Ralph Waldo Emerson and the State." Ph.D. diss., Minnesota University, 1934.

773 _____. "Emerson as a Critic of Fiction." Philological Quarterly, 15 (January, 1936), 30-45.

774 _____. "Emerson and Communism." New England Quarterly, 10 (June, 1937), 243-261.

775 FLETCHER, Edward G. "Emerson's 'Days.'" Explicator, 5 (April, 1947), no. 41.

776 FLETCHER, Richard M. "Emerson's Nature and Goethe's Faust." American Notes & Queries, 12 (1974), 102.

777 FLEWELLING, R. T. "Emerson and the Middle Border." Personalist, 16 (September, 1935), 295-309.

778 _____. "Emerson and Adolescent America." Personalist, 20 (October, 1939), 343-352.

779 FLOWER, B. O. "The Poet as a Philosopher." Arena, 39 (March, 1908), 323-331.

780 FLUGEL, F. "Pages from an Autograph Collection." University of California Chronicle, 28 (October, 1926), 351-353.

781 FOERSTER, Norman. "Emerson as a Poet of Nature." PMLA, 37 (September, 1922), 599-614.

782 _____. Nature in American Literature. New York: Russell & Russell, 1923, 1958. Emerson, pp. 37-68.

783 _____. "Emerson on the Organic Principle of Art." PMLA, 41 (March, 1926), 193-208.

784 _____. American Criticism: A Study in Literary Theory from Poe to the Present. Boston: Houghton, Mifflin, 1928. Emerson, pp. 52-110.

785 _____, ed. American Prose and Poetry, 4th ed. 2 vols. Boston: Houghton, Mifflin, 1962. Emerson, vol. I, pp. 439-531.

786 _____. American Prose and Poetry, 5th ed. Boston: Houghton, Mifflin, 1970. Emerson, pp. 400-474.

787 _____, and Robert P. Falk, eds. Eight American Writers. New York: W. W. Norton, 1963. "Emerson," by Stephen E. Whicher, pp. 173-408.

788 FORD, G. S. "The American Scholar Today." School and Society, 40 (November 17, 1934), 641-651.

789 FORD, Nick Aaron. "Henry David Thoreau: Abolitionist." New England Quarterly, 19 (September, 1946), 359-371.

790 FORD, Worthington C. "Mr. Emerson Was Present." Proceedings of the Massachusetts Historical Society, 62 (1930), 130-138.

791 FORSYTHE, Robert S. "Emerson and Moby-Dick." Notes & Queries, 177 (December 23, 1939), 457-458.

792 FOSTER, Charles H. "Ralph Waldo Emerson's Theory of Poetry." Ph. D. diss., University of Iowa, 1939. Published as Emerson's Theory of Poetry. Iowa City: Iowa University Press, 1939.

793 _____. "Emerson as American Scripture." New England Quarterly, 16 (March, 1943), 91-105.

794 FOSTER, Edward. The Civilized Wilderness. New York & London: Macmillan, 1975. Contains remarks on Emerson, pp. 118-123 and passim, on the idealization of the middle class.

795 FOSTER, Elizabeth, ed. The Confidence Man by Herman Melville. New York: Hendricks House, 1954. Emerson, pp. lxxiii, and 351-354.

796 FOSTER, Grace R. "The Natural History of the Will." American Scholar, 15 (Summer, 1946), 277-287.

797 FOSTER, Henry J. "Emerson's Poetry." Primitive Methodist Quarterly, 21 (April, 1899), 293-304.

798 FOY, Rena L. W. "The Philosophy of Ralph Waldo Emerson and Its Educational Implications." Ph. D. diss., University of Texas, 1962. Education.

799 FRANCIS, Richard Lee. "Archangel in the Pleached Garden: Emerson's Poetry." English Literary History, 33 (December, 1966), 461-472.

800 _____. "The Architectonics of Emerson's Nature." American Quarterly, 19 (Spring, 1967), 39-52.

801 _____. "Circumstances and Salvation: The Ideology of the Fruitlands Utopia." American Quarterly, 25 (1973), 202-234.

802 _____. "The Evolution of Emerson's Second 'Nature.'" American Transcendental Quarterly, 21 (1974), 33-35.

803 FRANKE, Kuno. German Ideals of Today. Boston: Houghton, Mifflin, 1907. "Emerson and the German Personality," pp. 93-126.

804 FREE, W. J. "E. A. Robinson's Use of Emerson." American Literature, 38 (March, 1966), 69-84.

805 FREEDMAN, Florence. "Emerson Giving Joy: Summer of 1855." Walt Whitman Review, 21 (1975), 162-163.

806 FRENCH, Daniel C. "From a Scholar's Workshop." Independent, 74 (February 13, 1913), 366-368.

807 _____. "A Sculptor's Reminiscences of Emerson." Art World, 1 (October, 1916), 44-47.

808 FRENIERE, E. A. "Emerson and [Theodore] Parker Letters in the Jackson Papers." ESQ, 22 (1961), 46-48.

809 FRIDEN, Georg. "Transcendental Idealism in New

England." Neuphilologische Mitteilungen (Finland), 69 (1968), 256-271. In English.

810 FRIEDRICH, Gerhard G. "The Idea of Internationalism in Ralph Waldo Emerson." Ph.D. diss., University of Minnesota, 1952.

811 _____. "Emerson's 'Brahma.'" American-Germanic Review, 19 (Fall, 1953), 29.

812 _____. "A Note on Emerson's Parnassus." New England Quarterly, 27 (Spring, 1954), 397-399.

813 FROMM, Harold. "Emerson and Kierkegaard: The Problem of Historical Christianity." Massachusetts Review, 9 (1968), 741-752.

814 FROST, Robert. "A Masque of Reason" (1945), in The Complete Poems of Robert Frost. New York: Henry Holt, 1959. Pp. 587-606. Comment on Emerson's "Uriel": "the greatest Western poem yet."

815 _____. "A Poet, Too, Must Learn the Magic Way to Poetry." New York Times, March 21, 1954, p. 1. Comments on "Brahma."

816 _____. "On Emerson." Daedalus, 88 (Fall, 1959), 712-718.

817 FROTHINGHAM, Octavius Brooks. Transcendentalism in New England. New York: Putnam's Sons, 1876. Reprinted New York: Harper's, 1959.

818 FRYE, Prosser H. Literary Reviews and Criticisms. New York & London: Putnam's Sons, 1908. "Emerson and the Modern Reports," pp. 291-312.

819 FULLER, Margaret (Ossoli). "Review of Emerson's Essays: Second Series." New York Daily Tribune, December 7, 1844. Reprinted in Konvitz, Recognition (1972), pp. 20-25.

820 _____. Memoirs of Margaret Fuller Ossoli, ed. Ralph Waldo Emerson, W. H. Channing, and James Freeman Clarke. Boston: Osgood, 1852.

821 _____. Woman in the Nineteenth Century, ed. Arthur B. Fuller. Boston: Jewett, 1855. Reprinted, with new Intro. by Bernard Rosenthal, New York: W. W. Norton, 1971.

822 _____. At Home and Abroad, ed. Arthur B. Fuller (Boston, 1856). Reprinted Port Washington, N. Y.: Kennikat Press, 1976.

823 _____. "Modern British Poets," in Art, Literature, and the Drama, ed. Arthur B. Fuller. Boston: Brown, Laggard, & Chasi, 1860.

824 _____. Love Letters of Margaret Fuller, 1845-1846 (New York, 1903). Reprinted Port Washington, N. Y.: Kennikat Press, 1975.

825 FURNESS, Horace H., ed. Records of a Lifelong Friendship, 1807-1882: Letters of Ralph Waldo Emerson and William Henry Furness. Boston: Houghton, Mifflin, 1910.

826 GABRIEL, Ralph H. The Course of American Democratic Thought. New York: Ronald Press, 1940. "Emerson and Thoreau," pp. 39-51.

827 GAGNON, Ray. "Thoreau: Some Negative Considerations." Thoreau Society Bulletin, 121 (1972), 5-7. Contains remarks on Emerson.

828 GALE, Robert. Barron's Simplified Approach to Ralph Waldo Emerson and Transcendentalism. Woodberry, N. Y.: Barron's, 1966.

829 GARDELLA, Raymond. "In Emerson, Consciousness Is King." ESQ, 50 Supplement (1968), 5-9.

830 _____. "The Tenets and Limitations of Emerson's All-Conscious Man." American Benedictine Review, 21 (1970), 375-388.

831 GARDINER, Harold C., S. J., ed. American Classics Reconsidered: A Christian Appraisal. New York: Scribner's, 1958. "The Era of the Half-Gods in

American Literature," pp. 1-14. Also contains "Ralph Waldo Emerson, 1803-1882: The Single Vision," by Robert S. Pollock, pp. 15-58.

832 GARMON, Gerald M. "Emerson's 'Moral Sentiment,' and Poe's 'Poetic Sentiment.'" Poe Studies, 6 (1973), 19-21.

833 GARNETT, Richard. Life of Emerson. London: Scott Publishers, 1888. (Great Writers Series.)

834 _____. "The Secret of Emerson." Living Age, 231 (November 16, 1901), 455-458. Also in Literature, 9 (September 21, 1901), 274-276.

835 GARRISON, Joseph Marion, Jr. "John Burroughs as a Literary Critic: A Study Emphasizing His Treatment of Emerson, Whitman, Thoreau, Carlyle, and Arnold." Ph.D. diss., Duke University Press, 1962. DA, 23 (1963), 3372-3373.

836 GARROD, H. W. "Emerson." New England Quarterly, 3 (January, 1930), 1-24.

837 _____. Poetry and the Criticism of Life. London: Oxford University Press, 1931. Emerson, pp. 85-107.

838 GASKINS, A. F. "The Concept of Correspondence in the Works of Wallace Stevens and Ralph Waldo Emerson." West Virginia University Philological Papers, 15 (1966), 62-69.

839 GASS, S. B. "Emerson and the Forgotten Man." Outlook, 150 (September 5, 1928), 729-731.

840 GAVIN, William. "Chaadayev and Emerson: Two Mystic Pragmatists." Russian Review, 32 (April, 1973), 119-130.

841 GAY, Robert M. Emerson: A Study of the Poet as Seer. New York: Doubleday, 1928.

842 GAYATONDE, S. N. "The Oriental Outlook of Emerson's Philosophy." The Ayran Path, 38 (March, 1967), 109-113.

843 GELPI, Albert J. Emily Dickinson: The Mind of the Poet. Cambridge, Mass.: Harvard University Press, 1965. Emerson, pp. 60-62 and passim.

844 _____. The Tenth Muse: The Psyche of the American Poet. Cambridge, Mass.: Harvard University Press, 1975. Emerson, pp. 57-111.

845 _____. "Emerson: The Paradox of Organic Form," in Levin, David, ed., Emerson: Prophecy, Metamorphosis, and Influence (1975), pp. 149-170. Shorter form of item 844.

846 GELPI, Donald Louis, S. J. "Emerson's Philosophy of Religious Experience," Ph.D. diss., Fordham University, 1970. Philosophy. DA, 31 (1971), 5461A.

847 GERBER, John C. Emerson's Economics. Chicago: University of Chicago Press, 1941. Derived from "Ralph Waldo Emerson's Economics." Ph.D. diss., University of Chicago, 1941.

848 _____. "Emerson and the Political Economists." New England Quarterly, 22 (September, 1949), 336-357.

849 GERSTER, Patrick G. "Aesthetic Individualism: Key to the Alienation of the American Intellectual. Studies in Ralph Waldo Emerson, Henry David Thoreau, and Walt Whitman." Ph.D. diss., University of Minnesota, 1970. History. DA, 31 (1971), 4673A.

850 GESELBRACHT, Raymond H. "The Ghosts of Andrew Wyeth: The Meaning of Death in the Transcendentalist Myth of America." New England Quarterly, 47 (1974), 13-29.

851 GIBSON, William M., and George Arms, eds. Twelve American Writers. New York: Macmillan, 1962. Emerson, pp. 1-78.

852 GILES, E. "A Study of Emerson's Essay on Education." Journal of Education, 68 (June 25, 1908), 28.

853 GILMAN, Albert, and Roger Brown. "Personality and

Style in Concord," in Simon and Parsons, eds., Transcendentalism and Its Legacy (1966), pp. 87-122.

854 GILMAN, Margaret. "Baudelaire and Emerson." Romanic Review, 24 (October, 1943), 211-222. In English.

855 GILMAN, William, et al., eds. Journals and Miscellaneous Notebooks of Ralph Waldo Emerson, 12 vols. Cambridge, Mass.: Harvard University Press, 1960-1976. Work in progress on a proposed 16 volumes.

856 _____. "How Should Journals Be Edited?" Early American Literature, 6 (1971), 73-83. On editing Emerson's Journals and Miscellaneous Notebooks.

857 _____, ed. Selected Writings of Ralph Waldo Emerson. Signet Classic, 1976.

858 GILMORE, A. G. "Was Emerson a Poet?" Christian Science Monitor, May 26, 1937, p. 6.

859 GIRGUS, Sam. "The Scholar as Prophet: Brownson vs. Emerson and the Modern Need for Moral Humanism." Midwest Quarterly, 17 (1975), 88-99.

860 GITTLEMAN, Edwin. Jones Very: The Effective Years, 1833-1840. New York: Columbia University Press, 1967. Emerson, pp. 162-167, 232-252 and passim.

861 GLICK, Wendell. "The Moral and Ethical Dimensions of Emerson's Aesthetic." ESQ, 55 (1969), 13-14.

862 _____. "Thoreau Rejects an Emerson Text." Studies in Bibliography (Virginia University Bibliographical Society), 25 (1972), 213-216.

863 GLICKSBERG, C. J. "Bryant on Emerson the Lecturer." New England Quarterly, 12 (September, 1939), 530-534.

864 GLICKSBERG, Charles I. "The Lost Self in Modern Literature." Personalist, 43 (Autumn, 1962), 527-538.

865 GODDARD, Harold Clarke. Studies in New England Transcendentalism. New York: Columbia University Press, 1908. Reprinted New York: Hillary House, 1960. Derived from "Studies in New England Transcendentalism." Ph.D. diss., Columbia University, 1908. Emerson, pp. 63-81 and passim.

866 _____. "Transcendentalism," in Trent, William P., et al., eds., The Cambridge History of American Literature (1917, 1944), vol. I, pp. 326-348.

866a _____, ed. Essays: First and Second Series. New York: Macmillan, 1926.

867 _____. Alphabet on the Imagination. Atlantic Highlands, N.J.: Humanities Press, 1974. Previously unpublished essays. Emerson, pp. 131-135, 209-224 (Expansion of Introduction to Essays), and passim. [Goddard died in 1950.]

868 GOGGIO, Emilio. "Emerson's Interest in Italy." Italica, 17 (September, 1940), 97-103.

869 GOHDES, Clarence F. "Whitman and Emerson." Sewanee Review, 37 (January-March, 1926), 79-93.

870 _____. "Some Remarks on Emerson's 'Divinity School Address.'" American Literature, 1 (March, 1929), 27-31.

871 _____. The Periodicals of American Transcendentalism. Durham, N.C.: Duke University Press, 1931.

872 _____. "A Gossip on Emerson's Treatment of Beauty." Open Court, 45 (May, 1931), 315-320.

873 _____, ed. Uncollected Lectures of Ralph Waldo Emerson. New York: W.E. Rudge, 1932.

874 _____. "Emerson's English Audience." Christian Science Monitor, November 6, 1944, p. 7.

875 _____. American Literature in Nineteenth Century England. Carbondale: Southern Illinois University Press, 1944. Emerson, pp. 132-134, 142-145.

876 _____. Bibliography Guide to Study of Literature in the United States, 3d ed. Durham, N. C.: Duke University Press, 1970.

877 GONNAUD, Maurice. "Emerson's 'Days' in French." ESQ, 14 (1959), 16-17. In French with headnote in English.

878 _____. Individu et société dans l'oeuvre de Ralph Waldo Emerson. Paris: Didier, 1964. Derived from 500-page Ph.D. diss., Sorbonne, Paris, 1964.

879 _____. "Le Message d'Emerson." Les Langues Modernes, 60 (May-June, 1966), 265-271.

880 _____. "The Humane Seer: Humor and Its Avatars in Emerson." American Transcendental Quarterly, 22 (1974), 79-85.

881 _____. "Emerson and the Imperial Self: A European Critique," in Levin, David, ed., Emerson: Prophecy, Metamorphosis, and Influence (1975), pp. 107-128.

882 GOODMAN, Paul. "Note on a Remark of Seami." Kenyon Review, 20 (August, 1958), 547-553. Discusses "The Concord Hymn" as an occasional poem.

883 GOODNIGHT, S. "Emerson's Opinion of Goethe." German-American Annals, 1 (May, 1903), 243-256.

884 _____. "German Literature in American Magazines Prior to 1846." Bulletin of the University of Wisconsin Philology and Literature Series, no. 4, 1908.

885 GORDON, G. A. "Emerson as a Religious Influence." Atlantic, 91 (May, 1903), 577-587.

886 GORDON, Jan B. "Emerson's 'The Snow Storm' and an 1835 Journal." ESQ, 47 (1967), 42-48.

887 GORDON, John D. "Ralph Waldo Emerson, 1803-1882: Catalogue of an Exhibition from the Berg Collection." Bulletin of the New York Public Library, 57 (August/September, 1953), 392-408, 433-460.

888 GORELY, Jean. "Emerson's Theory of Poetry." Poetry Review, 22 (July-August, 1931), 263-273.

889 _____. "Emerson Takes the Road." Christian Science Monitor, August 22, 1944, p. 6. A walking tour of 1823.

890 GOREN, Leyla. "Elements of Brahmanism in the Transcendentalism of Emerson." ESQ, 34 (Supplement, 1964). Reprint of a book published in Germany in 1959.

891 GOSSE, Edmund C. "Has America Produced a Poet?" Forum, 6 (October, 1888), 176-186.

892 GOSTWICK, Joseph. Handbook of American Literature (1856). Reprinted Port Washington, N. Y.: Kennikat Press, 1976.

893 GOUGEON, Leonard G. "The Forgotten God: A Study of Ralph Waldo Emerson as Man and Myth." Ph.D. diss., Massachusetts University, 1973. DA, 35 (1974), 2940A-2941A.

894 GRAY, Henry David. Emerson: A Statement of New England Transcendentalism as Expressed in the Philosophy of Its Chief Exponent. Palo Alto, Calif.: University of Stanford Press, 1917. Reprinted New York: Frederick Ungar, 1958. Based on his same title. Ph.D. diss., Columbia University, 1904.

895 GRAY, Leonard B. "Emerson and Thoreau." Unity (January-February, 1952), 88-92.

896 _____. "Emerson." ESQ, 13 (1958), 88-92. Poem about Emerson.

897 GREENBERGER, Evelyn Barish. "The Phoenix on the Wall: Consciousness in Emerson's Early and Late Journals." American Transcendental Quarterly, 21 (1974), 45-46. Also in Neufeldt, Leonard N., ed., Ralph Waldo Emerson: New Appraisals (1974), pp. 45-56.

898 GREENLEAF, Richard. "Emerson and Wordsworth." Science and Society, 22 (Summer, 1958), 218-230. Comments on poem "Brahma."

899 GREENOUGH, C. N., ed. Emerson's Works. 5 vols.

New York: Hearst's International Library Co., 1914.

900 GREGG, Edith W., ed. One First Love: Letters of Ellen Tucker Emerson to Ralph Waldo Emerson. Cambridge, Mass.: Harvard University Press, 1962. Letters of Emerson to Ellen seem to have been lost.

901 GRIERSON, Francis. "Emerson and Unitarianism," in The Celtic Temperament and Other Essays. London and New York: John Lane, 1913. Pp. 85-89.

902 GRIFFIN, William J. "Thoreau's Reaction to Horatio Greenough." New England Quarterly, 30 (December, 1957), 508-512.

903 GRIFFITH, Clark. "'Emersonianism' and 'Poeism': Some Versions of the Romantic Sensibility." Modern Language Quarterly, 22 (June, 1961), 125-134.

904 ———. "Caves and Cave Dwellers: The Study of a Romantic Image." Journal of English and Germanic Philology, 62 (1963), 551-568.

905 ———. "Robert Frost and American Nature." American Quarterly, 20 (1968), 21-37.

906 GRISWOLD, Rufus Wilmot. The Prose Writers of America with a Survey of the History, Condition, and Prospects of American Literature. Philadelphia: Carey and Hart, 1847.

907 GRONEWALD, B. F. "Emerson at Middletown in Connecticut." ESQ, 11 (1958), 55-56.

908 GROSS, John J. "Religion and Community in the American Renaissance." ESQ, 44 (1966), 59-64.

909 GROSS, Seymour L. "Emerson and Poetry." South Atlantic Quarterly, 54 (January, 1955), 82-94. Contains comment on "Each and All," and "The Rhodora."

910 GROSS, Theodore L. "Under the Shadow of Our Swords: Emerson and the Heroic Ideal." Bucknell

Review, 17 (1969), 22-34. Also in Gross, Theodore, The Heroic Ideal in American Literature (Riverside, New Jersey: Free Press, 1971). Emerson one of five figures.

911 GROVER, E. O. "Why Not Professors of Books? A Selling Tip from Ralph Waldo Emerson." Publishers' Weekly, November 30, 1929, pp. 2591-2593.

912 GRUNDY, Ernest. "Ralph Waldo Emerson and Scottish Common-Sense Philosophy." Ph.D. diss., University of Denver, n. d.

913 GUERARD, Albert. "Prometheus and the Aeolian Lyre." Yale Review, 33 (March, 1944), 482-497.

914 GUERNSEY, Alfred Hudson. Ralph Waldo Emerson: Philosopher and Poet. New York: Appleton, 1881.

915 GWYNN, Frederick, Ralph W. Condee, and Arthur O. Lewis, Jr., eds. The Case for Poetry. Englewood Cliffs, N. J.: Prentice-Hall, 1954. Emerson, pp. 138-140.

916 HADLEY, Arthur I. "Parnassus." Yale Literary Magazine, 75 (March, 1910), 329.

917 HAGBOLT, Peter. "Emerson's Goethe." Open Court, 46 (April, 1932), 234-244.

918 HAIG, R. L. "Emerson and William Hunter's Museum." New England Quarterly, 26 (June, 1953), 255-257.

919 _____. "Emerson and the 'Electric Word' of John Hunter." New England Quarterly, 28 (Spring, 1955), 394-397.

920 HALE, E. E. "Some Emerson Memories." Outlook, 66 (December 29, 1900), 1045-1046.

921 HALL, Arethusa. Life and Character of the Rev. Sylvester Judd (1854). Reprinted Port Washington, N. Y.: Kennikat Press, 1975. Only novelist associated with the Transcendentalist movement.

922 HALL, Bolton. "Emerson the Anarchist." Arena, 37 (April, 1907), 400-404.

923 HALLECK, Reuben C. A History of American Literature. New York: American Book Co., 1911. Emerson, pp. 178-193.

924 HANSEN, Arlen Jay. "Emerson's Poetry of Thought." Ph. D. diss., University of Iowa, 1969. DA, 30 (1970), 3944A.

925 _____. "Emerson and Porphyry's Life of Plotinus." ESQ, 18 (1972), 184-185.

926 HANSEN, Chadwick C. "Ralph Waldo Emerson's Nature: Gospel of Transcendentalism," in Hendrick George, ed., American Renaissance: The History and Literature of an Era (1961), pp. 39-61.

927 HARDING, Walter. "More Uncollected Emerson Letters." ESQ, 13 (1958), 34-36.

928 _____. Emerson's Library. Charlottsville: University Press of Virginia, 1967.

929 _____, ed. "Reminiscences of Augusta Bowers French." Thoreau Society Bulletin, 130 (1975), 5-7.

930 _____, ed. "Concord by A. Monroe." Thoreau Society Bulletin, 133 (1975), 1-3.

931 HARDY, Evelyn. "Emerson's Name." Times Literary Supplement, 1 (April, 1965), 255.

932 HARNETT, Louise Katherine. "Emerson and the Bhagavad Gita." The Ariel, 7 (May, 1903), 15-23.

933 HARONTUNIAN, Joseph. Piety Versus Moralism: The Passing of New England Theology (New York, 1932). Reprinted Gloucester, Mass.: Peter Smith Publishers, c. 1965. "The Unitarian Revolt," pp. 177-219.

934 HARRIS, R. T. "Nature: Emerson and Mill." Western Humanities Review, 6 (Winter, 1951-1952), 1-13.

935 HARRIS, William Torrey. "Ralph Waldo Emerson." Atlantic 50 (August, 1882), 238-252.

936 _____. "The Dialectic Unity in Emerson's Prose." Journal of Speculative Philosophy, 18 (1884), 195-202.

937 _____. "Emerson's Philosophy of Nature," in Sanborn, Franklin B., ed., The Genius and Character of Emerson (1885), pp. 339-362.

938 _____. "Emerson's 'Brahma' and the Bhagavad Gita." Poet Lore, 1 (June, 1889), 253-259.

939 HARRISON, John S. The Teachers of Emerson. New York: Sturgis & Walton, 1910.

940 HART, Beatrice. Seven Great American Poets. Boston: Silver, Burdett, 1901. Emerson, pp. 51-82.

941 HARTER, Carol Clancey. "Emerson's Rhetorical Failure in 'Love.'" ESQ, 69 (1972), 227-233.

942 HARTWIG, G. H. "Emerson on Historical Christianity." Hibbert Journal, 37 (April, 1939), 405-412.

943 _____. "An Immortal Friendship." Hibbert Journal, 38 (October, 1939), 102-114. Carlyle and Emerson.

944 HASKINS, David Greene. Ralph Waldo Emerson: His Maternal Ancestors with Some Reminiscences of Him. Boston: Cupples, Upham, 1887. Reprinted Port Washington, N. Y.: Kennikat Press, 1970. Also printed in American Transcendental Quarterly, 15 (1972), Part III.

945 HASTINGS, A. Louise. "Emerson in Cincinnati." New England Quarterly, 11 (September, 1938), 443-469.

946 _____. "Emerson's Journal at the West, 1850-1853: or Emerson's First Trip to the Mississippi Valley." Ph.D. diss., Indiana University, 1942.

947 _____. "Transcendentalism and the 'Almanacks' of Mary Moody Emerson." ESQ, 6 (1957), 9.

948 HAVILAND, T. P. "Two Emerson Letters." American Literature, 23 (March, 1951), 127-128.

949 HAWORTH, Helen E. "Emerson's Keats." Harvard Library Bulletin, 19 (1971), 61-70.

950 HAY, Stephen H. "Rabindranath Tagore in America." American Quarterly, 14 (Fall, 1962), 439-463. Emerson, Thoreau, Whitman: modern interest in India.

951 HAZARD, Lucy L. "Emerson's Reputation in Hawaii." English Journal, 8 (February, 1919), 101-104.

952 _____. The Frontier in American Literature. New York: Crowell, 1927. Reprinted New York: Frederick Ungar, 1967. Emerson, passim.

953 HEATON, Katherine May. "Emerson and Puritanism." Ph.D. diss., University of Iowa, 1940.

954 HECKER, Isaac T. "Two Prophets of This Age." Catholic World, 47 (1888), 684-693. Emerson and Arnold.

955 HEDGE, Frederic Henry. "Emerson, the Philosopher and Poet." Literary World, 11 (May 22, 1880), 176.

956 _____. "Memorial Address on Emerson," in Allen, J. H., ed., Our Liberal Movement in Theology. Boston: Roberts Publishers, 1882. Pp. 211-218.

957 HEDGES, William L. "A Short Way Around Emerson's Nature." Transactions of the Wisconsin Academy of Sciences, Arts, and Letters, 44 (1956), 21-27.

958 _____. "From Franklin to Emerson," in Lemay, J. A. Leo, ed., The Oldest Revolutionary: Essays on Benjamin Franklin in Memory of Theodore Hornberger. Philadelphia: University of Pennsylvania Press, 1976. Pp. 139-156.

959 HEITMAN, P. "How Europe Looked to Emerson." Current Literature, 51 (July, 1911), 100-101.

960 _____. "Emerson in the High School." English

Journal, 7 (March, 1918), 203-206.

961 HELMICK, E. T. "Emerson's 'Uriel' as Poetic Theory." American Transcendental Quarterly, 1 (1969), 35-38.

962 HENDRICK, George. "Emerson and Gandhi." ESQ, 2 (1956), 6-7.

963 _____. "The Influence of Thoreau's 'Civil Disobedience' on Gandhi's Satyagraha." New England Quarterly, 29 (December, 1956), 462-471.

964 _____. "Tolstoy's Quotations from Emerson in the Cycle of Reading." ESQ, 8 (1957), 29-31.

965 _____. "Influence of Thoreau and Emerson on Gandhi's Satyagraha." Gandhi Marg., 3 (July, 1959), 165-178.

966 _____, ed. American Renaissance: The History and Literature of an Era. Berlin: Diesterweg, 1961. In English; a collection of critical essays.

967 _____. "William Sloane Kennedy Looks to Emerson and Thoreau." ESQ, 26 (1962), 28-31.

968 HENNELLY, Mark. "Ishmael's Nightmare and the American Eve." American Imago, 30 (Fall, 1973), 274-293.

969 HENNESSEY, Helen. "The Dial: Its Poetry and Poetic Criticism." New England Quarterly, 31 (1958), 66-87.

970 HENNEY, Thomas G. "The Craft of Genius: A Study of Ralph Waldo Emerson's Poetic Development, 1823-1846." Ph.D. diss., Princeton, 1946.

971 HENRY, Myrtle. "Independence and Freedom as Expressed and Interpreted by Ralph Waldo Emerson." Negro History Bulletin, 6 (May, 1943), 173-174.

972 HERAUD, John A. "A Response from America." Monthly Magazine, 2 (September, 1839), 344-352. Reprinted in part in Sealts and Ferguson, eds., Emerson's Nature (1969), pp. 99-101.

973 HERNANDEZ, F. "Emerson's 'Days.'" Explicator, 33 (Fall, 1975), item 44.

974 HERNDON, Jerry A. "St. Paul and Emerson's 'Self-Reliance.'" American Transcendental Quarterly, 1 (1969), 90.

975 HERTZ, R. N. "Victory and the Consciousness of Battle: Emerson and Carlyle." Personalist, 45 (January, 1964), 60-71.

976 HICKS, Granville, ed. "Letters to William Francis Channing." American Literature, 2 (November, 1930), 294-298.

977 _____. "A Conversation in Boston." Sewanee Review, 39 (April-June, 1931), 129-141.

978 _____. "Emerson as Letter Writer." Virginia Quarterly Review, 15 (1939), 643. Review of Ralph Rusk, ed., Letters of Ralph Waldo Emerson (1939), 6 vols.

979 HIGGINSON, Thomas Wentworth. "Ralph Waldo Emerson," in Contemporaries. Boston: Houghton, Mifflin, 1899. Pp. 1-22.

980 _____, ed. "Walks with Ellery Channing." Atlantic, 90 (July, 1902), 27-34. Extracts from manuscript journals of Emerson.

981 _____. "The Personality of Emerson." Outlook, 74 (May 23, 1903), 221-227.

982 HIGHET, Gilbert. The Powers of Poetry. New York: Oxford University Press, 1960. "Emerson, the Aloof American," pp. 98-105.

983 HILL, David Whitten. "Emerson's Search for the Universal Symbol." Ph.D. diss., Indiana University, 1971. DA, 32 (1971), 2689A.

984 HILL, J. Arthur. Emerson and His Philosophy. London: W. Rider & Son, 1919.

985 HILLBRUNER, Anthony. "Emerson: Democratic Egalitarian." Central States Speech Journal, 10 (Winter, 1959), 25-30.

986 HILLESHEIM, James W., and George D. Merrill, eds. Theory and Practice in History of American Education. Pacific Palisades, Calif.: Goodyear, 1971. Emerson, pp. 191-193.

987 HOAR, Jay S. "A Study of Emerson's English Traits." Northern New England Review, 1 (1973), 48-57.

988 HOAR, Victor. "Emerson's 'The Young American.'" Canadian Association of American Studies, 3 (Spring-Summer, 1967), 3-18.

989 HOCH, David G. "'History' as Art: 'Art' as History." ESQ, 69 (1972), 288-293.

990 HOCHFIELD, George, ed. Selected Writings of the American Transcendentalists. New York: New American Library, 1966. (Signet Classic.)

991 HODGES, Robert. "Public Sentiment and Poetic Diction." Vis-a-Vis, 3 (1975), 15-19. On "Concord Hymn."

992 HOELTJE, Hubert H. "Ralph Waldo Emerson in Iowa." Iowa Journal of History and Politics, 25 (April, 1927), 236-276.

993 ———. "Emerson in Minnesota." Minnesota History, 2 (June, 1930), 145-159.

994 ———. "Emerson's Venture in Western Land." American Literature, 2 (January, 1931), 438-440.

995 ———. "Ralph Waldo Emerson in Virginia." Ph.D. diss., Iowa University, 1932.

996 ———. "Emerson in Virginia." New England Quarterly, 5 (October, 1932), 753-768. Address of 1876.

997 ———. "Emerson, Citizen of Concord." American Literature, 11 (January, 1940), 367-378.

998 ———. Sheltering Tree: The Friendship of Emerson and Alcott. Durham, N.C.: Duke University Press, 1943. Reprinted Port Washington, N.Y.: Kennikat Press, 1972.

999 HOEVELER, James Kimball. "The Endless Cycle: Visual Perception and Literary Expression in the Writings of Henry David Thoreau." Ph.D. diss., University of Pittsburgh, 1974. DA, 35 (1974), 2270A.

1000 HOFFMAN, Frederick J. The Twenties. New York: Viking Press, 1955. "Emerson, Whitman, and the Silhouette of Sweeney," pp. 123-131.

1001 HOFFMAN, Michael J. "The Anti-Transcendentalism of Moby-Dick." Georgia Review, 23 (1969), 3-16. Reprinted in The Subversive Vision (1972), pp. 87-100.

1002 _____. The Subversive Vision: American Romanticism in Literature. Port Washington, N.Y.: Kennikat Press, 1972. Emerson, as given and passim.

1003 _____. "From Analogism to Transcendentalism: Emerson's Nature and the Struggle for Symmetry," in The Subversive Vision (1972), pp. 30-46.

1004 _____. "From Analogism to Transcendentalism: Thoreau, the Individual versus the Institution," in The Subversive Vision (1972), pp. 46-58.

1005 HOGAN, Marjorie. "The Philosophy of Ralph Waldo Emerson." Scholastic, 1 (May 19, 1947), 50-51.

1006 HOLLIS, C. C. "A New England Outpost, as Revealed in Some Unpublished Letters of Emerson, Parker, and Alcott to Ainsworth Spafford." New England Quarterly, 38 (1965), 65-85.

1007 HOLLOWAY, John. The Victorian Sage: Studies in Argument. New York: Macmillan, 1953. Reprinted Hamden, Conn.: Archon Books, 1962. "Carlyle," pp. 21-85.

1008 HOLLS, F. W., ed. Correspondence between Ralph Waldo Emerson and Herman Grimm. Anonymous in The Atlantic, 1903, and in book form. Reprinted Port Washington, N.Y.: Kennikat Press, 1971.

1009 HOLMAN, C. Hugh. "Hemingway and Emerson: Notes

on the Continuity of an Aesthetic Tradition." Modern Fiction Studies, 1 (August, 1955), 12-16.

1010 HOLMES, Eugene D., ed. with Notes and Intro. Selected Essays and Addresses. New York: Macmillan, 1908.

1011 HOLMES, Oliver Wendell. Ralph Waldo Emerson. Boston: Houghton, Mifflin, 1885. (American Men of Letters series.)

1012 HOPKINS, Vivian C. "The Aesthetic Theory of Ralph Waldo Emerson." Ph.D. diss., Michigan, 1943.

1013 _____. "The Influence of Goethe on Emerson's Aesthetic Theory." Philological Quarterly, 27 (October, 1948), 325-344.

1014 _____. Spires of Form: A Study of Emerson's Aesthetic Theory. Cambridge, Mass.: Harvard University Press, 1951.

1015 _____. "Emerson and Cudworth, Plastic Nature and Transcendental Art." American Literature, 23 (March, 1951), 80-89.

1016 _____. "Emerson and Bacon." American Literature, 29 (January, 1958), 408-430.

1017 _____. "Two Unpublished Emerson Letters." New England Quarterly, 33 (December, 1960), 502-506.

1018 _____. "Emerson and the World of Dreams." American Transcendental Quarterly, 9 (1971), 56-69. Also in Carlson, Eric W., and J. Lasley Dameron, eds., Emerson's Relevance Today: A Symposium (1971), pp. 56-69.

1019 HORNOR, L. A. "Emerson, Poet or Philosopher?" Mind, 12 (August, 1903), 327-331.

1020 HORTON, Rod W., and Herbert W. Edwards. Backgrounds of American Literary Thought, 2d ed. New York: Appleton-Century-Crofts, 1967. "Unitarianism and Transcendentalism," pp. 108-121.

1021 HOTSON, Clarence P. "A Background for Emerson's

Poem 'Grace.'" New England Quarterly, 1 (April, 1928), 124-132. Also in The New-Church Magazine, 47 (1928), 219-225.

1022 _____. "Emerson's Philosophical Sources for 'Swedenborg,'" New Philosophy, 21 (1928), 482-516.

1023 _____. "Ralph Waldo Emerson and Swedenborg." Ph.D. diss., Harvard, 1929.

1024 _____. "Emerson's Biographical Sources for 'Swedenborg.'" Studies in Philology, 26 (January, 1929), 23-36.

1025 _____. "Emerson and the Doctrine of Correspondence." New-Church Review, 36 (January, April, July, and October, 1929), 47-59, 173-186; 304-316, 435-448. Four articles.

1026 _____. "Sampson Reed, a Teacher of Emerson." New England Quarterly, 2 (April, 1929), 249-277.

1027 _____. "Emerson's Title for Swedenborg." New-Church Life, 44 (July, 1929), 390-398.

1028 _____. "Emerson and the 'New-Church Quarterly Review.'" New-Church Magazine, 48 (July-September, October-December, 1929), 169-183, 239-253.

1029 _____. "Early Influence of Swedenborg in Europe." New-Church Review, 37 (January, 1930), 16-34.

1030 _____. "Swedenborg's Influence in America to 1830." New-Church Review, 37 (April, 1930), 188-207.

1031 _____. "Emerson and the Swedenborgians." Studies in Philology, 27 (July, 1930), 517-545.

1032 _____. "Emerson and Swedenborg." New-Church Messenger, 160 (September, 1930), 274-277.

1033 _____. "Corrections as to Emerson's Sources for 'Swedenborg.'" New Philosophy, 34 (January, 1931), 309.

1034 _____. "George Bush and Emerson's 'Swedenborg.'" The New-Church Magazine, 50 (January-March, April-June, 1931), 22-34, 98-108.

1035 _____. "George Bush: Teacher and Critic of Emerson." Philological Quarterly, 10 (October, 1931), 369-383.

1036 _____. "Emerson, Swedenborg, and B. F. Barret." New-Church Magazine, 50 (October-December, 1931), 244-252; also 51 (January-March, 1932), 33-43.

1037 _____. "Review of 'The Periodicals of American Transcendentalism,' by Clarence Gohdes." New-Church Review, 39 (January, 1932), 111-115.

1038 _____. "Emerson's Sources for 'Swedenborg.'" New-Church Messenger, 162 (February, 1932), 89-94.

1039 _____. "Emerson's Boston Lecture on Swedenborg." New-Church Magazine, 51 (April-June, 1932), 91-101.

1040 _____. "Professor Bush's Reply to Emerson on Swedenborg." New-Church Magazine, 51 (July-September, October-December, 1932), 175-184, 213-223.

1041 _____. "Emerson's Manchester Lecture on Swedenborg." New-Church Magazine, 52 (January-March, 1933), 48-58.

1042 _____. "A Salford Reply to Emerson's Manchester Lecture on Swedenborg." New-Church Magazine, 52 (July-September, October-November, 1933), 174-185, 232-243.

1043 _____. "Coleridge's 'Hamlet' and Emerson's 'Swedenborg.'" New-Church Magazine, 53 (1934), 99-112.

1044 _____. "The Christian Critics and Mr. Emerson." New England Quarterly, 11 (March, 1938), 29-47.

1045 HOURIHAN, Paul. "The Inner Dynamics of the Emerson-Thoreau Relationship." Ph.D. diss., Boston University Graduate School, 1967. DA, 28 (1967), 1787A-1788A.

1046 _____. "Ambiguities in the Emerson Sage-Image: The Facts of His Novel Reading." Humanities Association Bulletin, 22 (1971), 44-55.

1047 HOWARD, Besse D. "The First French Estimate of Emerson." New England Quarterly, 10 (September, 1937), 447-463. See also item 17.

1048 HOWARD, Leon, et al., eds. American Heritage. 2 vols. New York: D. C. Heath, 1955. Emerson, vol. I, pp. 610-679.

1049 _____. Literature and the American Tradition. New York: Doubleday, 1960. Emerson, pp. 136-155.

1050 HOWE, Daniel Walker. The Unitarian Conscience: Harvard Moral Philosophy, 1805-1861. Cambridge, Mass.: Harvard University Press, 1970. Emerson, passim.

1051 HOWE, Julia Ward. Margaret Fuller (Boston, 1883). Reprinted New York: Greenwood Press, 1975. Emerson, passim.

1052 _____. "Emerson's Relation to Society," in Sanborn, ed., Genius and Character of Emerson (1885), pp. 286-309.

1052a _____. "Emerson as I Knew Him." Critic, 42 (May, 1903), 411-413.

1053 HOWE, M. A. DeWolf. "Did Anything Happen to Emerson's Memory?" Saturday Review of Literature, 31 (January 2, 1942), 5-6.

1054 HOWELLS, William Dean. Literary Friends and Acquaintances (1900), ed. David F. Hiatt and Edwin H. Cady. Bloomington: Indiana University Press, 1968. Emerson, pp. 55-60 and passim.

1055 _____. "Impressions of Emerson." Harper's Weekly, 47 (May 16, 1903), 784.

1056 HUBACH, R. R. "Emerson's Lectures in Springfield, Illinois, in January, 1853." American Notes & Queries, 6 (February, 1947), 164-167.

1057 HUBBELL, George S. A Concordance to the Poems of Ralph Waldo Emerson. New York: H. W. Wilson, 1932. Based on Collected Works, vol. IX, Edward W. Emerson, ed., 1903.

1058 HUBBELL, Jay B. The South in American Literature: 1607-1900. Durham, N. C.: Duke University Press, 1954. Emerson, pp. 375-385.

1059 _____. Who Are the Major American Writers? Durham, N. C.: Duke University Press, 1972. Emerson, pp. 35-47 and passim.

1060 HUBNER, Charles William. "Emerson the Poet." Book-Lover, 14 (May-June, 1903), 107-108.

1061 HUDSON, H. R. "Concord Books." Harper's Magazine, 51 (June, 1875), 18-32. Reprinted in American Transcendental Quarterly, 16 (1972), 29-43.

1062 HUDSON, J. W. "The Religion of Emerson." Sewanee Review, 28 (April, 1920), 203-212.

1063 HUDSPETH, Robert N. "A Perennial Springtime: Channing's Friendship with Emerson and Thoreau," in Cook, Reginald, ed., Themes, Tones, and Motifs in the American Renaissance (1968), 30-36.

1064 HUGGARD, W. A. "Ralph Waldo Emerson and the Problem of War and Peace." University of Iowa Humanities Studies, no. 5 (1958), I-76. Derived from Ph.D. diss., University of Iowa, 1937.

1065 _____. "Emerson's Philosophy of War and Peace." Philological Quarterly, 22 (October, 1943), 370-375.

1066 _____. "Emerson's Glimpse of the Divine." Personalist, 36 (Spring, 1955), 167-176.

1067 HUGHES, James. "The Dialectic of Death in Poe, Dickinson, Emerson, Whitman." Ph.D. diss., University of Pennsylvania, 1969. DA, 31 (1970), 1280A.

1068 HUMMEL, Hermann. "Emerson and Nietzsche." New England Quarterly, 19 (March, 1946), 63-84.

1069 HUNTER, Doreen. "America's First Romantics: Richard Henry Dana, Sr., and Washington Allston." New England Quarterly, 45 (1972), 3-30.

1070 HURD, Charles, ed. A Treasury of Great American Speeches. New York: Hawthorn Books, 1959. Emerson, pp. 106-108.

1071 HUTCH, R. A. "Ralph Waldo Emerson: The Birth of a Seer," in Reynolds, F. E., and D. Capps, eds., The Biographical Process. The Hague: Mouton, 1976. Pp. 187-200.

1072 HUTCHISON, William R. The Transcendental Ministers: Church Reform in the New England Renaissance. New Haven, Conn.: Yale University Press, 1959. "Ripley, Emerson, and the Miracles Question," pp. 64-82. Reprinted in Barbour, ed., American Transcendentalism (1973), pp. 179-209.

1073 HUTH, Hans. Nature and the Americans: Three Centuries of Changing Attitudes. Berkeley: University of California Press, 1957. Emerson, pp. 87-100. Reprinted Lincoln: University of Nebraska Press, 1972.

1074 HYDER, Clyde K. "Emerson on Swinburne: A Sensational Interview." Modern Language Notes, 48 (March, 1933), 180-182.

1075 IGLESIAS, Antonio. "An Open Letter to Emerson." Saturday Review, 36 (August 15, 1953), 21, 35-36.

1076 IHRIG, Mary Alice. "Emerson's Transcendental Vocabulary: An Expositional Analysis and Concordance to Seven-Word Clusters in His Prose, Volumes I and II." Ph.D. diss., University of North Carolina, 1972. DA, 34 (1973), 2565A.

1077 ILLUMINATA, Sister Mary. "Emerson's Poetics." ESQ, 14 (1959), 13-16.

1078 Index to Early American Periodical Literature, 1728-1870. New York: New York University Press, 1942. "Ralph Waldo Emerson," no. 4, 40 pages, bibliography.

1079 IRELAND, Alexander. Ralph Waldo Emerson: His Life, Genius, and Writings. London: Simpkin, Marshall, 1882. Reprinted Port Washington, N. Y.: Kennikat Press, 1972.

1080 IRELAND, Robert Emerson. "The Concept of Providence in the Thought of W. E. Channing, Ralph Waldo Emerson, Theodore Parker, and Orestes A. Brownson: Study in Mid-Nineteenth Century American Intellectual History." Ph.D. diss., University of Maine, 1971. DA, 34 (1972), 703A.

1081 IRIE, Yukio. "Emerson as a Monist." American Literary Review, 24 (March, 1958), 1-9.

1082 _____. "Emerson's 'Days' in Japanese." ESQ, 11 (1958), 48-49.

1083 _____. "Why the Japanese People Find a Kinship with Emerson and Thoreau." ESQ, 27 (1962), 63-82.

1084 _____. "Emerson and Quakerism." Studies in English Literature (Tokyo), English number (1963), 63-82.

1085 _____. Emerson and Quakerism. Tokyo: Kenkyusha, 1967.

1086 IRVINE, Leigh H. "Poe and Emerson." The Coming Age, 3 (February, 1900), 172-174.

1087 IRWIN, John T. "The Symbol of the Hieroglyphics in the American Renaissance." American Quarterly, 26 (1974), 103-126.

1088 IVES, Charles. Essays Before a Sonata. New York: Knickerbocker Press, 1920. Reprinted New York: W. W. Norton, 1961. Emerson, pp. 11-45.

1089 JACKSON, Holbrook. Dreamers of Dreams: The

Rise and Fall of Nineteenth Century Idealism. London: Faber & Faber, 1948. Emerson, pp. 169-210.

1090 JACKSON, Paul R. "Henry Miller, Emerson, and the Divided Self." American Literature, 43 (1971), 231-241.

1091 JACKSON, S. L., translator. "A Soviet View of Emerson." New England Quarterly, 19 (June, 1946), 236-243.

1092 JAFFE, Adrian H. "An Earlier French Estimate of Emerson." New England Quarterly, 26 (March, 1953), 100-102.

1093 _____. "Emerson and Sartre: Two Parallel Theories of Responsibility." Comparative Literature Studies, 1 (1964), 113-117.

1094 JAMES, Henry, Sr. The Literary Remains of the Late Henry James, Sr., ed. William James. Boston: Osgood Publishers, 1885. Emerson, pp. 293-302.

1095 JAMES, Henry, Jr. Partial Portraits. London & New York: Macmillan, 1888, 1905. Emerson, pp. 1-33.

1096 JAMES, William. Memories and Studies. New York: Longmans, Green, 1911. "Address at the Emerson Centenary in Concord," pp. 19-34.

1097 JAMIESON, P. F. "Emerson's Transcendental Mountain." Appalachia, 31 (1957), 313-319.

1098 _____. "A Note on Emerson's 'Adirondacks.'" New England Quarterly, 31 (March, 1958), 88-90.

1099 _____. "Emerson in the Adirondacks." New York History, 39 (July, 1958), 215-237.

1100 JANTZ, Harold S. "German Thought and Literature in New England, 1620-1820." Journal of English and Germanic Philology, 41 (1942), 1-45.

1101 JENSON, Sid. "The Compassionate Seer: Wallace Stegner's Literary Artist." Brigham Young University Studies, 14 (Winter, 1974), 248-262.

1102 JOHNSON, Charles Frederick. Three Americans and Three Englishmen. New York: Whittaker, 1886. Emerson, pp. 174-212.

1103 _____. Outline History of English and American Literature. New York: American Book Co., 1900. Emerson, pp. 490-498. Comments on "The Concord Hymn," "The Problem," and "The Rhodora."

1104 JOHNSON, Ellwood. "Emerson's Psychology of Power." Rendevous, 5 (1969), 13-25.

1105 JOHNSON, Gerald W. "Emerson's Scholar: A New Chapter of His Biography." Key Reporter, 23 (July, 1958), 2-3.

1106 JOHNSON, Jane. "Whitman's Changing Attitude Toward Emerson." PMLA, 73 (September, 1958), 452.

1107 JOHNSTON, Kenneth G. "The Organic Tradition in Industrial America: A Study of Ralph Waldo Emerson and Frank Lloyd Wright." Ph.D. diss., University of Minnesota.

1108 JONES, Howard Mumford. The Iron String. Cambridge, Mass.: Harvard University Press, 1950.

1109 _____. Emerson Once More: The Ware Lecture. Boston: Beacon Press, 1953.

1110 _____, ed. with Intro. Emerson's English Traits. Cambridge, Mass.: Harvard University Press, 1966

1111 _____, ed. Emerson on Education: Seven Essays. New York: Teachers College Press, 1966.

1112 _____. Belief and Disbelief in American Literature. Chicago: University of Chicago Press, 1967. "Transcendentalism and Emerson," pp. 48-69.

1113 _____, Ernest E. Leisy, and Richard M. Ludwig, eds. Major American Writers, 3d ed. New York:

Harcourt, Brace, 1952. Emerson, pp. 372-484.

1114 JONES, Joseph. "Emerson's 'Days.'" Explicator, 4 (April, 1946), item 47.

1115 _____. "Emerson and Bergson on the Comic." Comparative Literature, 1 (Winter, 1949), 63-72.

1116 _____. "Emerson and Whitman 'Down Under': Their Reception in Australia and New Zealand." ESQ, 42 (1966), 35-46.

1117 JONES, William C. "Walt Whitman, The New England Transcendentalists, and the Mexican War." Ph.D. diss., University of Minnesota, 1971.

1118 JORDON, C. B. "At Emerson's Grave." Outlook, 74 (May 2, 1903), 30.

1119 JORDON, Leah E. "The Fundamentals of Ralph Waldo Emerson's Literary Criticism." Ph.D. diss., University of Pennsylvania, 1945. Published in 37-page summary, Philadelphia: University of Pennsylvania Press, 1945.

1120 JORGENSON, Chester E. "Emerson's 'Paradise Under the Shadow of Swords.'" Philological Quarterly, 11 (July, 1932), 274-292.

1121 JOYAUX, Georges J. "Victor Cousin and American Transcendentalism." French Review, 29 (1958), 117-130. Reprinted in Barbour, ed., American Transcendentalism (1973), pp. 125-138.

1122 JUGARU, Bunshō. A Bibliography of Ralph Waldo Emerson in Japan from 1878 to 1935. Kyoto: Sunward Press, 1947. 1-xx, 1-70 pages. Review in American Literature, May, 1949. Reprinted in ESQ, 46 (1967), 53-89.

1123 JYOTI, D. D. "'Mystical' and 'Transcendental' Elements in Some Modern English and American Writers in Relation to Indian Thought: Ralph Waldo Emerson, H. D. Thoreau, E. M. Forster, T. S. Eliot, and Aldous Huxley." Ph.D. diss., London, 1956-1957.

1124 KAISER, Leo M. "On Some Latin Quotations in Emerson." American Transcendental Quarterly, 13 (1972), 37.

1125 KAIYALA, Marguerite La Voy. "The Poetic Development of Theodore Roethke in Relation to the Emersonian-Thoreauvian Tradition of Nature." Ph.D. diss., University of Washington, 1970. DA, 31 (1971), 3507A-3508A.

1126 KAMEI, Shunsuke. "Emerson, Whitman, and the Japanese in the Meiji Era: 1868-1912." ESQ, 29 (1962), 28-62.

1127 KAPLAN, Harold. Democratic Humanism and American Literature. Chicago & London: University of Chicago Press, 1972. "Emerson, 'The Double Consciousness,'" pp. 49-78.

1128 KARLSTETTER, Klaus. "J. D. Salinger, Ralph Waldo Emerson, and the Perennial Philosophy." Moderna Språk, 63 (1969), 224-236. In English.

1129 KASDIN, Simon. Introduction to Prophetic Judaism. Parsippany, N. J.: Thunder Mountain Books, 1954.

1130 KASEGARA, Koh. "Emerson, Thoreau, Melville." Aoyama Journal of General Education, 5 (November, 1964), 15-24.

1131 KAZIN, Alfred. "Dry Light and Hard Expressions." Atlantic, 200 (July 1, 1957), 74-76.

1132 _____ and Daniel Aaron, eds. Emerson: A Modern Anthology. Boston: Little, Brown, 1959.

1133 KEARNS, F. E. "Emerson and the American Catholic Scholar." ESQ, 39 (1965), 63-68.

1134 KEATING, Jerome Francis. "Personal Identity in Jonathan Edwards, Ralph Waldo Emerson, and Alfred N. Whitehead." Ph.D. diss., Syracuse University, 1971. DA, 33 (1972), 5682A.

1135 KELLER, J. C. Literature and Religion. Rindge, New Hampshire: Richard R. Smith, 1956. Chapter on Emerson and Hawthorne.

1136 KELLER, Karl. "From Christianity to Transcendentalism: A Note on Emerson's Use of Conceit." American Literature, 39 (1967), 94-98.

1137 _____. "'The World Slickt up in Types': Edward Taylor as a Version of Emerson." Early American Literature, 5 (1970), 124-140.

1138 _____. "Emerson and the Anti-Imperialist Self." American Transcendental Quarterly, 18 (1973), 23-29.

1139 KENNEDY, Steele M. "Ralph Waldo Emerson's 'The American Scholar,' and Other Harvard Phi Beta Kappa Orations." Ph.D. diss., New York University, 1956.

1140 KENNEDY, William Sloane. "An Emerson Concordance: Being a Partial Index to Familiar Passages in His Poems." Literary World, 13 (July 15, 1882), 137-141.

1141 _____. "The Discarded Poems of Emerson." Literary World, 13 (October 7, 1882).

1142 _____. "Emerson's 'Brahma.'" Boston Evening Transcript, August 6, 1886.

1143 _____. "'Sartor,' 'Brahma,' and 'The Forest Hymn.'" Critic, 9 (February 4, 1888), 57-58.

1144 _____. "The Friendship of Whitman and Emerson." Poet-Lore, 7 (February, 1895), 71-74.

1145 _____. "Clews to Emerson's Mystic Verse." Poet-Lore, 11 (April-June, 1899), 243-250; 12 (January-March, April-June, 1900), 71-79, 270-283. Also in The American Author, June, 1903, pp. 194-230. Reprinted in Strauch, Carl, ed., Characteristics of Emerson: Transcendental Poet (1975), Appendix, pp. 2-20.

1146 KENT, C. W. "Emerson's Last Lecture." Book-Lover, May-June, 1903, pp. 103-104.

1147 KERN, Alexander C. "Emerson and Economics." New England Quarterly, 13 (December, 1940), 678-696.

1148 _____. "The Dark Side of Emerson's Optimism." ESQ, 10 (1958), 7-8.

1149 KERNAHAN, Coulson. "Is Emerson a Poet?" National Review, 36 (December, 1900), 523-536.

1150 _____. Wise Men and a Fool. London: Ward, Lock, 1901. "Emerson: A Poet Who Was Not a Poet," pp. 225-264.

1151 KEYES, Charlotte E. The Experimentor: A Biography of Ralph Waldo Emerson. New Haven, Conn.: College and University Press, 1962. For teenagers.

1152 KIM, Suk-Joo. "A Comparative Study of Emerson and Carlyle." The English Language and Literature (published by the English Literature Society of Korea), 11 (September, 1961), 66-75.

1153 KIMBALL, L. E. "Miss [Delia] Bacon Advances Learning." Colophon, 2 (Summer, 1937), 338-354.

1154 KING, D. R. "Emerson's 'Divinity School Address' and Sylvestor Judd's Margaret." ESQ, 47 (1967), 3-7.

1155 KINGSLEY, M. E. "Outline Study of Emerson's Essays." Education, 41 (October, 1920), 95-109.

1156 KINNE, E. W. "Hoosier Reactions to Emerson." Essex Institute of Historical Collections, 91 (January, 1955), 1-8.

1157 KINZIE, Mary. "Preface for Americans." Tri-Quarterly, 25 (1973), 5-8.

1158 KIRK, Russell. "Two Facets of the New England Mind: Emerson and Brownson." Month, 8 (October, 1952), 208-217.

1159 KLAMMER, Enno. "The Spiral Staircase in 'Self-Reliance.'" ESQ, 47 (1967), 81-83.

1160 KLEINFIELD, H. L. "The Structure of Emerson's Death." Bulletin of New York Public Library, 65 (January, 1961), 47-64.

1161 KLOECKNER, Albert J. "The Moral Sentiment: A Study of Ralph Waldo Emerson's Terminology." Ph. D. diss., Indiana, 1956.

1162 _____. "Intellect and Moral Sentiment in Emerson's Opinions of 'The Meaner Kinds' of Men." American Literature, 30 (November, 1958), 322-338.

1163 KNIGHT, Grant Cochran. American Literature and Culture. New York: Ray Lond & Richard R. Smith, 1932. Reprinted Chapel Hill: University of North Carolina Press, 1951. Emerson, pp. 175-192.

1164 KONVITZ, Milton R., ed. The Recognition of Ralph Waldo Emerson: Selected Criticism Since 1837. Ann Arbor: University of Michigan Press, 1972.

1165 _____, and Stephen E. Whicher, eds. Emerson: A Collection of Critical Essays. New York: Prentice-Hall, 1962. Preface by Stephen Whicher [written the day before he died].

1166 KOSTER, Donald. Transcendentalism in America. Boston: Twayne Publishers, 1975.

1167 KRAMER, Aaron. The Prophetic Tradition in American Poetry: 1835-1900. Rutherford, N. J.: Fairleigh Dickinson University Press, 1968. Based on Ph. D. diss., New York University, 1967.

1168 KREYMBORG, Alfred. Our Singing Strength: An Outline of American Poetry, 1620-1930. New York: Coward, McCann, 1929. "The Intoxicated Emerson," pp. 67-83.

1169 KRIEGE, Jack. "Emerson's 'Thoreau,' Last Paragraph." Explicator, 31 (1973), item 38.

1170 KRONMAN, Jeanne, ed. "Three Unpublished Lectures of Ralph Waldo Emerson." New England Quarterly, 19 (March, 1946), 98-110.

1171 KRUTCH, Joseph Wood, ed. with Intro. Henry David Thoreau. New York: American Book, 1948. (American Men of Letters series.) Emerson, pp. 41-51, 167-170 and passim.

1172 KUHN, Helmut. "Carlyle, Ally and Critic of Emerson." Emory University Quarterly, 4 (October, 1948), 171-180.

1173 KURTZ, S. Kenneth. "The Sources and Development of Emerson's Representative Men." Ph.D. diss., Yale, 1947.

1174 _____. "Emerson and Nature Today." ESQ, 10 (1958), 8-10.

1175 _____. "Emerson and Cooper: American Versions of the Heroic." ESQ, 42 (1966), 1-8.

1176 KWIAT, Joseph J. "Robert Henri and the Emerson-Whitman Tradition." PMLA, 71 (1956), 617-636.

1177 KYLE, Carol A. "Emerson's 'Uriel' as a Source for Frost." ESQ, 58 (1969), 111.

1178 LADU, Arthur I. "Channing and Transcendentalism." American Literature, 11 (May, 1939), 29-37.

1179 _____. "Emerson: Whig or Democrat." New England Quarterly, 13 (September, 1940), 419-441.

1180 _____. "The Political Ideas of Theodore Parker." Studies in Philology, 38 (1941), 106-123.

1181 LANDRETH, P. Studies and Sketches in Modern Literature: Periodical Contributions. Edinburgh: William Oliphant, 1861. Emerson, pp. 298-323.

1182 LA ROSA, Ralph C. "Bacon and the 'Organic Method' of Emerson's Early Lectures." English Language Notes, 8 (1970), 107-114.

1183 _____. "Emerson's Sententiae in Nature." ESQ, 58 (1970), 153-157.

1184 _____. "Emerson's Search for Literary Form: The Early Journals." Modern Philology, 69 (1971), 25-35.

1185 _____. "Invention and Imitation in Emerson's Early Lectures." American Literature, 44 (1972), 13-30.

1186 _____. "Necessary Truths: The Poetics of Emerson's Proverbs." Literary Monographs, 8 (1974), 129-192.

1187 LAUTER, Paul. "Ralph Waldo Emerson's Rhetoric." Ph.D. diss., Yale, 1958.

1188 _____. "Truth and Nature: Emerson's Use of Two Complex Words." Journal English Literary History, 27 (March, 1960), 66-85.

1189 _____. "Emerson's Revisions of Essays: First Series." American Literature, 33 (May, 1961), 143-158.

1190 _____. "Emerson Through Tillich." ESQ, 31 (1963), 49-55.

1191 LAWRENCE, D. H. "Emerson," in a Review of Stuart Sherman's Americans (1922). The Dial, May, 1923. Reprinted in Konvitz, ed., Recognition (1972), pp. 168-169.

1192 LAWTON, John H. "A Rhetorical Analysis of Representative Ceremonial Addresses of Ralph Waldo Emerson." Ph.D. diss., Iowa State, 1957.

1193 LAWTON, William Cranston. The New England Poets: A Study of Emerson, Hawthorne, Longfellow, Whittier, Lowell, and Holmes. New York: Macmillan, 1898. Emerson, pp. 21-47.

1194 _____. Introduction to the Study of American Literature. New York: Globe School Book, 1902. Emerson, pp. 122-138.

1195 LAZARUS, Emma. "On Being a Poet and Philosopher." Critic, 38 (May, 1901), 447-450.

1196 LE, Van-Diem. "Puritan Idealism and the Transcendental Movement." Ph.D. diss., University of Minnesota, 1960. DA, 21 (1961), 1929.

1197 LEARY, Lewis, ed. Articles on American Literature: 1900-1950. Durham, N. C.: Duke University Press, 1954. Emerson, pp. 86-95.

1198 ———, ed. Articles on American Literature: 1950-1967. Durham, N. C.: Duke University Press, 1968. Emerson, pp. 147-163.

1199 ———. American Literature: Study and Research Guide. New York: St. Martin's Press, 1976. Emerson, pp. 88-92.

1200 LEE, Gerald Stanley. "Emerson as a Poet." Critic, 42 (May, 1903), 416-429.

1201 LEE, Roland F. "Ralph Waldo Emerson and Christian Existentialism." Ph.D. diss., Ohio State University, 1952.

1202 ———. "Emerson Through Kierkegaard: Toward a Definition of Emerson's Theory of Communication." Journal of English Literary History, 26 (Spring, 1957), 229-248.

1203 ———. "Emerson's 'Compensation' as Argument and Art." New England Quarterly, 37 (Summer, 1964), 291-305.

1204 LEE, Vernon. "Emerson, Transcendentalist and Utilitarian." Contemporary Review, 67 (1895), 345.

1205 LEIDECKER, Kurt F. "Emerson and East-West Synthesis." Philosophy East and West, 1 (July, 1951), 40-50.

1206 ———. "Echoes of the East in the Wisest American." Visvabharati Quarterly, 18 (November, 1952-January, 1953), 218-232.

1207 LEIGHTON, Walter, L. French Philosophers and New England Transcendentalists. Charlottesville: University of Virginia Press, 1908. Reprinted New York: Greenwood Press, 1968. Based on Ph.D. diss., University of Virginia, 1908. Emerson, pp. 79-86.

1208 LEISY, E. E., and J. B. Hubbell, eds. "Doctoral Dissertations on Emerson." American Literature, 4 (January, 1933), 427-429; 19 (May, 1948), 178-180.

1209 LELIAERT, Richard Maurice. "Orestes A. Brownson (1803-1876): Theological Perspectives on His Search for the Meaning of God, Christology, and the Development of Doctrine." Ph.D. diss., Graduate Theological Union, 1974. DA, 35 (1974), 3108A.

1210 LENHART, Charmenz S. Musical Influence on American Poetry. Athens: University of Georgia Press, 1956. Emerson, pp. 109-114.

1211 LENTRICCHIA, Frank. "Coleridge and Emerson: Prophets of Silence, Prophets of Language." Journal of Aesthetics and Art Criticism, 32 (1973), 37-46.

1212 LERNER, Saul. "The Concepts of History, Progress and Perfectibility in Nineteenth Century American Transcendental Thought." Ph.D. diss., University of Kansas, 1966. History. DA, 28 (1968), 4097A.

1213 LE ROY, Gaylord C. "Emerson's 'Brahma.'" Explicator, 20 (December, 1961), item 29.

1214 LEVIN, David, ed. Emerson: Prophecy, Metamorphosis, and Influence. New York & London: Columbia University Press, 1975. (English Institue Essays, 1973-1974 sessions.)

1215 LEWIN, Walter. "Emerson." Bookman, 24 (June, 1903), 89-92.

1216 LEWIS, Albert E. "The Contribution of Ralph Waldo Emerson to American Education." Ph.D. diss., in education, Stanford University, 1943.

1217 ———. "Emerson and War." School and Society, 60 (August 12, 1944), 97-99.

1218 ———. "Words, Action, and Emerson." College English, 7 (October, 1945), 20-25.

1219 LEWIS, R. W. B. The American Adam: Innocence, Tradition, and Tragedy in the Nineteenth Century. Chicago: University of Chicago Press, 1955. Emerson, passim.

1220 LEWISOHN, Ludwig. Expression in America. New York: Harper & Brothers, 1932. Emerson, pp. 105-136.

1221 LIEBER, Todd M. Endless Experiments. Columbus: Ohio State University Press, 1973. "Emerson: Endless Experimenter," pp. 3-39.

1222 LIEBMAN, Sheldon W. "Emerson's Transformations in the 1820's." American Literature, 40 (1968), 133-154.

1223 ———. "The Development of Emerson's Theory of Rhetoric, 1821-1836." American Literature, 41 (1969), 178-206.

1224 ———. "Origins of Emerson's Early Poetics: His Reading in the Scottish Common Sense Critics." American Literature, 45 (1973), 23-33.

1225 ———. "Emerson's Discovery of the English Romantics, 1818-1836." American Transcendental Quarterly, 21 (1974), 36-44.

1226 LIN, Maurice Yaofu. "Children of Adam: Ginsberg, Ferlinghetti, and Snyder in the Emerson-Whitman Tradition." Ph.D. diss., University of Minnesota, 1972. DA, 34 (1973), 781A.

1227 LINDEMAN, Edouard C. "Emerson, Radical Democrat." Common Ground, 2 (1942), 3-6.

1228 ———. "Emerson's Pragmatic Mood." American Scholar, 16 (Winter, 1946-1947), 57-64.

1229 LINDNER, Carl Martin. "Ralph Waldo Emerson: The Conceptualization of Experience." Ph.D. diss., University of Wisconsin, 1970. DA, 31 (1970), 1233A-1234A.

1230 ———. "Robert Frost: 'In the American Grain.'" Colorado Quarterly, 22 (Spring, 1974), 469-479.

1231 _____. "Newtonianism in Emerson's Nature." ESQ, 77 (1974), 260-269.

1232 LINDQUIST, Vernon R. "Unpublished Emerson Letter Reveals a Bangor Friendship," in A Handful of Spice: A Miscellany of Maine Literature and History, ed. Richard S. Sprague. Orono: University of Maine Press, 1968. Pp. 155-157.

1233 LINSCOTT, Robert N., ed. with Notes and Intro. Journals of Ralph Waldo Emerson. New York: Random House, 1960. (Modern Library abridgement.)

1234 Literary World (Boston). Emerson Number, May 22, 1880. Contains: Bartol, Cyrus A., "Ralph Waldo Emerson the Man," 244; Higginson, T. W., "Emerson the Founder of a Literature," 245; Hedge, Frederic H., "Emerson the Philosopher and Poet," 247; Whitman, Walt, "Emerson's Books (the Shadows of them)," 249; Curtis, George W., "Mr. Emerson and The Dial," 251; Sanborn, Frank B., "Emerson and His Friends," 252; Hill, William B., "Emerson's College Days," 254; Cooke, George Willis, "Emerson's Literary Methods," 255; Bartlett, George B., "Mr. Emerson's Home," 256; Tributes by E. P. Whipple, Max Muller, A. P. Stanley, Henry W. Bellows, John G. Whittier, David Swing, 257; Table Talk, 258; A Bibliography of Emerson, 259-262.

1235 LLOYD, C. F. "Emerson as a Stimulant." Canadian Bookman, 18 (July, 1936), 1-3.

1236 LOCKWOOD, C. B. Philosophic Reminiscences--Memories of Emerson and Others: An Address. Unitarian Club, Washington, D. C., 1916. (pamphlet)

1237 LOCKWOOD, Francis C. "Ralph Waldo Emerson as a Philosopher." Ph.D. diss., Northwestern, 1896.

1238 LOMBARD, C. M. "Daniel Stern on Emerson." Notes & Queries, 3 (May, 1956), 217-218.

1239 LOMBARDO, Agostino. "Lombardo on Emerson and American Art." ESQ, 39 (1965), 28-34.

1240 LONG, Haniel. Walt Whitman and the Springs of

Courage. Sante Fe, N. M.: Writer's Editions, 1938. Emerson, pp. 16-25.

1241 LONG, William J. American Literature. Boston: Ginn, 1913. Emerson, pp. 318-338.

1242 LOOMIS, C. G. "Emerson's Proverbs." Western Folklore, 17 (October, 1958), 257-262.

1243 LOVEJOY, Arthur O. The Great Chain of Being: A Study in the History of an Idea. Cambridge, Mass.: Harvard University Press, 1936.

1244 _____. "The Meaning of Romanticism for the Historian of Ideas." Journal of the History of Ideas, 2 (1941), 257-278.

1245 _____. Essays in the History of Ideas. Baltimore: Johns Hopkins Press, 1948.

1246 LOWANCE, Mason, Jr. "From Edwards to Emerson to Thoreau: A Re-valuation." American Transcendental Quarterly, 18 (1973), 3-12.

1247 LOWELL, Amy. "Letter on Emerson and Whitman." New York Times, June 1, 1919.

1248 LOWELL, James Russell. "A Fable for Critics" (1848), in Charles Eliot Norton, ed., The Complete Writings of James Russell Lowell. 16 vols. Boston: Houghton, Mifflin, 1904. Vol. XII, pp. 17-87.

1249 _____. "Emerson, the Lecturer," in My Study Windows. Boston: Houghton, Mifflin, 1871. Pp. 375-384. Also in The Complete Writings (1904), vol. II, pp. 391-404.

1250 LOWRY, Howard Foster, and Ralph L. Rusk, eds. The Emerson-Clough Letters (Rowfant Club, 1934). Reprinted Hamden, Conn.: Shoe String Press, 1968.

1251 LUCKINGHAN, Brad. "The Pioneer Lecturer in the West: A Note on the Appearance of Ralph Waldo Emerson in St. Louis, 1852-1853." Missouri Historical Review, 58 (October, 1963), 70-88.

1252 LUDWIG, Richard. Literary History of the United States: Bibliographical Supplement II. New York: Macmillan, 1972. Bibliography on Transcendentalism and major figures.

1253 LUEDTKE, Luther Stephen. "German Reception and Criticism of Ralph Waldo Emerson." Ph.D. diss., Brown University, 1971. DA, 32 (1972), 5189A.

1254 _____. "First Notices of Emerson in England and Germany, 1835-1842." Notes & Queries, 22 (March, 1975), 106-107.

1255 LYDENBERG, John. "Emerson and the Dark Tradition." Critical Quarterly, 4 (Winter, 1962), 352-358.

1256 LYONS, Eleanor Joan. "The Parti-Colored Wheel: A Study of Emerson's Thought." Ph.D. diss., Virginia, 1967. DA, 28 (1968), 3642A-3643A.

1257 MABBOTT, Thomas Ollive. "Numismatic References to Three American Writers." Numismatist, 46 (November, 1933), 688.

1258 _____. "Poe and Emerson." Notes & Queries, 197 (December 20, 1952), 566.

1259 MABIE, Hamilton W. "Ralph Waldo Emerson in 1903." Harper's, 106 (May, 1903), 903-908.

1260 _____. "Emerson and Concord." Outlook, 74 (May 2, 1903), 18-29.

1261 _____. "How to Study Tennyson and Emerson." Ladies Home Journal, 25 (March, 1908), 32.

1262 _____. "Emerson and Concord," in Backgrounds of Literature. New York: Macmillan, 1912. Pp. 56-96.

1263 _____. "Emerson's Journals." Outlook, 106 (February 21, 1914), 418-420.

1264 McCLARY, Ben Harris. "Burroughs to Whitman on Emerson: An Unpublished Letter." ESQ, 43 (1966), 67-68.

1265 _____. "Earl Lytton to Alexander Ireland on Emerson." ESQ, 43 (1966), 70-73.

1266 McCORMICK, Edgar L. "Higginson, Emerson, and a National Literature." ESQ, 37 (1964), 71-74.

1267 _____. "To Encourage Understanding and Application of Basic Ideas of Emerson and Thoreau." Exercise Exchange, 3 (February, 1956), 11-12.

1268 McCORMICK, J. O. "Emerson's Theory of Human Greatness." New England Quarterly, 26 (Summer, 1953), 291-314.

1269 _____. "Emerson, Vico, and History," in Cheuse, A., and R. Koffler, eds., The Rarer Action: Essays in Honor of Francis Ferguson. New Brunswick, N. J.: Rutgers University Press, 1971. Pp. 320-332.

1270 McCUSKEY, Dorothy. Bronson Alcott: Teacher. New York: Macmillan, 1940. Reprinted New York: Arno Press, 1975. Emerson, passim.

1271 McDERMOTT, J. F. "Emerson at St. Louis, 1852: Some Unpublished Letters and Telegrams." ESQ, 6 (1957), 7-9.

1272 MacDONALD, Hugh P., ed. The Power of Emerson's Wisdom. New York: Pageant Press, 1954. Quotations gathered from essays.

1273 McDONALD, John J. "Emerson and John Brown." New England Quarterly, 44 (1971), 377-396.

1274 McDOWELL, Tremaine. "A Freshman Poem by Emerson." PMLA, 45 (March, 1930), 326-329.

1275 _____. William Cullen Bryant. New York: American Book, 1935. (American Writers series.) Emerson, passim.

1276 McELDERRY, Bruce R., Jr. "Wolfe and Emerson on

'Flow.'" Modern Fiction Studies, 2 (May, 1956), 77-78.

1277 _____. "Emerson's Second Address on the American Scholar." Personalist, 39 (August, 1958), 361-372.

1278 _____. "The Transcendental Hawthorne." Midwest Quarterly, 2 (Summer, 1961), 307-323.

1279 _____. "Emerson Resurgent." Personalist, 43 (January, 1962), 127-130.

1280 McELROY, John H., ed. "Emerson in the Land of the Dead." Modern Humanities Review, 36 (1975), 84-99. Letters from Egypt.

1281 McEUEN, Kathryn A. "Emerson's Rhymes." American Literature, 20 (March, 1948), 31-42.

1282 McFARLAND, Thomas. Coleridge and the Pantheist Tradition. Oxford, England: Clarendon Press, 1969. Emerson, pp. 44-45, 283-285 and passim.

1283 McGIFFERT, Arthur S. Young Emerson Speaks. Boston: Houghton, Mifflin, 1938. Reprinted Port Washington, N. Y.: Kennikat Press, 1971. Contains 25 unpublished sermons and other related material.

1284 McGILL, F. T., Jr. Channing of Concord: A Life of William Ellery Channing. New Brunswick, N. J.: Rutgers University Press, 1967. Emerson, passim.

1285 McGILL, Robert A. "Emerson's Letter to the Editor." ESQ, 6 (1957), 5-6.

1286 _____. "Ralph Waldo Emerson and His Audience." Ph.D. diss., University of Pennsylvania, 1959. DA, 20 (1959), 299-300.

1287 McKINSEY, Elizabeth. The Western Experiment: New England Transcendentalism in the Ohio Valley. Cambridge, Mass.: Harvard University Press, 1973. Undergraduate Honors Thesis.

1288 McLEAN, Andrew M. "Emerson's 'Brahma' as an Expression of Brahman." New England Quarterly, 42 (1969), 115-122.

1289 McMICHAEL, George, ed. Anthology of American Literature. 2 vols. New York: Macmillan, 1974. Emerson, vol. I, pp. 1266-1407.

1290 McMINN, G. R. "Emerson and Maeterlinck." Sewanee Review, 24 (July, 1916), 265-281.

1291 McMULLEN, Haynes. "Ralph Waldo Emerson and Libraries." Library Quarterly, 25 (April, 1955), 152-162.

1292 McNULTY, John Bard. "Emerson's Friends and the Essay on Friendship." New England Quarterly, 19 (September, 1946), 390-394.

1293 McQUISTON, Raymer. "The Relation of Ralph Waldo Emerson to Public Affairs." Humanistic Studies (Lawrence, Kan.), III, 1 (1923).

1294 MacRAE, David. "Emerson: A Personal Reminiscence." Spectator, 90 (June 20, 1903), 972.

1295 MacRAE, Donald E. "Ralph Waldo Emerson and the Fine Arts." Ph.D. diss., University of Iowa, 1934.

1296 _____. "Emerson and the Arts." Arts Bulletin, 20 (March, 1938), 79-95.

1297 McSHANE, Frank. "Walden and Yoga." New England Quarterly, 37 (September, 1964), 322-342.

1298 McWILLIAMS, Wilson Carey. The Idea of Fraternity in America. Berkeley: University of California Press, 1973. Emerson, pp. 280-300.

1299 MACY, John. The Spirit of American Literature. New York: Boni & Liveright, 1913. Emerson, pp. 45-76.

1300 _____, ed. American Writers on American Literature. New York: Horace Liveright, 1931. "Emerson," by Henry Hazlitt, pp. 81-96.

1301 MADDOX, L. H. "Emerson on Education." Educational Theory, 7 (January, 1957), 56-58.

1302 MAETERLINCK, Maurice. On Emerson and Other Essays, trans. M. J. Moses. New York: Dodd, Mead, 1912. Emerson, pp. 31-52.

1303 MAGNUS, Philip. "Emerson's Thoughts on Education." Nineteenth Century, 80 (December, 1916), 1198-1211.

1304 MAGOWAN, Robin. "The Horse of the Gods: Possession in 'Song of Myself.'" Walt Whitman Review, 15 (1969), 67-76.

1305 MAITRA, H. "Emerson from an Indian Point of View." Harvard Theological Review, 4 (October, 1911), 403-417.

1306 MALLOY, Charles. "An Interpretation of Emerson's 'Brahma.'" Journal of Practical Metaphysics, 1 (November, 1896), 31-36.

1307 _____. "'The Sphinx.'" Arena, 17 (1897), 399-415.

1308 _____. "'Mithridates.'" The Coming Age, 1 (February, 1899), 177-180.

1309 _____. "'The Apology.'" The Coming Age, 1 (March, 1899), 295-299.

1310 _____. "'The Amulet.'" The Coming Age, 1 (April, 1899), 413-417.

1311 _____. "Emerson's 'Brahma.'" The Coming Age, 1 (May, 1899), 535-543.

1312 _____. "'Days.'" The Coming Age, 1 (June, 1899), 629-634.

1313 _____. "'Etienne de la Boece.'" The Coming Age, 2 (July, 1899), 28-32.

1314 _____. "'Celestial Love.'" The Coming Age, 2 (August, 1899), 159-164; and (September, 1899), 285-291.

1315 _____. "'Monadnoc.'" The Coming Age, 2 (November, December, 1899), 479-485, 612-617; 3 (January, February, March, 1900), 59-64, 149-154, 250-274.

1316 _____. The Poems of Emerson. Privately reprinted from type of The Coming Age. Boston, 1899-1900. c. 200 pages.

1317 _____. "'Merlin.'" The Coming Age, 3 (April, May, 1900), 374-382, 495-499.

1318 _____. "'Saadi.'" The Coming Age, 3 (June, 1900), 55-58; 4 (July, 1900), 585-589.

1319 _____. "Emerson's Poems." Practical Ideals, 5 (May, 1903), 8-10.

1320 _____. "What Bearing upon Emerson's Poems Have Their Titles?" Poet-Lore, 14 (October, 1903), 65-79.

1321 _____. "'The Sphinx.'" Arena, 31 (February, March, April, May, 1904), 138-152, 272-283, 370-380, 494-507.

1322 _____. "'Days.'" Arena, 31 (June, 1904), 592-602.

1323 _____. "'The Problem.'" Arena, 32 (July, August, 1904), 39-47, 145-150.

1324 _____. "'Uriel.'" Arena, 32 (September, 1904), 278-283.

1325 _____. "'Bacchus,' One of the World's Greatest Poems." Arena, 32 (November, 1904), 504-512.

1326 _____. "'Hermione.'" Arena, 33 (January, February, March, 1905), 65-70, 182-187, 289-295.

1327 _____. A Study of Emerson's Major Poems [written 1897-1904]. Collected and ed. by Kenneth W. Cameron. Hartford: Transcendental Books, 1973. The critical articles collected are those cited in entries 1308-1327.

1328 MANSFIELD, Luther S. "The Emersonian Idiom and the Romantic Period in American Literature," in Strauch, Carl F., ed., Critical Symposium on American Romanticism, in ESQ, 35 (1964), 23-28.

1329 MANTENO, G. "Robert Frost's Linked Analogies." New England Quarterly, 49 (1974), 463-468.

1330 MARBLE, Annie Russell. "Emerson as a Public Speaker." Dial, 34 (May 16, 1903), 327-329.

1331 _____. "First Editions of Emerson." Critic, 42 (May, 1903), 430-436.

1332 _____. "Emerson, Poet and Thinker." Dial, 37 (December 1, 1904), 366.

1333 MARCHAND, Ernest. "Emerson and the Frontier." American Literature, 3 (May, 1931), 149-174.

1334 MARKS, Emerson R. "Victor Cousin and Emerson," in Simon, Myron, and Thonrton H. Parsons, eds., Transcendentalism and Its Legacy (1966), 63-86.

1335 MARRS, Suzanne. "Ralph Waldo Emerson and the 18th Century English Moralists." Ph.D. diss., University of Oklahoma, 1973. DA, 34 (1974), 5920A-5921A.

1336 MARSH, James. The Remains of the Rev. James Marsh, D. D. (1843). Reprinted Port Washington, N. Y.: Kennikat Press, 1975. Marsh considered a major catalyst in the development of American Transcendentalism.

1337 MARX, Leo. "The American Scholar Today." Commentary, 32 (1961), 48-53.

1338 MASON, August H. "Emerson's 'Terminus.'" Explicator, 4 (March, 1946), item 37.

1339 MASON, Gabriel Richard, ed. Great American Liberals. Boston: Starr King Press, 1956. Emerson, pp. 41-51.

1340 MASSON, T. L. "Emerson, the Radical." Bookman, 57 (June, 1923), 401-403.

1341 MASTERS, Edgar Lee, ed., with Intro. The Living Thoughts of Emerson. London: Cassell, 1941. Anthology of selections.

1342 MATERSON, Robert S. "Emerson and the Aeolian Harp." South-Central Bulletin, 23 (1963), 4-9.

1343 MATHEWS, J. Chesley. "Emerson's Knowledge of Dante." University of Texas Studies in English (1942), 22 (1942), 171-198.

1344 _____, ed. "Emerson's Translation of Dante's Vita Nuova." Harvard Library Bulletin, 11 (Spring, Autumn, 1957), 208-244; 346-352.

1345 MATHY, Francis. "The Three Johns: Portraits of Emerson, Thoreau, Hawthorne, and Holmes." English Language and Literature Studies (Hiroshima), 10 (1973), 163-181.

1346 MATLE, John H. "Emerson and Brook Farm." ESQ, 58 (1969), 84-88.

1347 MATTHEWS, Brander. An Introduction to the Study of American Literature. New York: American Book, 1896. Rev. ed., 1918. Emerson, pp. 93-109.

1348 MATTHIESSEN, Francis O. American Renaissance: Art and Expression in the Age of Emerson and Whitman. London & New York: Oxford University Press, 1941. Emerson, pp. 3-175.

1349 MAULSBY, David L. The Contribution of Ralph Waldo Emerson to Literature. Medford, Mass.: Tufts College, 1911. Based on Ph.D. diss., University of Chicago, 1909.

1350 MAURY, A. C. de P. P. "Friend of Emerson: Being a Little Memoir of Charles Mallory." Poet-Lore, 25 (May, 1915), 357-367.

1351 MAXFIELD-MILLER, Elizabeth. "Emerson and Elizabeth of Concord." Harvard Library Bulletin, 19 (1971), 290-306. Refers to Elizabeth Hoar in the Journals.

1352 MAYBERRY, George. "In Defense of Emerson." Science and Society, 2 (Spring, 1938), 257-259.

1353 MAYER, Frederick, ed. The Great Teachers. New York: Citadel Press, 1967. Emerson, pp. 235-246; includes "The American Scholar."

1354 MEAD, C. David. "Emerson's Scholar and the Scholars." Journal of Higher Education, 40 (November, 1969), 649-660.

1355 _____, ed. The American Scholar Today. New York: Dodd, Mead, 1970. A collection of criticism with bibliography.

1356 MEAD, David. "Ralph Waldo Emerson: Transcendental Traveler," in Yankee Eloquence in the Middle West: The Ohio Lyceum 1850-1870. East Lansing: Michigan State College Press, 1951. Emerson, pp. 24-61. Lectures in Ohio.

1357 MEAD, Edwin D. "Emerson's Ethics," in Sanborn, Franklin B., ed., The Genius and Character of Emerson (1885), pp. 233-285.

1358 _____. The Influence of Emerson. Boston: American Unitarian Association, 1903.

1359 _____. Emerson and Theodore Parker. Boston: American Unitarian Association, 1910. Pamphlet.

1360 MEAD, George H. Movements of Thought in the Nineteenth Century, ed. Merritt H. Moore. Chicago: University of Chicago Press, 1936. Emerson, p. 152 and passim.

1361 MEEKS, L. H. "The Lyceum in the Early West." Indiana Magazine of History, 29 (June, 1933), 87-95.

1362 MEESE, Elizabeth A. "Transcendental Vision: A History of the Doctrine of Correspondence and Its Role in American Transcendentalism." Ph.D. diss., Wayne State University, 1971. DA, 33 (1972), 6319A-6320A. Principally on Thoreau.

1363 _____. "Emerson: Transcendentalist. The Metaphysics of the Theme." American Literature, 47 (March, 1975), 1-20.

1364 MELTZER, Milton, ed. Thoreau: People, Principles, and Politics. New York: Hill & Wang, 1963. Emerson, passim.

1365 MELZ, C. F. "Goethe and America." College English, 10 (May, 1949), 425-431.

1366 MENCKEN, Henry L. "Unheeded Law-Giver," in Prejudices--First Series. New York: Knopf, 1919. Pp. 191-194.

1367 MENDENHALL, Mary. "A Transcendental Philosophy of Education--Thomas Carlyle and Ralph Waldo Emerson." Ph.D. diss., Yale, 1934.

1368 MESEROLE, Harrison T., et al., eds. American Literature: Tradition and Innovation. 2 vols. New York: D. C. Heath, 1969. Emerson, vol. I, pp. 929-1077.

1369 METCALF, John Calvin. American Literature. Atlanta: B. F. Johnson, 1914. Emerson, pp. 157-172.

1370 METZGER, Charles Reid. Emerson and Greenough: Transcendental Pioneers of an American Aesthetic. Berkeley: University of California Press, 1954. Reprinted New York: Greenwood Press, 1975.

1371 MEYER, A. N. "Do We Need Emerson Today?" Vital Speeches, 5 (February 15, 1939), 261-264.

1372 MICHAUD, Regis. "Emerson et Nietzsche." Revue Germanique, 6 (July-August, 1910), 414-421. In French.

1373 _____. "Emerson's Transcendentalism." American Journal of Psychology, 30 (January, 1919), 73-82.

1374 _____. Autour d'Emerson. Paris, 1924. In French.

1375 _____. L'esthetique d'Emerson: la nature, l'art, l'histoire. Paris, 1927. In French.

1376 _____. Emerson: The Enraptured Yankee, translated from the French by George Boas. New York: Harper & Brothers, 1930.

1377 MIDY, Godefroy. "Ralph Waldo Emerson's Philosophy of the Person." Ph.D. diss., Fordham University, 1971. Philosophy. DA, 32 (1971), 2140A.

1378 MIEHER, D. "New Appeal of Emerson to Youth." Scholastic, 32 (May 28, 1938), 21.

1379 MIGNON, Charles W., ed. "Emerson to Chapman: Four Letters About Publishing." ESQ, 73 (1973), 224-230. On Essays: Second Series and Poems.

1380 _____. "Starsown Poet, Abstemious Muse," in Strauch, Carl F., ed., Characteristics of Emerson: Transcendental Poet (1975), pp. 33-41.

1381 MILES, Josephine. The Continuity of Poetic Language: The Primary Language of Poetry in the 1740's and 1840's. Berkeley: University of California Press, 1950. Emerson, pp. 301-305.

1382 _____. "Emerson's Wise Universe." Minnesota Review, 2 (Spring, 1962), 305-313.

1383 _____. Ralph Waldo Emerson. Minneapolis: University of Minnesota, 1964. (University of Minnesota Pamphlets on American Writers series, no. 41.)

1384 _____. Style and Proportion. Boston: Little, Brown, 1967. Emerson, pp. 64-78.

1385 MILLER, F. DeWolfe. Christopher Pearce Cranch and His Caricature of New England Transcendentalists. Cambridge, Mass.: Harvard University Press, 1951.

1386 MILLER, James E., Jr. "Uncharted Interiors: The American Romantics Revisited." ESQ, 35 (1964), 35-36.

1387 _____. "The 'Classic' American Writers and the Radicalized Curriculum." College English, 31 (1970), 565-570.

1388 MILLER, J. Hillis. Poets of Reality. Cambridge, Mass.: University Press, 1965. Emerson, passim.

1389 MILLER, Lee W. "Ralph Waldo Emerson and the New Testament." Ph.D. diss., Louisiana State University, 1953.

1390 MILLER, Norman. "Emerson's 'Each and All' Concept: A Re-examination." New England Quarterly, 41 (1968), 381-392.

1391 MILLER, Perry. The New England Mind: The Seventeenth Century. New York: Macmillan, 1939. Emerson, passim.

1392 _____. "Jonathan Edwards to Emerson." New England Quarterly, 13 (December, 1940), 589-617. Reprinted with important changes in Errand into the Wilderness (1956), pp. 184-203.

1393 _____, ed. The Transcendentalists: An Anthology. Cambridge, Mass.: Harvard University Press, 1950.

1394 _____. "Emersonian Genius and the American Democracy." New England Quarterly, 26 (March, 1953), 27-44.

1395 _____. "Melville and Transcendentalism," in Hillway, Tyrus, ed., Moby-Dick Centennial Essays. Dallas: Southern Methodist University Press, 1953. Pp. 123-152. Also a shorter version in Virginia Quarterly Review, 29 (Autumn, 1953), 556-575.

1396 _____. Errand into the Wilderness. Cambridge, Mass.: Harvard University Press, 1956. Emerson, pp. 184-203.

1397 _____, ed. The American Transcendentalists: Their Prose and Poetry. New York: Doubleday, 1957. Shorter than item 1393, but contains some new material.

1398 _____, ed. Major Writers of America. 2 vols. New York: Harcourt Brace, 1962. "Emerson," by Newton Arvin, vol. I, pp. 477-591.

1399 _____. Margaret Fuller: American Romantic. New York: Random House, 1963.

1400 _____. Nature's Nation. Cambridge, Mass.: Harvard University Press, 1967. Posthumous essays.

1401 MILLS, John. "Memories of Ralph Waldo Emerson Visiting England." ESQ, 2 (1956), 15-16. Reprinted from Christian Science Monitor.

1402 MILNE, Gordon. "George William Curtis: Inheritor of the Transcendental Mantle." American Transcendental Quarterly, 18 (1973), 35-40.

1403 MILNES, Richard Monckton. "American Philosophy: Emerson's Works." Westminster Review, 33 (March, 1840), 345-372. Reprinted in part in Sealts and Ferguson, ed., Emerson's Nature (1969), pp. 102-105; also in Konvitz, ed., Recognition (1972), pp. 16-18.

1404 MINNICK, W. C. "Matthew Arnold on Emerson." Quarterly Journal of Speech, 37 (October, 1951), 332-336.

1405 MONDALE, Lester. "The Practical Mysticism of Ralph Waldo Emerson," in Stiernotte, Alfred P., ed., Mysticism and the Modern Mind. New York: Liberal Arts Press, 1959. Pp. 43-59.

1406 MONROE, Harriet. "Emerson in a Loggia." Poetry, 10 (September, 1917), 311-315.

1407 MONTEIRO, George. "Bibliographical Note on Four Emerson Letters." ESQ, 47 (1967), 15-16.

1408 MOODY, Marjory M. "The Evolution of Emerson as an Abolitionist." American Literature, 17 (March, 1945), 1-21.

1409 MOORE, C. L. "Master of Maxims." Dial, 34 (May 1, 1903), 293-295.

1410 MOORE, John B. "The Master of Whitman." Studies in Philology, 23 (March, 1926), 77-89.

1411 ———. "Emerson on Wordsworth." PMLA, 41 (March, 1926), 179-192.

1412 ———. "Thoreau Rejects Emerson." American Literature, 4 (November, 1932), 241-256.

1413 MORAN, Virginia. "Circle and Dialectic: A Study of Emerson's Interest in Hegel." Nassau Review, 1 (1969), 32-42.

1414 MORAVSKY, Maria. "Idol of Compensation." Nation, 108 (June 28, 1919), 1004-1005.

1415 MORE, Paul Elmer. "The Influence of Emerson," in Shelburne Essays: First Series. New York: Putnam's Sons, 1904. Pp. 71-84.

1416 ———. "Emerson," in Trent, William P., ed., Cambridge History of American Literature (1917), vol. I, pp. 349-363.

1417 MORLEY, John. Ralph Waldo Emerson: An Essay. New York: Macmillan, 1884. 53 pages. Also in Critical Miscellanies (1904), vol. I, pp. 293-347.

1418 MOSIER, Richard. The American Temper: Patterns of Our Intellectual Heritage. Berkeley: University of California Press, 1952. Emerson, passim, Book III, "The Romantic Mind," pp. 159-229.

1419 MOSLEY, J. R. "The Charm of Emerson." Arena, 34 (June, 1905), 31-38.

1420 MOSS, Sidney P. "Analogy: The Heart of Emerson's Style." ESQ, 39 (1965), 21-24.

1421 ———. "'Cock-a-Doodle-Doo,' and Some Legends in Melville Scholarship." American Literature, 40 (1968), 192-210.

1422 MOULTON, Charles Wells, ed. The Library of Literary Criticism. Buffalo, N. Y.: Moulton, 1904. Emerson, vol. VII, pp. 342-380. New ed., edited by Martin Tucker, Moulton's Library of Literary Criticism. New York: Frederick Unger, 1966. Emerson, vol. IV, pp. 3-26.

1423 MOWAT, R. B. "The England Emerson Saw from 'Americans in England.'" Christian Science Monitor, May 2, 1942, p. 8.

1424 MOYNE, Ernest J. "Thoreau and Emerson: Their Interest in Finland." Neuphilologische Mitteilungen (Helsinki), 70 (1969), 738-750.

1425 MUDGE, James. "Emerson, as a Poet." Methodist Review, 85 (January-February, 1903), 102-110.

1426 _____. "Chips from Emerson's Workshop." Methodist Review, 99 (September, 1917), 689-702.

1427 MUIR, John. "Forests of the Yosemite Park." Atlantic Monthly, 85 (April, 1900), 493-507. Emerson, pp. 505-507.

1428 MULQUEEN, James E. "Emerson and Stevens: Transcendentalism and Radical Transcendentalism." Ph.D. diss., Purdue University, 1970. DA, 31 (1971), 5418A.

1429 _____. "Is Emerson's Work Central to the Poetry of Emily Dickinson?" Emily Dickinson Bulletin, 24 (1973), 211-220.

1430 _____. "Emersonian Transcendentalism: Over-Soul or Over-Self?" Tennessee Studies in Literature, 21 (1977), 21-27.

1431 MUMFORD, Lewis. The Golden Day. New York: Boni & Liveright, 1926. "Emerson, The Morning Star," pp. 85-106.

1432 _____. "Have Courage! An Essay in Praise of Emerson." American Heritage, 20 (1969), 104-111.

1433 _____. Interpretations and Forecasts: 1922-1972. New York: Harcourt Brace Jovanovich, 1973. "Emerson: The Morning Star," pp. 17-34. "Emerson's Journals," pp. 103-109.

1434 MUNSTERBERG, Hugo. "Emerson as Philosopher." Harvard Psychological Studies, 2 (1906).

1435 MURDOCK, C. A. "Emerson in California."

Pacific Unitarian, 11 (May, 1903), 263-268.

1436 MURPHY, Walter H., ed. "A Letter by Emerson" (to J. R. Leeson, May 17, 1870). American Literature, 36 (March, 1964), 64-65.

1437 MURRAY, D. M. "Emerson's Language as 'Fossil Poetry.'" New England Quarterly, 29 (June, 1956), 204-215.

1438 MYERS, Henry Alonzo. Are Men Equal? An Inquiry into the Meaning of American Democracy. New York: G. P. Putnam's, 1945. Reprinted Ithaca, N. Y.: Great Seal Books, 1955. Emerson, pp. 37-46 and passim.

1439 MYERSON, Joel A., ed. "Lowell on Emerson: A New Letter from Concord in 1838." New England Quarterly, 44 (1971), 649-652. Sent to Nathan Hale, Jr.; it is uncomplimentary of Emerson's "Divinity School Address."

1439a _____. "A History of The Dial (1840-1844)." Ph.D. diss., Northwestern University, 1971. DA, 32 (1971), 4573A. First complete study of The Dial and its contributors, 647 pp.

1440 _____. "A Calendar of Transcendental Club Meetings." American Literature, 44 (1972), 197-207.

1441 _____. "Margaret Fuller's 1842 Journal: At Concord with the Emersons." Harvard Library Bulletin, 21 (1973), 320-340.

1442 _____. "Practical Editions: Ralph Waldo Emerson's 'The American Scholar.'" Proof, 3 (1973), 379-394.

1443 _____. "An Unpublished Interview with Emerson in 1867." South Atlantic Bulletin, 39 (1974), 89-94.

1444 _____. "Eight Lowell Letters from Concord in 1838." Illinois Quarterly, 38 (1975), 20-42.

1445 _____. "Two Unpublished Reminiscences of Brook

Farm." New England Quarterly, 48 (1975), 253-260.

1446 _____. "An Ungathered Sanborn Lecture on Brook Farm." American Transcendental Quarterly, 26 (1975), 1-11.

1447 NARASIMHAIAH, C. D., ed. Indian Response to American Literature. New Delhi: U. S. Education Foundation, 1967. "Emerson," by B. Damodar Rao, pp. 15-27.

1448 NAYLOR, L. H. "Emerson and an Italian Carriage Driver of 1833." ESQ, 1 (1955), 3-4.

1449 NEILSON, W. A. "The American Scholar Today." The American Scholar, 5 (Spring, 1936), 149-163.

1450 NELSON, Carl. "The Rhetoric of Emerson's Hindu 'Heroism.'" ESQ, 69 (1972), 258-264.

1451 NELSON, Ernest. "About Emerson." Poetry, 11 (December, 1917), 166-167.

1452 NELSON, Truman. "The Walden Pond of Ralph Waldo Emerson. ESQ, 13 (1958), 6-8.

1453 NEUFELDT, Leonard N. "The Severity of the Ideal: Emerson's 'Thoreau.'" ESQ, 58 (1970), 77-84.

1454 _____. "'Intellect': The Vital Mind, Emerson's Epistemology." Philological Quarterly, 50 (1971), 253-270.

1455 _____. "Emerson and the Civil War." Journal of English and Germanic Philology, 71 (1972), 502-513. Also paper read at Modern Language Association meeting, December 29, 1970.

1456 _____, ed. Ralph Waldo Emerson: New Appraisals, A Symposium. Hartford: Transcendental Books, 1973.

1457 _____. "The Law of Permutation: Emerson's

Mode." American Transcendental Quarterly, 21 (1974), 20-30.

1458 NEWBROUGH, George F. "Reason and Understanding in the Works of Theodore Parker." South Atlantic Quarterly, 47 (January, 1948), 64-75.

1459 NEWCOMER, Lee Robert. "Classical Mythology in the American Renaissance." Ph.D. diss., University of Utah, 1971. DA, 31 (1971), 4730A.

1460 NEWMAN, F. B. "Emerson and Buonarroti [i. e., Michelangelo]." New England Quarterly, 25 (December, 1952), 524-535.

1461 NEWTON, Annabel. Wordsworth in Early American Criticism. Chicago: University of Chicago Press, 1928. Emerson, pp. 145-152 and passim.

1462 NEWTON, R. H. "Emerson the Man." Arena, 30 (October, 1903), 359-376.

1463 NICHOL, John. American Literature, an Historical Sketch, 1620-1880. Edinburgh: Adam & Charles Black, 1882. Emerson, pp. 254-321, 465-466.

1464 NICOLL, William Robertson. "Ralph Waldo Emerson." North American Review, 176 (1903), 675-687.

1465 NICOLOFF, Philip L. "Ralph Waldo Emerson's Thought in English Traits." Ph.D. diss., Columbia University, 1959.

1466 _____. Emerson: On Race and History. New York: Columbia University Press, 1961. Based on English Traits.

1467 NICOLSON, Marjorie H. "James Marsh and the Vermont Transcendentalists." The Philosophical Review, 34 (January, 1925), 28-50.

1468 NILON, Charles H. Bibliography of Bibliography in American Literature. New York: Bowker, 1970. Emerson, pp. 78-80. Lists primary and secondary bibliographies.

1469 NIRENBERG, Morton. The Reception of American Literature in German Periodicals, 1820-1850. Heidelberg, West Germany: Carl Winter, 1970.

1470 NIVEN, Penelope Ellen. "Emerson's Lectures in English Literature: A Study of Critical Principles." M. A. Thesis, Wake Forest College, 1962.

1471 NORTHSTEIN, Ira O. "Emerson's Influence on the Religious Life of America." Lutheran Church Review, 27 (April, 1908), 282-287.

1472 NORTON, Andrews. "On the 'Divinity School Address.'" Boston Daily Advertiser, August 27, 1838. Reprinted in Konvitz, Recognition (1972), pp. 7-9.

1473 _____. A Disclosure on the Latest Form of Infidelity (1839). Reprinted Port Washington, N. Y.: Kennikat Press, 1975. Document issued by Unitarians against Transcendentalism.

1474 NORTON, Charles Eliot. "Review of May-Day and Other Pieces." North American Review, 105 (July, 1867), 325.

1475 _____, ed. Correspondence Between Ralph Waldo Emerson and Thomas Carlyle. Boston: Osgood, 1888. 2 vols.

1476 _____, ed. Letters from Ralph Waldo Emerson to a Friend: 1838-1853 (1899). Reprinted Port Washington, N. Y.: Kennikat Press, 1971. Letters to Samuel Gray Ward.

1477 _____. Letters of Charles Eliot Norton. Boston: Houghton, Mifflin, 1913. 2 vols. Emerson references in vol. I.

1478 NOTOPOULOS, James A. "Emerson in Greece." ESQ, 22 (1961), 42-43. Emerson discussed in Constantine Cavarnos's The Universe and Man in American Philosophy.

1479 NOYES, Alfred. Some Aspects of Modern Poetry. New York: Stokes, 1924. "The Poetry of Emerson," pp. 65-78.

1480 NULL, Jack. "Strategies of Imagery in 'Circles.'" ESQ, 69 (1972), 265-270.

1481 NYE, R. B. "Emerson in Michigan and the Northwest." Michigan Historical Magazine, 26 (Spring, 1942), 159-172.

1482 OBUCHOWSKI, Peter Anthony. "The Relationship of Emerson's Interest in Science to His Thought." Ph.D. diss., University of Michigan, 1969. DA, 30 (1970), 3914A-3915A.

1483 _____. "Emerson's Science: An Analysis." Philological Quarterly, 54 (1975), 624-632.

1484 O'CONNOR, William Van. "Emerson, Chapman, and Righteous Individualism." Revue des Langues Vivantes, 21 (November, 1955), 442-447.

1485 O'DANIEL, Therman B. "Emerson as a Literary Critic." College Language Association Journal, 8 (September and December, 1964; March, 1965), 21-43, 157-189, 246-272.

1486 ODELL, A. T. La Doctrine sociale d'Emerson. Paris, 1931. Contains extensive coverage of Emerson's views of slavery. In French.

1487 OLDS, Sharon Stuart Cobbs. "Emerson's Innovations in Prosody: Poems, 1847." Ph.D. diss., Columbia University, 1972. DA, 34 (1973), 330A.

1488 OLIVER, Egbert S. "Melville's Picture of Emerson and Thoreau in The Confidence Man." College English, 8 (November, 1946), 61-72.

1489 _____. "Emerson's 'Days.'" New England Quarterly, 19 (December, 1946), 518-524.

1490 _____. "'Cock-a-Doodle-Doo' and Transcendental Hocus-Pocus." New England Quarterly, 21 (June, 1948), 204-216.

1491 _____. "The Asia in Emerson's Mind." Korean

Survey, 2 (May, 1953), 10-12.

1492 _____. "The Rise of American Understanding in Asia." United Asia (Bombay), 9 (June, 1957), 149-156.

1493 _____. "Emerson's Almost Perfect Orator: Edward Taylor." Today's Speech, 8 (April, 1960), 20-22.

1494 OLMERT, K. Michael, ed. "Cranch on Emerson: A Letter Re-edited." American Transcendental Quarterly, 13 (1972), 31-32.

1495 OLSSON, K. A. "Fredrika Bremer and Ralph Waldo Emerson." Swedish Pioneer Historical Quarterly, 2 (August, 1951), 39-42.

1496 ONDERDONK, James Lawrence. History of American Verse, 1610-1897. Chicago: McClurg, 1901. Emerson, pp. 301-316.

1497 ORDON, Edmund. "Mickiewicz and Emerson," in Bugelski, B. R., ed., Mickiewicz and the West: A Symposium (1956) (University of Buffalo Studies, no. 23).

1498 ORIANS, George Harrison. A Short History of American Literature, Analyzed by Decades. New York: Crofts, 1940. Emerson, pp. 145-146.

1499 ORR, John. "Transcendentalism in New England." International Review, 13 (October, 1882), 381-398.

1500 ORTH, Michael. "The Prose Style of Henry Thoreau." Language and Style, 7 (1974), 36-52. Compare with article on Emerson and Thoreau by Donald Ross, Jr. (item 1674).

1501 ORTH, Ralph H. "Ralph Waldo Emerson's Encyclopedia." Ph.D. diss., University of Rochester, 1960.

1502 _____. "Emerson Lectures in Vermont." Vermont Historian 33 (1965), 395-399.

1503 _____. "Emerson, Thoreau, and Transcendentalism." Fortnightly, 108 (1974), 3-17.

1504 OSBORNE, Clifford H. "Ralph Waldo Emerson's Reading." Ph.D. diss., University of Indiana, 1936.

1505 OSGOOD, Hamilton. "Maeterlinck and Emerson." Arena, 15 (March, 1896), 563-573.

1506 OSGOOD, Samuel. "Emerson." The Western Messenger, 2 (January, 1837), 385-393. Reprinted in Sealts and Ferguson, eds., Emerson's Nature (1969), pp. 77-80.

1507 OSTRANDER, Gilman M. "Emerson, Thoreau, and John Brown." Mississippi Valley Historical Review, 39 (March, 1953), 713-726.

1508 OTIS, William Bradley. American Verse, 1625-1807. New York: Moffat, Yard, 1909. Emerson, passim.

1509 OVERSTREET, Harry. The Mature Mind. New York: W. W. Norton, 1949. Emerson, p. 138 and passim.

1510 OVERSTREET, M. M. "Emerson on English Traits." Saturday Review of Literature, 20 (August 26, 1939), 9.

1511 PACKER, Barbara Lee. "Emerson's Apocalypse of Mind." Ph.D. diss., Yale University, 1973. DA, 34 (1974), 7241A-7242A.

1512 PADOVER, Saul K. "Ralph Waldo Emerson: The Moral Voice in Politics." Political Science Quarterly, 74 (Spring, 1959), 334-350.

1513 _____. The Genius of America: Men Whose Ideas Shaped Our Civilization. New York: McGraw Hill, 1960. "The American as Philosopher: Ralph Waldo Emerson," pp. 179-195.

1514 PAGE, Curtis Hidden, ed. The Chief American Poets. Boston: Houghton, Mifflin, 1905. Emerson, pp. 663-667.

1515 PAINTER, F. V. N. Introduction to American

Literature, rev. ed. Boston: Sibley, 1916. Emerson, pp. 208-226.

1516 PANCOAST, Henry S. An Introduction to American Literature, 2d ed., rev. New York: Henry Holt, 1912. Emerson, pp. 164-178.

1517 PANEK, LeRoy Lad. "Emerson's 'Compensation': Commerce, Law, and Physics." ESQ, 69 (1972), 218-221.

1518 PARAMANANDA, swāmi. Emerson and Vedanta, 2d ed. Boston: Vedanta Center, 1918. Reprinted from the Vedanta monthly, The Message of the East.

1519 PARIS, Bernard J. "Emerson's 'Bacchus.'" Modern Language Quarterly, 23 (June, 1962), 150-159.

1520 PARKER, Hershel. "Melville's Satire of Emerson and Thoreau: An Evaluation of the Evidence." American Transcendental Quarterly, 7 (1970), 61-67.

1521 _____. "Melville's Satire of Emerson and Thoreau: Corrections." American Transcendental Quarterly, 9 (1971), 70.

1522 _____, ed. The Confidence Man by Herman Melville. New York: W. W. Norton, 1971. (Norton Critical edition.) Has section on Melville and the Transcendentalists, pp. 254-263.

1523 PARKER, Theodore. A Discourse of Matters Pertaining to Religion (Boston, 1842). Reprinted New York: Arno Press, 1976.

1524 _____. "The Writings of Ralph Waldo Emerson: A Review of Emerson's Essays." Massachusetts Quarterly Review, 3 (March, 1850), 200-255. Reprinted in Parker's Works, centenary ed. (1907). Also reprinted in part in Konvitz, ed., Recognition (1972).

1525 _____. Life and Correspondence of Theodore Parker, ed. John Weiss. New York: D. Appleton, 1863. "Theodore Parker's Experience as a

Minister," vol. II, pp. 447-513.

1526 ———. "Lecture on Transcendentalism," in The World of Matter and the Spirit of Man. Boston: American Unitarian Association, 1907. Also in Works, Centenary Edition (1907).

1527 PARKES, Henry Bamford. "The Puritan Heresy." Hound and Horn, 1932. Reprinted in The Pragmatic Test. San Francisco: Colt Press, 1941. Pp. 10-62. Emerson, pp. 39-62.

1527a ———. "Emerson." Hound and Horn, 5 (July-September, 1933), 581-601.

1528 ———. The American Experience. New York: Random House, 1947. Emerson, pp. 188-192.

1529 PARRINGTON, Vernon Louis. Main Currents in American Thought. 3 vols. New York: Harcourt, Brace, 1939. "Ralph Waldo Emerson: Transcendental Critic," in vol. II, The Romantic Revolution in America, pp. 386-399.

1530 PARTRIDGE, Elinore Hughes. "Emerson: A Stylistic Analysis of His Prose." Ph.D. diss., University of California at Davis, 1970. DA, 31 (1971), 6564A.

1531 PATMORE, Coventry. Principle in Art. London: George Bell & Sons, 1889. Emerson, pp. 125-133.

1532 PATTEE, Fred Louis. A History of American Literature, rev. ed. New York: Silver Burdett, 1909. Emerson, pp. 208-220. Early college text; original edition, 1896.

1533 ———. "Emerson's 'Self-Reliance.'" Chautauquan, 30 (March, 1900), 628-633.

1534 ———. Side Lights on American Literature. New York: Century, 1922. Emerson, passim. See Chapter on Bryant.

1535 PAUL, Sherman. "The Angle of Vision, and the Arc of the Circle: 'Correspondence' in Ralph Waldo Emerson's Transcendental Vision." Ph.D. diss., Harvard, 1950.

1536 _____. Emerson's Angle of Vision: Man and Nature in American Experience. Cambridge, Mass.: Harvard University Press, 1952.

1537 _____. The Shores of America: Thoreau's Inward Exploration. Urbana: University of Illinois Press, 1958. Emerson, pp. 200-300 and passim.

1537a _____, ed. with Intro. Nature, the Conduct of Life, and Other Essays. New York: E. P. Dutton, 1963. Pp. v-xi.

1538 _____, ed. Six Classic American Writers. Minneapolis: University of Minnesota Press, 1970. "Ralph Waldo Emerson," by Josephine Miles, pp. 86-121.

1539 _____. Repossessing and Renewing: Essays in the Green America Tradition. Baton Rouge: Louisiana State University Press, 1976. "Emerson's Essays," pp. 1-13.

1540 PAULITS, Brother F. Joseph. "Ralph Waldo Emerson's Concept of Good and Evil." Ph.D. diss., Pittsburgh, 1955. DA, 15 (1955), 1063-1064.

1541 PAYNE, Leonidas. History of American Literature. Chicago: Rand McNally, 1919. Emerson, pp. 157-168. Early college text.

1542 _____. "Poe and Emerson." Texas Review, 7 (October, 1921), 54-69.

1543 PAYNE, William M. Leading American Essayists. New York: Holt, 1910. Reprinted Freeport, N.Y.: Books for Libraries Press, 1968. "Life and Literary Works of Emerson," pp. 135-240.

1544 PEACOCK, Markham L., Jr. The Critical Opinions of William Wordsworth. Baltimore: Johns Hopkins Press, 1950. Emerson, passim.

1545 PEAKE, Charles. "'Sweeney Erect' and the Emersonian Hero." Neophilologues, 44 (1960), 54-61.

1546 PEARCE, Roy Harvey. "On the Continuity of American Poetry." Hudson Review, 10 (Winter, 1957-

1958), 518-539. Emerson, pp. 524-527.

1547 _____. "Frost's Momentary Stay." Kenyon Review, 23 (Spring, 1961), 258-273.

1548 _____. The Continuity of American Poetry. Princeton, N. J.: Princeton University Press, 1961. Emerson, pp. 153-164.

1549 PEARSALL, Robert. "Carlyle and Emerson: Horses and Revolutions." South Atlantic Quarterly, 55 (April, 1956), 179-191.

1550 PECK, H. W. "Emerson's 'Brahma': The Poet-Philosopher in the Presence of Deity." Arena, 33 (April, 1905), 375-376.

1551 PECK, Harry Thurston. Studies in Several Literatures. New York: Dodd, Mead, 1909. Emerson, pp. 133-145.

1552 PECK, W. E. "A Lost Poem of Emerson?" Southwest Review, 12 (July, 1927), 304-305. "To the Sea," published in 1818.

1553 PECKHAM, Morse, ed. Essays: First and Second Series. Columbus, Ohio: Merrill, 1969. Facsimile reproduction.

1554 _____. "Emerson's Prose." American Transcendental Quarterly, 21 (1974), 64-74.

1555 _____. Romanticism and Behavior. Columbia: University of South Carolina Press, 1976. "An Introduction to Emerson's Essays," pp. 126-138.

1556 PERKINS, Elizabeth. "Emerson and Charles Harpur." Australian Literary Studies (Tasmania), 6 (1973), 82-88.

1557 PERRIS, George H., ed. with Intro. and Critical Notes. Emerson. London: George Bell & Sons, 1910. A collection of essays by Ralph Waldo Emerson.

1558 PERRY, R. Bliss. The American Spirit in Literature. New Haven, Conn.: Yale University Press,

1918. Emerson, pp. 119-130.

1559 _____. "Emerson's Most Famous Speech," and "Emerson's 'Savings Bank,'" in In Praise of Folly and Other Papers. Boston: Houghton, Mifflin, 1923. Pp. 81-129. See also Perry's "Emerson's 'Savings Bank.'" Nation, 99 (September, 24, 1914), 371-373. Refers to Journals.

1560 _____, ed. The Heart of Emerson's Journals. Boston: Houghton, Mifflin, 1926. Reprinted New York: Dover Press, 1958.

1561 _____. Emerson Today. Princeton, N. J.: Princeton University Press, 1931. Reprinted Hamden, Conn.: Shoe String Press, 1969.

1562 _____, ed. The Heart of Emerson's Essays. Boston & New York: Houghton, Mifflin, 1933.

1563 _____. The Thought and Character of William James, 2 vols. Boston: Houghton, Mifflin, 1935. Reprinted Westport, Conn.: Greenwood Press, 1974. Emerson, vol. I, chapters 3-5.

1564 PERRY, T. A. "Emerson, the Historical Frame and Shakespeare." Modern Language Quarterly, 9 (December, 1948), 440-447.

1565 PERSONS, Stow. American Minds: A History of Ideas. New York: Henry Holt, 1958. "Emerson as a Transcendentalist," pp. 209-213.

1566 PETERSON, Edith. "Emerson's 'Brahma.'" Orient/West, 8 (1963), 53-55.

1567 PETTIGREW, Richard C. "Milton in the Work of Ralph Waldo Emerson, James Russell Lowell, and Oliver Wendell Holmes." Ph.D. diss., Duke University, 1930.

1568 _____. "Emerson and Milton." American Literature, 3 (March, 1931), 45-69.

1569 PHELPS, William Lyon. "American Philosopher." Ladies Home Journal, 40 (April, 1923), 23 ff.

PHILLIPS, George Searle   see   SEARLE, January

1570 PICHT, Douglas R. "Robert Henri and the Transcendental Spirit." Research Studies, 36 (1968), 50-56.

1571 PINSKER, Sanford. "Emerson's Anti-Essay: The Dissolving Rhetoric of 'Intellect.'" ESQ, 69 (1972), 284-287.

1572 POCHMANN, Henry A. "The Emerson Canon." University Toronto Quarterly, 12 (July, 1943), 478-484.

1573 _____. "Emerson and the St. Louis Hegelians." Anglo-German Review, 10 (February, 1944), 14-17.

1574 _____. New England Transcendentalism and St. Louis Hegelianism. Philadelphia: Carl Schurz, 1948. Emerson, pp. 53-65.

1575 _____. German Culture in America: 1600-1900. Madison: University of Wisconsin Press, 1957. Emerson, pp. 153-207.

1576 POIRIER, Richard. A World Elsewhere. New York: Oxford University Press, 1966. "Self and Environment," pp. 3-49. "Is There an I for an Eye?" Pp. 50-92.

1577 _____, et al., eds. American Literature. 2 vols. Boston: Little, Brown, 1970. Emerson, vol. I, pp. 438-534.

1578 POLLIN, Burton R. "Poe's Use of D'Israeli's Curiosities to Belittle Emerson." Poe Newsletter, 3 (1970), 38.

1579 _____. "Emerson's Annotations in the British Museum Copy of The Dial." Studies in Bibliography, 24 (1971), 187-195.

1580 POLLITT, J. D. "Ralph Waldo Emerson's Debt to John Milton." Marshall Review, 3 (1939), 13-21.

1581 POLLOCK, Robert C. "A Re-Appraisal of Emerson." Thought, 32 (Spring, 1957), 86-132.

1582 _____. "Single Vision," in Gardiner, Harold C., ed., American Classics Reconsidered: A Christian Appraisal (1958), pp. 15-58.

1583 POMEROY, Ralph S. "Ralph Waldo Emerson as a Public Speaker." Ph.D. diss., Stanford University, Speech, 1960.

1584 POMMER, Henry F. "Literature as Religion." Modern Churchman, 2 (July, 1958), 34-43.

1585 _____. "The Contents and Basis of Emerson's Belief in Compensation." PMLA, 77 (June, 1962), 248-253.

1586 _____. Emerson's First Marriage. Carbondale: Southern Illinois University Press, 1967.

1587 PORTE, Joel. "Emerson and Thoreau: Transcendentalists in Conflict." Ph.D. diss., Harvard, 1962.

1588 _____. "Nature as Symbol: Emerson's Noble Doubt." New England Quarterly, 37 (December, 1964), 453-476.

1589 _____. Emerson and Thoreau: Transcendentalists in Conflict. Middletown, Conn.: Wesleyan University Press, 1966.

1590 _____. "Emerson, Thoreau, and the Double Consciousness." New England Quarterly, 41 (March, 1968), 40-50.

1591 _____. "Transcendental Antics," in Levin, Harry, ed., Veins of Humor. Cambridge, Mass.: Harvard University Press, 1972. Pp. 167-183.

1592 _____. "The Problem of Emerson," in Engel, Monroe, ed., Uses of Literature. Cambridge, Mass.: Harvard University Press, 1973. Pp. 85-114.

1593 PORTER, Carolyn Jane. "Form and Process in American Literature." Ph.D. diss., Rice, 1972. DA, 34 (1973), 1291A. Chapter on Emerson's conflict to reject established forms and the recognition that such rejection makes formlessness harmful to human needs.

1594 PORTER, Charlotte, and Helen Archibald Clarke. "Each and All." Poet-Lore, 6 (May, 1894), 273-276.

1595 PORTER, Lawrence C. "Transcendentalism: A Self-Portrait." New England Quarterly, 35 (March, 1962), 27-47.

1596 PORTER, M. Gilbert. "John Updike's 'A & P,' the Establishment, and an Emersonian Cashier." English Journal, 61 (November, 1972), 1155-1158.

1597 PORTNAY, Howard N. "Emerson, Melville, and 'The Poet.'" Junction (Brooklyn College), 1 (1973), 172-175.

1598 POTTER, C. F. "The Hindu Invasion of America." Modern Thinker, 1 (March, 1932), 16-23.

1599 POTTER, Russell. "'Ladies and Gentlemen, Mr. Emerson.'" Saturday Review, 39 (March 10, 1956), 9-10, 40-41.

1600 POUND, Louise. "Emerson as a Romanticist." Mid-West Quarterly, 2 (January, 1915), 184-195.

1601 POWELL, Thomas. The Living Authors of America. New York: Stringer and Townsend, 1850. Emerson, pp. 49-77. Good early article, principally on poetry.

1602 POWER, Julia. Shelley in America in the Nineteenth Century. Lincoln: University of Nebraska Press, 1940. Emerson, passim.

1603 PRESSLEY, Ruth Peyton. "Whitman's Debt to Emerson." Ph.D. diss., University of Texas, 1930.

1604 PRITCHARD, John Paul. Return to the Fountains. Durham: Duke University Press, 1942. Reprinted New York: Octagon Books, 1966. "Emerson's Debt to Aristotle," pp. 44-60.

1605 _____. Criticism in America. Norman: University of Oklahoma Press, 1956. Emerson, pp. 43-56.

1606 PROCTOR, Edna. "Ralph Waldo Emerson." National, 34 (July, 1911), 477.

1607 PULOS, C. E. "Walden and Emerson's 'The Sphinx.'" American Transcendental Quarterly, 1 (1969), 7-11.

1608 PURDY, Vivian. "Emerson and Oriental Philosophy." Southern University Bulletin, 43 (Fall, 1956), 57-69.

1609 QUINN, Arthur Hobson, ed. Emerson's Essays. New York: Charles Scribner's Sons, 1920.

1610 QUINN, Patrick F. "Emerson and Mysticism." American Literature, 21 (1950), 397-414.

1611 ———. "Poe's 'Eureka' and Emerson's Nature." ESQ, 31 (1963), 47.

1612 RANDEL, William P., ed. "A Late Emerson Letter." American Literature, 12 (January, 1941), 496-497.

1613 RANDS, William B. "Transcendentalism in England, New England, and India." Contemporary Review, 29 (c. 1896), 469-488.

1614 RAO, Adapha R. "Ralph Waldo Emerson's Attitude Toward Humanitarian Reform." Ph.D. diss., University of Wisconsin, 1964. DA, 25 (1965), 2519.

1615 RAO, B. Damodar. "Emerson and the Principles of Literature." Literary Criterion (India), 5 (1962), 39-47.

1616 ———. "Conceptual Enactment: Emerson's Literary Performance." American Studies Research Centre Newsletter (India), 10 (1966), 26.

1616a ———. "Emerson," in Narasimhaiah, ed. Indian Response (1967), pp. 15-27.

1617 RAPIN, René. "Emerson's English Traits, Chap. IX."

Explicator, 11 (November, 1952), item 9.

1618 RAY, Gordon Norton, Leon Edel, et al., eds. Masters of American Literature. Boston: Houghton, Mifflin, 1959. Emerson, pp. 237-364.

1619 RAYAPATI, Jacob P. Rao. "Early American Interest in Vedic Literature and Vedantic Philosophy." Ph.D. diss., University of Pennsylvania, 1970. DA, 32 (1971), 397A.

1620 _____. Early American Interest in Vedanta. New York: Asia Publishing House, 1973. "Early Vedic Readings by American Transcendentalists," pp. 93-106.

1621 REAVER, J. Russell. "Ralph Waldo Emerson's Use of Imagery as Seen in the Study of His Poetry." Ph.D. diss., Ohio State, 1942.

1622 _____. Emerson as Mythmaker. Gainsville: University of Florida Press, 1954.

1623 _____. "Emerson's Use of Proverbs." Southern Folklore Quarterly, 27 (December, 1963), 280-299.

1624 _____. "Mythology in Emerson's Poems." ESQ, 39 (1965), 56-63.

1625 _____. "Emerson on the Psychic Potential." American Transcendental Quarterly, 9 (1971), 52-55.

1626 REDDING, Mary W. Edrich [see also Edrich]. "Emerson's 'Instant Eternity': An Existential Approach," in Carlson, Eric W. and J. Lasley Dameron, eds., Emerson's Relevance Today (1971), pp. 43-52. Also in American Transcendental Quarterly, 9 (1971), 43-52.

1627 REDPATH, James, ed. Echoes of Harper's Ferry (1860). Reprinted New York: Arno Press, 1976.

1628 REED, Sampson. Observations on the Growth of the Mind, 5th ed. (Boston, 1859). Reprinted New York: Arno Press, 1976.

1629 REGAN, Robert Alton. "Updike's Symbol of the

Center." Modern Fiction Studies, 20 (1974), 77-96.

1630 REID, Alfred S. "Emerson and Bushnell as Forerunners of Jamesian Pragmatism." Furman Studies, 13 (November, 1965), 18-30.

1631 _____. "Emerson's Prose Style: An Edge to Goodness." ESQ, 60 (1970), 37-42. Also in Strauch, Carl F., ed., Style in the American Renaissance (1970), pp. 37-42.

1632 _____. "Emersonian Ideas in the Youth Movement of the 1960's." American Transcendental Quarterly, 9 (1971), 12-16.

1633 REILLY, John M. "'Threnody' and the Traditional Funeral Elegy." ESQ, 47 (1967), 17-19.

1634 REIN, Irving Joseph. "The New England Transcendentalists: Rhetoric of Paradox." Ph.D. diss., University of Pittsburgh, 1966. DA, 27 (1967), 3149A.

1635 REITEN, Sister Paula. "Emerson's 'The Snow-Storm.'" Explicator, 22 (January, 1964), item 39.

1636 REUBEN, Paul P. "Dynamics of New England Transcendentalism in Benjamin Orange Flowers' Arena, 1889-1909." Ph.D. diss., Bowling Green State University, 1970.

1637 REYNOLDS, Michael S. "Whitman's Early Prose and 'The Sleepers.'" American Literature, 41 (1969) 406-411. Relates to Emerson and Swedenborg.

1638 RHINELANDER, Philip H. "Education and Society." The Key Reporter, 34 (Autumn, 1968), 2-4.

1639 RHYS, Ernest, ed. Conduct of Life, Nature, and Other Essays. New York: E. P. Dutton, 1908. New ed. edited by Sherman Paul, 1963. (Everyman's Library Edition.)

1640 _____, ed. English Traits, Representative Men, and Other Essays. New York: E. P. Dutton, 1908. (Everyman's Library Edition.)

1641 _____, ed. Society and Solitude and Other Essays. New York: E. P. Dutton, 1912. (Everyman's Library Edition.)

1642 RICE, Allen T., ed. Essays from the North American Review. London: Nimmo & Bain, 1880. "'Milton,' July, 1838," by Emerson, pp. 99-123.

1643 RICHARD, Blakeney, J. "Emerson and Berkeleian Idealism." ESQ, 59 (1970), 90-96.

1644 RICHARDSON, Charles Francis. American Literature, 1607-1885. New York: G. P. Putnam's, 1887-1889.

1645 RICHARDSON, L. N. "What Rutherford B. Hayes Liked in Emerson." American Literature, 17 (March, 1945), 22-32.

1646 RICHMOND, Mrs. H. L. "Ralph Waldo Emerson in Florida." Florida Historical Quarterly (October, 1939), 75-93. Relates Emerson's Meeting with Achille Murat.

1647 RICKMAN, H. P., ed. Pattern and Meaning in History: Thoughts on History and Society. New York: Harper's, 1961. Also published as Meaning in History: Wilhelm Dilthey's Thoughts on History and Society. London: George Allen, 1961.

1648 RIDER, Daniel E. "Music Philosophy and Practice of the New England Transcendentalists." Ph.D. diss., Minnesota, 1962.

1649 RIDGELY, J. V. "Whitman, Emerson, and Friend." Columbia Library Columns, 10 (November, 1960), 15-19.

1650 RIEPE, Dale. "Emerson and Indian Philosophy." Journal of History of Ideas, 28 (January-March, 1967), 115-122.

1651 _____. The Philosophy of India and Its Impact on American Thought. Springfield, Ill.: Charles C. Thomas, 1970. Emerson, Chapters 1 and 2.

1652 RILEY, I. Woodbridge. American Thought from Puritanism to Pragmatism. New York: Holt, Rinehart, 1915. Revised, 1941. Reprinted Gloucester, Mass.: Peter Smith, 1959. Emerson, pp. 140-171.

1653 RIPLEY, George. "Philosophic Thought in Boston," in Memorial History of Boston. Boston: Osgood, 1880.

1654 ROBERTS, A. J., and C. J. Weber. "Emerson's Visits to Waterville College." Colby Mercury, 5 (April 1, 1934), 41-45.

1655 ROBERTS, J. Russell. "Seventeenth Century Contributions to Ralph Waldo Emerson's Thought." Ph.D. diss., Washington, Philosophy, 1940.

1656 _____. "Emerson's Debt to the Seventeenth Century." American Literature, 21 (November, 1949), 298-310.

1657 ROBERTSON, Eric S. Life of Henry Wadsworth Longfellow. London: W. Scott, 1887. Reprinted Port Washington, N. Y.: Kennikat Press, 1975. Emerson, Chapter 13, pp. 171-177.

1658 ROBERTSON, John M. Modern Humanists: Sociological Studies of Carlyle, Mill, Emerson, Arnold, et al. London: Sonnenschein, 1891, 1895. Reprinted Port Washington, N. Y.: Kennikat Press, 1970.

1659 ROBINSON, David. "The Romantic Quest in Poe and Emerson: 'Ulalume' and 'The Sphinx.'" American Transcendental Quarterly, 26 (1975), 26-30.

1660 ROBINSON, Edwin Arlington. "Letter to D. G. Mason." Yale Review (June, 1936), 861. Remarks on the experience of reading Emerson.

1661 ROCKWELL, Kiffin Ayres. "Emerson's 'Hamatreya'-- Another Guess." ESQ, 33 (1963), 24.

1662 ROGERS, Jane E. "The Transcendental Quest in Emerson and Melville." Ph.D. diss., Pittsburgh, 1973. DA, 35 (1974), 1632A.

1663 ROLLINS, Henry B. "Ralph Waldo Emerson and

Practical Affairs." Ph.D. diss., North Carolina, 1956.

1664 ROSA, Alfred E. "Charles Ives: Music, Transcendentalism, and Politics." New England Quarterly, 44 (1971), 433-443.

1665 _____. "Emerson and the Salem Lyceum." Essex Institute of Historical Collections, 110 (1974), 75-85.

1666 ROSE, Edward J. "Emerson and King Arthur." ESQ, 33 (1963), 49-51.

1667 _____. "Melville, Emerson, and the Sphinx." New England Quarterly, 36 (June, 1963), 249-258.

1668 ROSENBERRY, Edward H. "Israel Potter, Benjamin Franklin, and the Doctrine of Self-Reliance." ESQ, 28 (1962), 27-29.

1669 ROSENFELD, Alvin H. "Emerson and Whitman: Their Personal and Literary Relationships." Ph.D. diss., Brown University, 1967. DA, 28 (1968), 3197A.

1670 ROSENTHAL, Bernard. "The Dial, Transcendentalism and Margaret Fuller." English Language Notes, 8 (1970), 28-36.

1671 _____, ed. Woman in the Nineteenth Century, by Margaret Fuller, orig. ed. by Arthur B. Fuller. Boston: Jewett, 1855. Reprinted New York: W. W. Norton, 1971.

1672 ROSS, Donald, Jr. "Emerson's 'Brahma.'" ESQ, 39 (1965), 42-43.

1673 _____. "Composition as a Stylistic Feature." Style, 4 (1970), 1-10.

1674 _____. "Emerson and Thoreau: A Comparison of Prose Styles." Language and Style, 6 (1973), 185-195.

1675 _____. "Emerson's Stylistic Influence on Whitman,'" in Strauch, Carl F., ed., Characteristics of Emerson: Transcendental Poet (1975), pp. 41-51. Also in American Transcendental Quarterly, 25 (1975), 41-51.

1676 ROSS, William Michael. "The Shifting Viewpoint: A Key to the Thought and Art of Emerson's Essays." Ph.D. diss., Fordham University, 1972. DA, 34 (1973), 285A.

1677 ROTHSTEIN, Eric, ed. George Eliot, DeQuincey, and Emerson. Madison: University of Wisconsin Press, 1976. "Necessary Truths: The Poetics of Emerson's Proverbs," by Ralph C. LaRosa.

1678 ROUNTREE, Thomas J., ed. Critics on Emerson. Coral Gables, Fla.: University of Miami Press, 1973.

1679 ROVIT, Earl. "James and Emerson: The Lesson of the Master." The American Scholar, 33 (1964), 434-440.

1680 _____. "Emerson: A Contemporary Reconsideration." The American Scholar, 41 (1972), 429-438.

1681 ROWE, H. D. "Emerson as Quoter: Notes on 'Eloquence' and 'Art and Criticism.'" New England Quarterly, 29 (June, 1956), 233-234.

1682 ROYCE, Josiah. The Religious Aspect of Philosophy: A Critique of the Bases of Conduct and of Faith. Boston: Houghton, Mifflin, 1885.

1683 _____. The Spirit of Modern Philosophy. Boston & New York: Houghton, Mifflin, 1892.

1684 _____. William James and Other Essays on the Philosophy Life. New York: Macmillan, 1911. Emerson, p. 8 and passim.

1685 RUCHAMES, Louis. "Two Forgotten Addresses by Ralph Waldo Emerson." American Literature, 28 (January, 1957), 425-433. Addresses deal with abolition of slavery. First printed in National Anti-Slavery Standard, July 16, 1846; and The Liberator, August 17, 1849.

1686 _____. "Emerson's Second West Indian Emancipation Address." New England Quarterly, 28 (September, 1965), 383-388.

1687 RUCKER, Mary E. "Emerson's 'Friendship' as Process." ESQ, 69 (1972), 234-248.

1688 RULAND, Richard. The Re-Discovery of American Literature. Cambridge, Mass.: Harvard University Press, 1967. Emerson, pp. 237-272. Analysis of F. O. Matthiessen's discussion of Emerson in American Renaissance.

1689 RUSK, Ralph L., ed. Letters of Ralph Waldo Emerson. 6 vols. New York: Columbia University Press, 1939.

1690 _____. "Review of Emerson the Essayist by Kenneth Walter Cameron." American Literature, 17 (January, 1946), 272-274.

1691 _____. Life of Ralph Waldo Emerson. New York: Scribner's, 1949.

1692 _____. "Emerson and the Stream of Experience." English Journal, 42 (April, 1953), 181-187; also in College English, 14 (April, 1953), 373-379.

1693 _____. "The Abiding Dignity of Man as Man." New York Times Book Review, May 24, 1953, pp. 1, 23.

1694 _____. "Emerson in Salem." Essex Institute of Historical Collections, 94 (July, 1958), 194-195.

1695 RUSSELL, John D. "Emerson's 'Brahma.'" Explicator, 20 (December, 1961), item 29.

1696 RUSSELL, Phillips. Emerson: The Wisest American. New York: Blue Ribbon Books, 1929.

1697 RUST, R. Dilworth. "Vision in Moby-Dick." ESQ, 33 (1963), 73-74.

1698 RYAN, Alvan S. "The Critique of Transcendentalism: Orestes A. Brownson," in Gardiner, ed., American Classics Reconsidered (1958), pp. 98-120.

1699 _____. "Frost and Emerson: Voice and Vision." Massachusetts Review, 1 (Fall, 1959), 5-23.

1700 _____. "Emerson's 'The American Scholar.'" Explicator, 18 (June, 1960), item 53.

1701 SADLER, M. E. "Emerson's Influence on Education." Education Review, 26 (December, 1903), 457-463.

1701a ST. CLAIR, F. Y. "Emerson's 'Chiser, the Fountain of Life.'" Philological Quarterly, 26 (January, 1947), 81-84. Relates to essay "Persian Poetry."

1702 _____. "Emerson Among the Siphars." American Literature, 19 (March, 1947), 73-77. Relates to early fictional tale, "Organ," 1822.

1702a SAINTSBURY, George. A History of Criticism. New York: Dodd, Mead, 1904. "Emerson as Critic," pp. 632-634.

1703 SAKAMOTO, Masayuki. An Introduction to the American Renaissance: Emerson, Thoreau, Whitman. Tokyo: Kenkyusha, 1969. Emerson, pp. 25-72.

1704 SAKMANN, Paul. Emerson's Geisteswelt. Stuttgart, 1927. In German.

1705 SALOMON, Louis B. "A Walk with Emerson on the Dark Side." Costerus, 6 (1972), 121-135.

1706 SALTER, William M. "Emerson's Views on Reform." New England Magazine, 4 (July, 1891), 656-664.

1707 _____. "Emerson's Views of Society and Reform." International Journal of Ethics, 13 (1903), 414.

1708 SAMS, Henry W., ed. Autobiography of Brook Farm. Englewood Cliffs, N. J.: Prentice-Hall, 1958. Emerson, pp. 221-226 and passim. Collection of critical essays; contains good bibliography.

1709 SANBORN, Franklin Benjamin. "Emerson, The Poet-Philosopher." The American, 4 (May 6, 1882), 54.

1710 _____, ed. The Genius and Character of Emerson. Lectures at the Concord School of Philosophy. Boston: Osgood, 1885. Reprinted Port Washington, N. Y.: Kennikat Press, 1970. Contains notable essays by friends of Emerson in the Concord School of Philosophy.

1711 _____. "Emerson Among the Poets," in The Genius and Character of Emerson (1885), pp. 173-214.

1712 _____. "Emerson and His Friends in Concord." New England Magazine, 4 (December, 1890), 411-431. Reprinted in American Transcendental Quarterly, 13 (1972), 53-62.

1713 _____. "The Emerson-Thoreau Correspondence." Atlantic Monthly, 59 (May, 1892), 557-596.

1714 _____. "The Maintenance of a Poet." Atlantic Monthly, 86 (December, 1900), 819-825.

1715 _____. Ralph Waldo Emerson, edited by M. A. DeWolfe Howe. Boston: Small, Maynard, 1901. Beacon Biographies Series.

1716 _____. "Emerson, Thoreau, Channing." Springfield Republican, July 2, 1902, p. 14.

1717 _____. "Emerson and Contemporary Poets." Critic, 42 (May, 1903), 413-416.

1718 _____. The Personality of Emerson. Boston: Goodspeed, 1903. Personal reminiscences of Emerson from 1853.

1719 _____. "A Concord Notebook." Critic, 47 (October and November, 1905), 349-356, 444-451.

1720 _____. "Theodore Parker and Ralph Waldo Emerson." Critic, 48 (September, 1906), 273-281.

1721 _____. "Emerson in Ancestry and in Life," in

Recollections of Seventy Years. 2 vols. Boston: R. G. Badger, 1909. Vol. II, pp. 420-440.

1722 SANDEEN, Ernest E. "Ralph Waldo Emerson's Americanism." Ph.D. diss., Iowa, 1940.

1723 _____. "Emerson as an American," in Critical Studies in Arnold, Emerson, and Newman, ed. by Joseph E. Baker. Iowa City: University of Iowa Press, 1942. Pp. 63-118.

1724 SANDERS, William. "Emerson and Melville: The Oversoul and the Underworld." Junction, 2 (1973), 25-29.

1725 SANFORD, Charles L. "Emerson, Thoreau, and the Hereditary Duality." ESQ, 54 (1968), 36-43. Also in Cook, Reginald L., ed., Themes, Tones, and Motifs ... (1968), pp. 36-43.

1726 SAN JUAN, Epifanio, Jr. "Explication of Emerson's 'Each and All.'" ESQ, 43 (1966), 106-109.

1727 _____. "Symbolic Significance in the Poems of Emerson." St. Louis Quarterly, 4 (1966), 37-54.

1728 SANTAS, Constantine. "Emerson's Theory of the Hero." Ph.D. diss., Northwestern University, 1971. DA, 32 (1971), 3329A.

1729 SANTAYANA, George. Interpretations of Poetry and Religion. New York: Scribner's, 1900. Emerson, pp. 217-233.

1730 _____. "The Genteel Tradition in American Philosophy," in The Winds of Doctrine. New York: Scribner's, 1913. Pp. 186-215.

1731 _____. Little Essays from the Writings of George Santayana, ed. L. P. Smith. New York: Scribner's, 1920. Emerson, pp. 199-203.

1732 SAXENA, P. K. "A Note on Emerson and 'Ex oriente lux.'" Literary Criterion (India), 6 (1965), 48-55.

1733 SCHAMBERGER, John Edward. "Emerson's Concept of the 'Moral Sense': A Study of Its Sources and

and Its Importance to His Intellectual Development." Ph.D. diss., University of Pennsylvania, 1969. DA, 31 (1970), 1292A.

1734 _____. "Emerson's Reading of D. Stewart and P. Price at Harvard." ESQ, 18 (1972), 179-183.

1735 SCHAPPES, Morris, ed. "The Letters of Emma Lazarus: 1868-1885." Bulletin of the New York Public Library, 53 (July, August, September, 1949), 315-334, 367-386, 419-446.

1736 SCHEICK, William J. "Emerson's 'Prudence': Language as the Organizing Principle." ESQ, 69 (1972), 249-257.

1737 _____. "Aspiring to the Highest: Imagery in Emerson's 'The American Scholar.'" Notre Dame English Journal, 8 (1973), 34-42.

1738 SCHILLER, Andrew. "Gnomic Structure in Emerson's Poetry." Papers of the Michigan Academy of Sciences and Art Literature, 40 (1955), 313-320.

1739 SCHING, A. "French Origins of American Transcendentalism." American Journal of Psychology, 29 (January, 1918), 50-65.

1740 SCHLABACK, Anne V. "A Critical Study of Some Problems Derived from Hawthorne's Novels and Emerson's Representative Men." Ph.D. diss., University of Wisconsin, 1947.

1741 SCHLESINGER, Arthur M., Jr. "Jacksonian Democracy and Literature," from The Age of Jackson. Boston: Little, Brown, 1945. Pp. 369-391.

1742 SCHLICHENMAIER, Carol. "The Poetic Theory of Emerson, Poe, and T. S. Eliot." Ph.D. diss., University of Miama, 1963.

1743 SCHNEIDER, Herbert W. The Puritan Mind. New York: Henry Holt, 1930. Reprinted Ann Arbor: University of Michigan Press, 1958. Emerson, pp. 257, 263, and passim.

1744 _____. A History of American Philosophy. New

York: Columbia University Press, 1946. Emerson, pp. 280-286.

1745 _____. "American Transcendentalism's Escape from Phenomenology," in Simon, Myron, and Thornton H. Parsons, eds., Transcendentalism and Its Legacy (1966), pp. 215-228.

1746 SCHNEIDER, Richard John. "The Balanced Vision: Thoreau's Observations of Nature." Ph.D. diss., University of California at Santa Barbara, 1973. DA, 34 (1974), 5929A.

1747 SCHORER, C. E. "Emerson and the Wisconsin Lyceum." American Literature, 24 (January, 1953), 462-475.

SCHORER, Mark see SHORER, Mark

1748 SCHORTEMEIER, F. E. "Indianapolis Newspaper Accounts of Ralph Waldo Emerson." Indiana Magazine of History, 49 (1953), 307-312.

1749 SCHOTT, Rolf. "Ralph Waldo Emerson." Neue Schweizer Rundschau, 21 (May, 1953), 33-38.

1750 SCHOTTLAENDER, Rudolf. "Two Dionysians: Emerson and Nietzsche." South Atlantic Quarterly, 39 (July, 1940), 330-343.

1751 SCHRADER, Allen. "Emerson to Salinger to Parker." Saturday Review, 42 (April 11, 1959), 52, 58.

1752 SCHULTZ, Arthur R., and Henry A. Pochmann. "George Ripley: Unitarian, Transcendentalist, or Infidel?" American Literature, 14 (March, 1942), 1-19.

1753 SCHWARTZ, Arthur. "The American Romantics: An Analysis." ESQ, 35 (1964), 39-44.

1754 SCOTT, Eleanor B. "Emerson Wins the Nine Hundred Dollars." American Literature, 17 (March, 1945), 78-85. Western lecture tour of 1856.

1755 SCOTT, Leonora C. The Life and Letters of Christopher P. Cranch. Boston: Houghton, Mifflin, 1917. Emerson, pp. 49-65.

1756 SCUDDER, Townsend, III. "Ralph Waldo Emerson in England." Ph.D. diss., Yale, 1932.

1757 _____. "Emerson's British Lecture Tour, 1847-1848," 2 parts. American Literature, 7 (March and May, 1935), 15-36, 166-180.

1758 _____. "Emerson in Dundee." American Scholar, 4 (Summer, 1935), 331-344.

1759 _____. "Emerson in London and the London Lectures." American Literature, 8 (March, 1936), 22-36.

1760 _____. "A Chronological List of Emerson's Lectures on His British Lecture Tour of 1847-1848." PMLA, 51 (March, 1936), 243-248.

1761 _____. "Incredible Recoil: A Study in Aspiration." American Scholar, 5 (Winter, 1936), 35-48.

1762 _____. Lonely Wayfaring Man: Emerson and Some Englishmen. London & New York: Oxford University Press, 1936.

1763 _____. "The Human Emerson." Saturday Review of Literature, 20 (June 10, 1939), 15, 34.

1764 SEAGER, Allan. They Worked for a Better World. New York: Macmillan, 1939. Emerson, pp. 56-75.

1765 SEALTS, Merton M., Jr., and Alfred R. Ferguson, eds. Emerson's "Nature": Origin, Growth, and Meaning. New York: Dodd, Mead, 1969. Contains 1836 text, passages from Journals, early reviews, criticism, and bibliography. Also drawings by C. P. Cranch.

1766 _____. "Emerson on the Scholar, 1833-1837." PMLA, 85 (1970), 185-195.

1767 _____. "Emerson on the Scholar, 1838: A Study of 'Literary Ethics,'" in Falk, Robert P., ed., Literature and Ideas in America (1975), pp. 40-57.

1768 SEARLE, January [pseud. for George Searle Phillips]. Emerson: His Life and Writings. London: Holyoake, 1855. First life of Emerson, 48 pp.

1769 SEARS, Clara E. Bronson Alcott's Fruitlands. Boston: Houghton, Mifflin, 1915.

1770 SEBOUHIAN, George. "'Experience': An Approach to Content and Method." ESQ, 47 (1967), 75-78.

1771 ———. "The Emersonian Idealism of Henry James." Ph.D. diss., Ohio State, 1972. DA, 34 (1973), 739A.

1772 SHACKFORD, Martha Hale. Talks on Ten Poets, Wordsworth, to Moody. New York: Bookman Associates, 1958. "Emerson, 'Woodnotes': 1840-1841," pp. 60-67.

1773 SHAFFER, R. B. "Emerson and His Circle: Advocates of Functionalism." Journal of the Society of Architectural History, 8 (July-December, 1948), 17-20.

1774 SHANLEY, J. Lyndon, ed. The Making of Walden, with the Text of the First Version. Reprinted Chicago: University of Chicago Press, 1958.

1775 SHAPIRO, Fred C. "The Transcending Margaret Fuller." Ms., 1 (November, 1972), 36-39.

1776 SHAPIRO, Karl Jay, ed. American Poetry, vol. 4 of American Literary Forms, ed. William Van O'Connor. New York: Thomas Y. Crowell, 1960.

1777 ———. Essay on Rime. New York: Reynal & Hitchcock, 1945. Emerson, p. 30. An essay in verse.

1778 SHARMA, Mohan Lal. "Emerson's 'Hamatreya.'" Explicator, 26 (1968), item 63.

1779 ———. "Emerson's Multilingual Coinage 'Hamatreya.'" Word Study, 44 (1968), 6-8.

1780 SHAW, Charles Gray. "Emerson, the Nihilist." International Journal of Ethics, 25 (October, 1914), 68-86.

1781 SHEA, Daniel B. "Emerson and the American Metamorphosis," in Levin, David, ed., Emerson ... (1975), pp. 29-56.

1782 SHEPARD, Odell, ed. The Heart of Thoreau's Journals. Boston: Houghton, Mifflin, 1927.

1783 ———. Henry Wadsworth Longfellow. New York: American Book, 1934. Emerson, passim.

1784 ———. Pedlar's Progress: The Life of Bronson Alcott. Boston: Little, Brown, 1937.

1785 ———, ed. Journals of Bronson Alcott. Boston: Little, Brown, 1938.

1786 SHEPHARD, G. F. "Emerson's Attitude Toward the Classics." Education, 54 (June, 1934), 626-628.

1787 ———. "Emerson's Attitude Toward the Fine Arts." Education, 55 (December, 1934), 223-225.

1788 ———. "Emerson and Natural Science." Education, 59 (June, 1939), 590-594.

1789 SHERMAN, Stuart Pratt, ed. with Intro. Essays and Poems by Emerson. New York: Scribner's, 1921.

1790 ———. "The Emersonian Liberation," in Americans. New York: Scribner's, 1922. Pp. 62-121. The original introduction to Essays and Poems by Emerson (1921).

1791 SHERWOOD, Donald Guthrie. "Emerson's Attitudes Toward the Drama and Theater from 1803 through 1850." Ph.D. diss., University of Indiana, 1943.

1792 SHORER, Mark, et al., eds. Criticism: The Foundation of Modern Literary Judgment, rev. ed. New York: Harcourt, Brace, 1958. Orig. ed., 1948. [Author's name may be given as Schorer.]

1793 SHUKLA, Kamal Kant. "Emerson and Hindu Thought." Ph.D. diss., Wayne State University, 1973. DA, 34 (1974), 7246A.

1794 SHUSTER, G. N. "Ancient Vision and the Newer

Needs: Philosophy of Emerson." Catholic World, 106 (March, 1918), 733-741.

1795 SILL, Edward Rowland. "The Prose and Verse of Emerson." Overland Monthly, 4 (October, 1884), 434-443.

1796 SILLEN, Samuel. "Emerson at War." New Masses, 47 (May 25, 1943), 22-24.

1797 _____. "The Living Emerson." Masses and Mainstream, 6 (May, 1953), 28-35.

1798 SILVER, Mildred. "Ralph Waldo Emerson and the Idea of Progress." Ph.D. diss., University of Iowa, 1938.

1799 _____. "Emerson and the Idea of Progress." American Literature, 12 (March, 1940), 1-19.

1800 SILVER, Rollo G. "Emerson as Abolitionist." New England Quarterly, 6 (March, 1933), 154-158.

1801 _____. "Ellery Channing's Collaboration with Emerson." American Literature, 7 (March, 1935), 84-86.

1802 _____. "Mr. Emerson Appeals to Boston." American Book Collector, 6 (May-June, 1935), 209-219. Anti-slavery lecture given in 1855.

1803 SIMISON, B. D. "The Letters of Ralph Waldo Emerson: Addenda." Modern Language Notes, 55 (June, 1955), 425-427.

1804 SIMON, Julius. "Ralph Waldo Emerson in Deutschland: 1852-1932." Ph.D. diss., Giessen, 1937; published Berlin, 1937.

1805 SIMON, Myron, and Thornton H. Parsons, eds. Transcendentalism and Its Legacy. Ann Arbor: University of Michigan Press, 1966. Collection of essays on Emerson and others.

1806 SIMONDS, Arthur Beaman. American Song: A Collection of Representative American Poems. New York: G. P. Putnam's, 1894. Criticism of Emerson's poems, pp. 39-43.

1807 SIMONDS, William E. A Student's History of American Literature. Boston: Houghton, Mifflin, 1909. Emerson, pp. 157-177.

1808 SIMPSON, Lewis P. "Emerson and the Myth of New England's Intellectual Lapse." ESQ, 10 (1958), 28-31.

1809 _____. "The Telescope and the Transparent Eyeball." South Atlantic Bulletin, 36 (1971), 30-31.

1810 _____. "The Crises of Alienation in Emerson's Early Thought." American Transcendental Quarterly, 9 (1971), 35-43.

1811 _____. The Man of Letters in New England and the South. Baton Rouge: Louisiana State University Press, 1973. Emerson, pp. 62-85.

1812 SINGH, Man M. "Ralph Waldo Emerson and India." Ph.D. diss., University of Pennsylvania, 1947.

1813 SISK, John P. "Beatniks and Tradition." Commonweal, 70 (April 17, 1959), 75-77.

1814 SKARD, Sigmund. The Study of American Literature. Philadelphia: University of Pennsylvania Press, 1949. Pamphlet: Inaugural Lecture at the American Institute, University of Oslo.

1815 SLATER, Joseph. "An Introduction to the Correspondence of Carlyle and Emerson." Ph.D. diss., Columbia University, 1956.

1816 _____, ed. with Intro. Emerson and Carlyle Correspondence. New York: Columbia University Press, 1964.

1817 _____. "Two Sources for Emerson's First Address on West Indian Emancipation." ESQ, 43 (1966), 106-109, and ESQ, 44 (1966), 97-100.

1818 _____. "Emerson's Praedials." American Literature, 38 (May, 1966), 235-236. Relates to "Emancipation West Indies Address."

1819 SLOAN, J. M. "Carlyle and Emerson." Living Age, 309 (May 21, 1921), 486-489.

1820 SLOAN, J. M., Jr. "'The Miraculous Uplifting': Emerson's Relationship with His Audience." Quarterly Journal of Speech, 52 (1966), 10-15.

1821 SMALLEY, George Washburn. "A Visit to Ralph Waldo Emerson," and "Emerson in England," in Anglo-American Memories. New York & London: Putnam's, 1911, 1912. Pp. 51-73.

1822 SMART, George K. "A Note on 'Emerson and Communism.'" New England Quarterly, 10 (December, 1937), 772-773. Refers to article by John T. Flanagan.

1823 SMITH, Duane E. "Romanticism in America: The Transcendentalists." Review of Politics, 35 (1973), 302-325.

1824 SMITH, G. J. "Emerson and Whitman." Conservator, 14 (June, 1903), 53-55.

1825 SMITH, Henry Nash. "Emerson's Problem of Vocation--A Note on 'The American Scholar.'" New England Quarterly, 12 (March, 1939), 52-67.

1826 _____. Virgin Land: The American West as Symbol and Myth. Cambridge, Mass.: Harvard University Press, 1950 and 1971. Emerson, pp. 3, 44, 77, and passim.

1827 _____. "The American Scholar Today." Southwest Review, 48 (Summer, 1963), 191-199.

1828 SMITH, H. Shelton. "Was Theodore Parker a Transcendentalist?" New England Quarterly, 37 (June, 1964), 147-170.

1829 SMITH, Huntington, ed. The Emerson Birthday Book. New York: Thomas Y. Crowell, 1905. Contains 365 quotations from essays and poems.

1830 SMITH, John W. "Ralph Waldo Emerson's English Traits: A Critical and Annotated Study." Ph.D. diss., University of Texas, 1957.

1831 SMITH, L. W. "Ibsen, Emerson, and Nietzsche: The Individualists." Popular Science Monthly, 78 (February, 1911), 147-157.

1832 SMITH, Orren H., ed. with Notes and Suggestions for Study. The American Scholar, Self-Reliance, and Compensation. New York: American Book, 1911.

1833 SNIDER, Denton J. The Life of Emerson. St. Louis, 1921. Reprinted Philadelphia: Richard West, 1969. Related to St. Louis Hegelians.

1834 SNUGGS, Henry L. "Emerson and Ben Jonson." South Atlantic Bulletin, 21 (January, 1956), 8. Abstract of a talk given at MLA meeting, December, 1955.

1835 SOCIAL Circle in Concord, eds. Centenary of Ralph Waldo Emerson. Boston: Riverside Press, 1903. Contains addresses by LeBaron Russell Briggs, Samuel Hoar, Charles Eliot Norton, Thomas W. Higginson, William James, and others.

1836 SOWD, David H. "Emerson's Correspondence with Peter Kaufman." Ph.D. diss., Bowling Green, 1973. DA, 34 (1974), 7204A.

1837 _____. "Peter Kaufman's Correspondence with Emerson." ESQ, 75 (1974), 91-100.

1838 SOWDER, William Jacob. "Ralph Waldo Emerson's Reputation in English Periodicals from 1840 through the Turn of the Century." Ph.D. diss., University of Kentucky, 1956. DA, 21 (1961), 2721-2722.

1839 _____. "Emerson's Early Impact on England." PMLA, 77 (December, 1962), 561-576.

1840 _____. "Emerson's Rationalist Champions: A Study in the British Periodicals." New England Quarterly, 37 (June, 1964), 147-170.

1841 _____. Emerson's Impact on the British Isles and Canada. Charlottsville: University of Virginia Press, 1966.

1842 _____. "Ralph Waldo Emerson's Reviewers and Commentators: 19th Century Periodical Criticism." ESQ, 53 (1968), 1-51. Also printed in book form, Hartford: Transcendental Books, 1968.

1843 SPENCER, Benjamin T. The Quest for Nationality. Syracuse, N. Y.: Syracuse University Press, 1957. Emerson, pp. 158-163 and passim. Stresses need for a national literature.

1844 SPENCER, Clare Bennett. "Orestes Brownson: On Civil Religion, Conflicts in the Evolution of a Concept of National Faith." Ph.D. diss., Case Western Reserve University, 1973. DA, 34 (1974), 5047A.

1845 SPILLER, Robert E., et al., eds. Literary History of the United States. New York: Macmillan, 1948. Emerson, vol. I, pp. 358-387; Emerson bibliography, vol. III, pp. 492-501.

1846 ———. The Cycle of American Literature. New York: Macmillan, 1955. Emerson, pp. 47-66.

1847 ———. "Emerson Is Easy to Teach." ESQ, 10 (1958), 10-11.

1848 ———. "From Lecture into Essay: Emerson's Method of Composition." Literary Critic, 5 (1962), 28-38.

1849 ———, ed. Selected Essays, Lectures, and Poems of Ralph Waldo Emerson. New York: Washington Square Press, 1965.

1850 ———. "Ralph Waldo Emerson: Man Thinking," in The Oblique Light. New York: Macmillan, 1968. Pp. 111-147.

1851 ———. "Emerson and Humboldt." American Literature, 42 (1971), 546-548. Letters.

1852 STAEBLER, Warren. Ralph Waldo Emerson. New York: Twayne Publishers, 1973. Review by Wallace E. Williams, American Literature, 47 (1975), 123-124.

1853 ———. "Review of Sealts, ed., Journals and Miscellaneous Notebooks of Ralph Waldo Emerson, Vol. X, 1847-1848." American Literature (1974), 400-402.

1854 STAFFORD, John. The Literary Criticism of "Young America": A Study of the Relationship of Politics and Literature. Berkeley: University of California Press, 1952.

1855 STAFFORD, W. T. "Emerson and the James Family." American Literature, 24 (January, 1953), 433-461.

1856 STAGEBERG, Norman C., and Wallace L. Anderson, eds. Poetry as Experience. New York: American Book, 1952. Reprints remarks on "The Snow Storm" from F. O. Matthiessen, American Renaissance (1941). Pp. 485-486.

1857 STALLKNECHT, Newton. Strange Seas of Thought. Bloomington: University of Indiana Press, 1958. Principally about Wordsworth; Emerson, passim.

1858 STALLMAN, Robert W., et al., eds. American Literature: Readings and Critiques. New York: G. P. Putnam's, 1961. Emerson, pp. 185-237. Contains good criticism.

1859 STANSBERRY, Gloria Jean. "'Let Wild Birds Sing: A Study of the Bird Imagery in the Writings of Henry David Thoreau." Ph.D. diss., Kent State University, 1973. DA, 35 (1974), 417A.

1860 STANTON, Michael N. "The Startled Muse: Emerson and Science Fiction." Extrapolation, 16 (December, 1974), 64-66. Asimov's "Nightfall" and Emerson's Nature.

1861 ———. "The Education at 'College of Fools': References to Emerson's 'Self-Reliance' in The Invisible Man." Notes on Contemporary Literature, 4 (1974), 13-15.

1862 STANTON, Robert. "The Trial of Nature: An Analysis of The Blithedale Romance." PMLA, 76 (December, 1961), 528-538.

1863/4 STAPLETON, Laurence. "Emerson and the Freedom of the Reader," in The Elected Circle. Princeton, N. J.: Princeton University Press, 1973. Pp. 166-194.

1865/6 STAUFFER, Donald B. A Short History of American Poetry. New York: E. P. Dutton, 1974. Emerson, pp. 93-113.

1867 STEARNS, A. W. "Four Emerson Letters to Dr. Daniel Parker." Tuftonian, 1 (November, 1940), 6-9.

1868 STEARNS, Frank Preston. "Emerson as a Poet." Unitarian Review, 36 (October, 1891), 259-270.

1869 _____. The Real and the Ideal in Literature. Boston: J. G. Cupples, 1892. "Sonnet, 'R. W. E.'" p. 147; "Emerson as a Poet," pp. 148-167; "A Poetic Autobiography," pp. 168-186.

1870 _____. "Emerson and the Great Poets." A Centennial Contribution. 8 pp. pamphlet.

1871 STEDMAN, Edmund C. Poets of America. Boston: Houghton, Mifflin, 1885. Emerson, pp. 133-179.

1872 _____. The Nature and Elements of Poetry. Boston: Houghton, Mifflin, 1892. Reprinted Upper Saddle River, N. J.: Gregg Press, 1970. Emerson, passim.

1873 _____, ed. An American Anthology, 1787-1900. Boston: Houghton, Mifflin, 1902.

1874 STEEVES, Harrison R., ed. "An Ungarnered Emerson Item: 'The Garden of Plants.'" Nation, 100 (May 20, 1915), 563-564.

1875 _____. "Bibliographical Notes on Emerson." Modern Language Notes, 32 (November, 1917), 431-434. Comments on "uncollected" writings other than in Bigelow.

1876 _____. "Emerson Bibliography," in Trent, William P., ed. Cambridge History of American Literature. New York: Macmillan, 1917. Vol. I, pp. 551-566.

1877 STEIN, William Bysshe, ed. Two Brahman Sources of Emerson and Thoreau. New York: Scholars' Facsimiles and Reprints, 1967. Rajah R. Roy, trans., Texts of the Veds, London, 1832; and William Ward, A View of the History, Literature, and Mythology of the Hindoos, vol. II, London, 1822.

1878 _____. "A Bibliography of Hindu and Buddhist Literature Available to Thoreau through 1854." ESQ, 47 (1967), 52-56. Lists some 75 Oriental texts, English and French translations of Veda, Epic, Purana, Kanya, etc.

1879 _____. "Emerson's 'History': The Rhetoric of Cosmic Consciousness." ESQ, 69 (1972), 199-206.

1880 _____, J. D. Russell, Marilyn Baldwin, and G. C. LeRoy. "Emerson's 'Brahma': Four Explications." Explicator, 20 (December, 1961), item 29.

1881 STEINBRINK, Jeffrey. "Novels of Circumstance and Novels of Character: Emerson's View of Fiction." ESQ, 75 (1974), 101-114.

1882 STEN, Christopher W. "Bartleby the Transcendentalist: Melville's Dead Letter to Emerson." Modern Language Quarterly, 35 (1974), 30-44.

1883 STENBERG, J. J. "Emerson and Oral Discourse," in Studies in Rhetoric and Public Speaking in Honor of James Albert Winans by Pupils and Colleagues. New York, 1925. Reprinted New York: Russell, c. 1961. Pp. 153-180.

1884 STENERSON, D. C. "Emerson and the Agrarian Tradition." Journal of History of Ideas, 14 (January, 1953), 95-115.

1885 STEPHEN, Leslie. "Emerson." National Review, 36 (February, 1901), 882-898.

1886 _____. Studies of a Biographer. London: Duckworth, 1902. Emerson, vol. IV, pp. 130-167.

1887 STERN, Milton R., and Seymour Gross, eds. American Literature Survey. 4 vols. New York: Viking Press, 1962. Emerson, vol. II, pp. 250-370.

1888 STEVENS, David M. "Emerson on the Saxon Race:

A Manuscript Fragment Related to English Traits." ESQ, 47 (1967), 103-105.

1889 STEVENSON, Burton. "The Mouse-Trap." Colophon, 5 (December, 1934), 19.

1890 _____. "More About the Mouse-Trap." Colophon, 6 (Summer, 1935), 71-86.

1891 STEWART, Randall. "The Concord Group." Sewanee Review, 44 (October-December, 1936), 434-446.

1892 _____. "Emerson, Asset or Liability?" Tennessee Studies in Literature, 2 (1957), 33-40. Expanded in American Literature and Christian Doctrine. Baton Rouge: Louisiana State University Press, 1958. "The Deification of Man," pp. 43-72.

1893 _____ and Dorothy Bethuram, eds. Concord Idealism, in Masterpieces of American Literature. New York: Scott, Foresman, 1954. Emerson, pp. 3-69 and 258-288.

1894 _____ and _____, eds. American Poetry, in Masterpieces of American Literature. New York: Scott, Foresman, 1964. Emerson, pp. 53-84.

1895 STILLMAN, William J. "The Philosopher's Camp: Emerson, Agassiz, Lowell, and Others in the Adirondacks." Century Magazine, 46 (August, 1893), 598-606.

1896 STOEHR, Taylor. "'Eloquence Needs No Constable': Alcott, Emerson, and Thoreau on the State." Canadian Review of American Studies, 5 (1974), 81-100.

1897 _____. "Transcendental Attitudes Toward Communitism and Individualism." ESQ, 20 (1974), 65-90.

1898 STOLLER, Leo. "Thoreau's Doctrine of Simplicity." New England Quarterly, 29 (December, 1956), 443-461.

1899 STONE, Vida Reed. "Emerson, Revealer of Truth." New Outlook, 10 (May, 1957), 12-16.

1900 STORM, Melvin G., Jr. "The Riddle of 'The Sphinx':
Another Approach." ESQ, 62 (1971), 44-48.

1901 STOVALL, Floyd. "The Optimism Behind Robinson's
Tragedies." American Literature, 10 (March,
1938), 1-23.

1902 _____. "The Value of Emerson Today." College
English, 3 (February, 1942), 442-454.

1903 _____. American Idealism. Norman: University
of Oklahoma Press, 1943. Emerson, pp. 37-54.

1904 _____, ed. The Development of American Literary
Criticism. Chapel Hill: University of North
Carolina Press, 1955. "Changing Attitudes in Early
American Literary Criticism," by Harry H. Clark,
pp. 15-73.

1905 _____, ed. Eight American Authors. New York:
Modern Language Association, 1956, 1963. Emerson, pp. 47-99. Extensive listing of critical
sources. Rev. ed., New York: W. W. Norton,
1971, James Woodress, ed. [q.v.--item 2161].

1906 STOWELL, Robert E. "Poetry About Thoreau: 19th
Century." Thoreau Society Bulletin, 112 (1970),
1-3.

1907 STRATTON, Clarence. "Emerson's Rhymes." Word
Study, December, 1944, pp. 2-4. Replies in
Word Study, April, 1945, pp. 7-8.

1908 STRAUCH, Carl F. "The Background of Emerson's
'Boston Hymn.'" American Literature, 14 (March,
1942), 36-47.

1909 _____. "Emerson at Lehigh." Lehigh Alumni
Bulletin, 29 (April, 1942), 15-16.

1910 _____. "Gérando: A Source for Emerson."
Modern Language Notes, 58 (January, 1943), 64-67.
Relates to poetry, W. IX, 353.

1911 _____. "Critical and Variorum Edition of the
Poems of Ralph Waldo Emerson." Ph.D. diss.,
Yale, 1946. DA, 26 (1965), 2226. Studies 46
poems.

1912 _____. "Emerson's Phi Beta Kappa Poem." New England Quarterly, 23 (March, 1950), 65-90.

1913 _____. "The Manuscript Relationships of Emerson's 'Days.'" Philological Quarterly, 29 (April, 1950), 199-208.

1914 _____. "The Date of Emerson's 'Terminus.'" PMLA, 65 (1950), 360-370.

1915 _____. "The Daemonic and Experimental in Emerson." Personalist, 33 (Winter, 1952), 40-55.

1916 _____. "Emerson as a Creator of Vignettes." Modern Language Notes, 70 (April, 1955), 274-278.

1917 _____. "The Sources of Emerson's 'Song of Nature.'" Harvard Library Bulletin, 9 (August, 1955), 300-334.

1918 _____. "The Year of Emerson's Poetic Maturity: 1834." Philological Quarterly, 34 (October, 1955), 353-377. Studies "The Rhodora," "Xenophon," "Each and All," and "The Snow Storm."

1919 _____. "Emerson's 'New England Capitalist.'" Harvard Library Bulletin, 10 (Spring, 1956), 245-254. An unpublished poem with analysis.

1920 _____. "The Importance of Emerson's Skeptical Mood." Harvard Library Bulletin, 11 (Winter, 1957), 117-139. Unpublished poem, "The Skeptic," with analysis.

1921 _____. "Emerson and the American Continuity." ESQ, 6 (1957), 1-5.

1922 _____. "Emerson's Sacred Science." PMLA, 73 (June, 1958), 237-250.

1923 _____. "The New Emerson Anthology and Modern Scholarship." ESQ, 13 (1958), 29-31.

1924 _____. "Emerson and the Longevity of the Mind." ESQ, 54 (1958), 60-68. Also in Cook, Reginald L., ed., Themes, Tones, and Motifs ... (1968), pp. 60-68.

1925 _____. "Emerson as Literary Middleman." ESQ, 18 (1960), 2-9.

1926 _____, ed. Critical Symposium on American Romanticism. ESQ, 35 (1964), 2-60.

1927 _____. "The Problem of Time and the Romantic Mode in Hawthorne, Melville, and Emerson," in Strauch, ed., Critical Symposium (1964), pp. 50-60.

1928 _____. "The Background and Meaning of the 'Ode Inscribed to W. H. Channing.'" ESQ, 42 Supplement (1966), 4-14.

1929 _____. "Emerson and the Doctrine of Sympathy." Studies in Romanticism, 6 (1967), 152-174.

1930 _____. "'Hatred's Swift Repulsions': Emerson, Margaret Fuller, and Others." Studies in Romanticism, 7 (1968), 65-103.

1931 _____. "Emerson Rejects Reed and Hails Thoreau." Harvard Library Bulletin, 16 (1968), 257-273. Analysis of unpublished poem, "S. R." (Sampson Reed).

1932 _____. "E[merson]'s Use of the Organic Method." ESQ, 55 (1969), 18-24.

1933 _____, ed. Style in the American Renaissance. Hartford: Transcendental Books, 1970.

1934 _____. "The Mind's Voice: Emerson's Poetic Styles." ESQ, 60 (1970), 43-59. Also in Strauch, ed., Style in the American Renaissance (1970), pp. 43-59.

1935 _____, ed. Characteristics of Emerson: Transcendental Poet: A Symposium. Hartford: Transcendental Press, 1975. Contains 8 unpublished essays on poems; also reprint of W. S. Kennedy's "Clews to Emerson's Mystic Verse." Also published as American Transcendental Quarterly, 25 (1975), 1-65, plus appendix.

1936 _____. "Emerson's Adaptation of Myth in 'The Initial Love,'" in Strauch, ed., Characteristics ... (1975), pp. 51-65.

1937 STRONG, Augustus H. American Poets and Their Theology. Philadelphia: Griffith & Rowland Press, 1916. Emerson, pp. 51-103.

1938 STUART, John A. "Ralph Waldo Emerson's Nature: Its Relation to Coleridge's Transcendental Idealism." Ph.D. diss., Northwestern, 1945.

1939 SUMMERLIN, Charles T. "The Possible Oracle: Three Transcendental Poets." Ph.D. diss., Yale, 1973. DA, 34 (1973), 3435A-3436A. Emerson, Thoreau, and Jones Very.

1940 SUPER, Robert H. "Emerson and Arnold's Poetry." Philological Quarterly, 33 (October, 1954), 396-403.

1941 SUTCLIFFE, Emerson G. "Emerson's Theories of Literary Expression." Ph.D. diss., University of Illinois, 1918. Published in University of Illinois Studies in Language and Literature, 8 (1923), 9-152.

1942 _____. "Whitman, Emerson, and the New Poetry." New Republic, 19 (May 24, 1919), 114-116.

1943 SUZUKI, Jakio. "Emerson's View of the Poet." Eigo Eibungakn Kenkya, 7 (February, 1962), 1-22. In English.

1944 SWIFT, Lindsay. Brook Farm (New York, 1900). Reprinted with Intro. by Joseph Schiffman. New York: Corinth Books, 1961.

1945 TACEY, W. S. "Emerson on Eloquence." Today's Speech, 6 (Spring, 1958), 23-27.

1946 TAFT, K. B. "The Byronic Background on Emerson's 'Good-Bye.'" New England Quarterly, 27 (December, 1954), 525-527.

1947 TANNER, Tony. "Saints Behold: The Transcendental Point of View," in The Reign of Wonder: Naivety and Reality in American Literature, by Tony Tanner. Cambridge, England: Cambridge University

Press, 1965. Reprinted in Barbour, Brian, ed., American Transcendentalism (1973), pp. 53-58.

1948 TANZY, C. E. "Browning, Emerson, and Bishop Blougram." Victorian Studies, 1 (March, 1958), 255-266.

1949 TAPPAN, Eva M., ed. A Friend in the Library: A Guide to Emerson, Hawthorne, Longfellow, et al. Boston: Houghton, Mifflin, 1909. Arranged by topics in 12 vols.

1950 TATE, Allen. Reactionary Essays in Poetry and Ideas. New York: Scribner's, 1936. Emerson, passim.

1951 TAYLOR, Walter Fuller. The Story of American Letters. Chicago: Henry Regnery, 1936. Emerson, pp. 134-145.

1952 TENNEY, Thomas A. "Emerson and the Encyclopaedia Americana." ESQ, 19 (1973), 219-223.

1953 TERWILLIGER, Ernest W. "The Individual and Ralph Waldo Emerson's Concept of Equality." Ph.D. diss., Cornell, 1954.

1954 THARP, Louise H. The Peabody Sisters of Salem. Boston: Little, Brown, 1949. Emerson, p. 35 and passim.

1955 THAYER, James B. A Western Journey with Emerson. Boston: Little, Brown, 1884. Reprinted Port Washington, N.Y.: Kennikat Press, 1971.

1956 THAYER, William Roscoe. The Influence of Emerson. Boston: Cupples, Upham, 1886.

1957 THOMAS, Bess. "Osman in America: A Study of the Contemporary Reputation of Emerson's Poetry, 1846-1882." Ph.D. diss., Yale, 1930.

1958 THOMPSON, Cameron. "John Locke and New England Transcendentalism." New England Quarterly, 35 (December, 1962), 435-457.

1959 THOMPSON, Frank Thornber. "Ralph Waldo Emer-

son's Debt to Wordsworth, Carlyle, and Coleridge."
Ph. D. diss., University of North Carolina, 1925.

1960 _____. "Emerson's Indebtedness to Coleridge."
Studies in Philology, 23 (January, 1926), 55-76.

1961 _____. "Emerson and Carlyle." Studies in Philology, 24 (July, 1927), 438-453.

1962 _____. "Emerson's Theory and Practice of Poetry." PMLA, 43 (December, 1928), 1170-1184.

1963 _____. "Emerson and Etienne Geoffroy St. Hilaire." Symposium, 5 (November, 1951), 216-229. Related to John Muir and science.

1964 THOMPSON, Lawrance Roger. Emerson and Frost: Critics of Their Times. Philadelphia: Philobiblon Club, 1940. Pamphlet, 45 pp.

1965 THOMPSON, Ralph. "Emerson and the Offering for 1829." American Literature, 6 (May, 1934), 151-157. Relates to early fictional tale, "Organ," 1822.

1966 THOMSON, James. Poems, Essays, and Fragments. London: Bertram Dobell, 1892. "Notes on Emerson," pp. 75-85.

1967 THORBURN, D., and G. H. Hartman, eds. Romanticism. Ithaca, N. Y.: Cornell University Press, 1973. "Emerson: The Glory and Sorrows of American Romanticism," by Harold Bloom, pp. 155-173.

1968 THOREAU, Henry David. Works. 20-vol. Walden Edition, Bradford Torrey and Francis H. Allen, eds. Boston: Houghton, Mifflin, 1906.

1969 _____. Works (1906), vol. VII, pp. 229-237. Comments on Emerson's poem "The Sphinx," in Journal for March, 1841.

1970 _____. The Heart of Thoreau's Journals, ed. Odell Shepard. Boston: Houghton, Mifflin, 1927.

1971 _____. Collected Poems, edited Carl Bode.

Chicago: Packard, 1943. Enlarged ed., Baltimore: Johns Hopkins Press, 1964.

1972 _____. Journals, vols. 7-20 of Works (1906). Boston: Houghton, Mifflin, 1949. Reprinted in two volumes, N. Y.: Dover, 1962.

1973 _____. Correspondence, ed. Walter Harding & Carl Bode. New York, 1958. Reprinted New York: Greenwood Press, 1975.

1974 _____. Selected Journals, ed. Carl Bode. Signet Classic, 1967.

1975 _____. The Annotated Walden, ed. Philip Van Doren Stern. New York: Clarkson N. Potter, 1970.

1976 _____. The Major Essays, ed. Jeffrey L. Duncan. New York: E. P. Dutton, 1972.

1977 _____. Henry David. The Variorum Walden, ed. Walter Harding. Boston: Twayne, 1975.

1978 THORP, Willard. "Emerson on Tour." Quarterly Journal of Speech, 16 (February, 1930), 19-34.

1979 THURIN, Erik Ingrar. "Love and Friendship: Emerson and the Platonic Tradition." Ph.D. diss., University of Minnesota, 1970. DA, 31 (1971), 5429A.

1980 _____. The Universal Autobiography of Ralph Waldo Emerson. Lund, Sweden: C. W. K. Gleerup, 1974.

1981 THWING, Charles Franklin. "Emerson's 'American Scholar,' Sixty Years After." Forum, 23 (August, 1897), 661-671.

1982 _____. "Education According to Emerson." School and Society, 2 (October 16, 1915), 551-553.

1983 _____. "'The American Scholar': Emerson's Phi Beta Kappa Address--1837." Hibbert Journal, 36 (October, 1937), 119-131.

1984 TIFFANY, Francis. "Transcendentalism: The New England Renaissance." Unitarian Review, 31 (1887), 111-114.

1985 TILTON, Eleanor M. "Emerson's Lecture Schedule, 1837-1838, Revised." Harvard Library Bulletin, 21 (1973), 382-399.

1986 _____. "Mr. Emerson--of Boston," in Bruccoli, Matthew J., ed., The Chief Glory of Every People: Essays on Classic American Writers. Carbondale: Southern Illinois University Press, 1973. Pp. 191-210.

1987 _____, ed. [Additional Letters of Emerson. A projected 3- or 4-volume set originally intended for publication about 1973; no further information available.]

1988 TIMPE, Eugene F. American Literature in Germany 1861-1872. Chapel Hill: University of North Carolina Press, 1964. Emerson, pp. 62-70.

1989 TINGLEY, Donald F. "Ralph Waldo Emerson on the Illinois Lecture Circuit." Journal of Illinois State Historical Society, 64 (1971), 192-205.

1990 TOKAHASHI, Norikane, ed. Emerson's Essays on Nature. Tokyo: Hokuseido Press, 1970. English texts, notes in Japanese.

1991 TOKUZA. "Ralph Waldo Emerson's Theory of Art." Parts I and II. Jimbun Shizen Kagaku Ronshyu [Studies in Humanities] (Tokyo College of Economics), 35 (1973), 1-119.

1992 TOLLES, Frederick B. "Emerson and Quakerism." American Literature, 10 (May, 1938), 142-165.

1993 TOLMAN, George. Mary Moody Emerson, ed. with a Preface by Edward W. Forbes. Privately printed, 1929.

1994 TORBERT, J. K. "Emerson and Swedenborg." Texas Review, 2 (April, 1917), 313-326.

1995 TOWNSEND, H. G. Philosophical Ideas in the United

States. New York: American Book, 1936. Emerson, passim.

1996 TRANQUILLA, Ronald Edward. "Henry David Thoreau and the New England Transcendentalists." Ph.D. diss., University of Pittsburgh, 1973. DA, 35 (1974), 1065A.

1997 TRAUBEL, Horace. With Walt Whitman in Camden. 3 vols. Boston: Small, Maynard, 1906-1914. Reprinted New York: Rowman & Littlefield, 1961. Vol. IV, ed. Sculley Bradley, 1953. Vol. V, ed. Gertrude Traubel, 1964.

1998 TRAVIS, Mildred K. "Echoes of Emerson in Melville's Plotinus Plinlimmon in Pierre." American Transcendental Quarterly, 14 (1972), 47-48.

1999 TRENT, William P. "Ralph Waldo Emerson." Bookman, 17 (June, 1903), 421-425.

2000 _____ and John Erskine. "Transcendentalists," in Great American Writers. New York: Henry Holt, 1912. Pp. 108-134.

2001 _____, et al., eds. Cambridge History of American Literature. 3 vols. New York: Macmillan, 1917. Reprinted 1944. Emerson by Paul Elmer More, vol. I, pp. 349-362.

2002 TRICOMI, Albert H. "The Rhetoric of Aspiring Circularity in Emerson's 'Circles.'" ESQ, 69 (1972), 271-283.

2003 TRUEBLOOD, D. E. "The Influence of Emerson's 'Divinity School Address.'" Harvard Theological Review, 32 (January, 1939), 41-56.

2004 TRYON, Shirley Esther. "'The One, the Many': Polarity in Ralph Waldo Emerson's Representative Men." Ph.D. diss., University of Virginia, 1969.

2005 TUCKER, Ellen Louisa. One First Love: Letters of Ellen Tucker to Ralph Waldo Emerson, ed. Edith W. Gregg. Cambridge, Mass.: Harvard University Press, 1962. Tucker was Emerson's future wife. His letters to her seem to have been lost.

2006   TUERK, Richard Carl. "Circle Imagery in the Prose of Emerson and Thoreau from Nature (1836) to Walden (1854)." Ph.D. diss., Johns Hopkins University, 1967. DA, 28 (1967), 1798A.

2007   _____. "Emerson's Nature: Miniature Universe." American Transcendental Quarterly, 1 (1969), 110-113.

2008   _____. "Emerson as Translator: 'The Phoenix.'" ESQ, 63 (1971), 24-26.

2009   _____. "Los Angeles' Reaction to Emerson's Visit to San Francisco." New England Quarterly, 44 (1971), 477-482.

2010   _____. "Emerson's Darker Vision: 'Hamatreya' and 'Days,'" in Strauch, Carl F., ed. Characteristics of Emerson (1975), pp. 28-33.

2011   TURK, R. T. "Emerson Hill." Staten Island History, 21 (April-June, 1960), 13-14. Home of William Emerson.

2012   TURNER, Arlin. "The Undergraduate Meets Emerson." ESQ, 10 (1958), 11-12.

2013   TURNER, Lorenzo Dow. Anti-Slavery Sentiment in American Literature Prior to 1865. Washington, D. C.: Association for the Study of Negro Life and History, 1929. Emerson, pp. 33-34 and passim.

2014   TURNER, Robert C. "The Influence of French Culture and Literature upon Ralph Waldo Emerson before 1850." Ph.D. diss., Yale, 1935.

2015   TURPIE, Mary C. "The Growth of Ralph Waldo Emerson's Thought." Ph.D. diss., University of Minnesota, 1943.

2016   _____. "A Quaker Source for Emerson's Sermon on the Lord's Supper." New England Quarterly, 17 (March, 1944), 95-101.

2017   TYRER, C. E. "Emerson as Poet." Manchester Quarterly, 3 (April, 1884), 105-128.

2018 TYRRELL, Alexander. "The Origins of a Victorian Best-Seller--An Unacknowledged Debt." Notes and Queries, 17 (1970), 347-349. Refers to Smiles' Self-Help, published in 1859.

2019 URBANSKI, Marie M. O. "Margaret Fuller's Woman in the Nineteenth Century." Ph.D. diss., University of Kentucky, 1973. DA, 35 (1974), 1636A.

2020 USTICK, W. L. "Emerson's Debt to Montaigne." Washington University Studies, 9 (1922), 245-262.

2021 VANCE, William S. "Carlyle in America Before Sartor Resartus." American Literature, 7 (January, 1936), 363-375.

2022 VAN CROMPHOUT, Gustaaf Victor. "Emerson's Eroica: A Study of His Idea of Greatness." Ph.D. diss., University of Minnesota, 1966. DA, 28 (1967), 246A-247A.

2023 _____. "Emerson and the Dialectics of History." PMLA, 91 (January, 1976), 54-65.

2024 VAN DOREN, Mark, ed. American Poets: 1630-1930. Boston: Little, Brown, 1932. Emerson, pp. 65-116.

2025 _____, ed. The Portable Emerson. New York: Viking Press, 1957.

2026 _____. Introduction to Poetry. New York: Hill & Wang, 1966, 1968. Emerson, pp. 90-93, 337-341.

2027 VAN NOSTRAND, A. D. Everyman His Own Poet: Romantic Gospels in American Literature. New York: McGraw-Hill, 1968. "Emerson's Strategic Retreat," pp. 28-43.

2028 VAN WESEP, H. B. "Ralph Waldo Emerson: Gentle

Iconoclast," in Seven Sages: The Story of American Philosophy. New York: Longmans Green, 1960. Pp. 61-127.

2029 VELLELA, Ellen. "Emerson and The Conduct of Life." English Review, 1 (1973), 6-27.

2030 VERY, Jones. Essays and Poems, ed. Ralph Waldo Emerson. Boston: Little and Brown, 1839. Reprinted New York: Arno Press, 1972.

2031 _____. Poems and Essays, rev. ed., with Preface by C. A. Bartol (Boston, 1886). Reprinted New York: Arno Press, 1976.

2032 VINCENT, Leon Henry. American Literary Masters. Boston: Houghton, Mifflin, 1906. Emerson, pp. 147-186.

2033 VIRTANEN, Reino. "Proust and Emerson." Symposium, 6 (May, 1952), 123-139.

2034 VITANZA, Victor J. "Melville's Redburn and Emerson's 'General Education of the Eye.'" ESQ, 21 (1975), 40-45.

2035 VOGEL, Dan. "Orville Dewey on Emerson's 'The Lord's Supper.'" ESQ, 31 (1963), 40-42.

2036 VOGEL, Stanley M. German Influences on the American Transcendentalists. New Haven, Conn.: Yale University Press, 1955. Emerson, pp. 172-176 and passim.

2037 WADE, Mason. Margaret Fuller: Whetstone of Genius. New York: Viking Press, 1940. Emerson, pp. 82-101.

2038 _____, ed. The Writings of Margaret Fuller. New York: Viking Press, 1941. Emerson, passim.

2039 WAGENKNECHT, Edward. Ralph Waldo Emerson: Portrait of a Balanced Soul. New York: Oxford University Press, 1974. Review by John Lydenberg, American Literature, 47 (March, 1975).

2040 WAGGONER, Hyatt H. "The Humanistic Idealism of Robert Frost." American Literature, 13 (November, 1941), 207-223.

2041 ———. "Emily Dickinson: The Transcendent Self." Criticism, 7 (1965), 297-334.

2042 ———. American Poets from the Puritans to the Present. Boston: Houghton, Mifflin, 1968. Emerson, pp. 90-114.

2043 ———. "'Grace' in the Thought of Emerson, Thoreau, and Hawthorne." ESQ, 54 (1969), 68-72. Also in Cook, Reginald L., ed., Themes, Tones, and Motifs in the American Renaissance (1969), pp. 68-72.

2044 ———. Emerson as Poet. Princeton, N.J.: Princeton University Press, 1974. Review by John C. Broderick, American Literature, 47 (January, 1976), 448-449.

2045 ———. "Works, Days, Poetry, and Imagination." American Transcendental Quarterly, 21 (1974), 30-32.

2046 WAGNER, Vern. "'No Tumult of Response': Emerson's Reception as a Lyceum Lecturer." Western Humanities Review, 6 (Spring, 1952), 129-135.

2047 WAHR, Frederick B. Ralph Waldo Emerson and Goethe. Ann Arbor, Mich.: George Wahr, 1915. Based on Ph.D. diss., University of Michigan, 1915.

2048 ———. "Emerson and the Germans." German Section of MLA of Central West and South, 33 (February, 1941).

2049 ———. "Emerson and Goethe," and "Emerson and the Germans." Reprinted Hartford: Transcendental Books, 1971. Also in American Transcendental Quarterly, 15 (1972), parts 1 and 2, pp. 5-59.

2050 WAITE, Robert G. "'Linked Analogies': The Symbolic Mode of Perception in Emerson and Melville." Ph.D. diss., University of Kentucky, 1973. DA, 34 (1974), 6668A-6669A.

2051 WALCUTT, Charles Child. American Literary Naturalism: A Divided Stream. Minneapolis: University of Minnesota Press, 1956. Emerson, pp. 10-11 and passim.

2052 _____. "Emerson's 'The Sphinx.'" Explicator, 31 (1972), item 20.

2053 WALKER, B. R. "Ralph Waldo Emerson: A Re-Evaluation." Crane Review, 6 (Winter, 1962), 121-135.

2054 WARD, J. A. "Emerson and 'The Educated Will': Notes on the Process of Conversion." English Literary History, 35 (December, 1967), 495-517.

2055 WARD, Julius Hammond. "Emerson in New England Thought." Andover Review, 8 (1887), 380-395.

2056 WARD, Robert Stafford. "Still 'Christians': Still 'Infidels.'" Southern Humanities Review, 2 (1968), 365-374.

2057 WARDERS, Donald F. "'The Progress of the Hour and the Day': A Critical Study of The Dial (1840-1844)." Ph.D. diss., University of Kansas, 1973. DA, 34 (1974), 7790A-7791A.

2058 WARFEL, Harry R. "Margaret Fuller and Ralph Waldo Emerson." PMLA, 50 (June, 1935), 576-594.

2059 WARREN, Austin. "The Concord School of Philosophy." New England Quarterly, 2 (April, 1929), 199-233.

2060 _____. The Elder Henry James. New York: Macmillan, 1934. "Emerson," Chapter III, pp. 39-54 and passim.

2061 _____. New England Saints. Ann Arbor: University of Michigan Press, 1956. "Emerson, Preacher to Himself," pp. 46-57.

2062 _____. The New England Conscience. Ann Arbor: University of Michigan Press, 1966. Emerson, pp. 105-107, 122-124 and passim.

2063 WASUNG, C. J. "Emerson Comes to Detroit." Michigan Historical Magazine, 29 (January, 1945), 59-72.

2064 WAYMAN, Virginia. "A Study of Emerson's Philosophy of Education." Education, 56 (April, 1936), 474-482.

2065 WEBSTER, Frank M. "Transcendental Points of View." Washington University Studies (St. Louis), 7 (April, 1920), 187-203.

2066 WEISS, Robert M. "The Image of Emerson in American Life and Thought." Ph.D. diss., University of Wisconsin, 1963.

2067 WELLEK, René. "The Minor Transcendentalists and German Philosophy." New England Quarterly, 25 (December, 1942), 652-680. Also in Barbour, Brian, ed., American Transcendentalism (1973), pp. 103-120.

2068 _____. "Emerson and German Philosophy." New England Quarterly, 16 (March, 1943), 41-62.

2069 _____. "Emerson's Literary Theory and Criticism," in Gustav Erdmann and Alfons Eichstaedt, eds., Worte und Werte-Bruno Markwardt zum 60. Geburtstag. Berlin: Walter de Gruyter, 1961. Pp. 444-456. Article in English.

2070 _____. Confrontations. Princeton, N. J.: Princeton University Press, 1965. Reprints "The Minor Transcendentalists and German Philosophy" (1942) and "Emerson and German Philosophy" (1943).

2071 _____. History of Modern Criticism. 4 vols. New Haven, Conn.: Yale University Press, 1965. Emerson, in The Age of Transition, vol. III, pp. 163-181 and 324-330.

2072 _____. "Irving Babbitt, Paul More, and Transcendentalism," in Simon, Myron, and Thornton H. Parsons, eds., Transcendentalism and Its Legacy (1966), pp. 185-203.

2073 WELLS, Henry W. The Modern American Way in

Poetry. New York: Russell & Russell, 1964. Emerson, pp. 56-66.

2074 WELLS, Ronald V. Three Christian Transcendentalists: James Marsh, Caleb Sprague Henry, and Frederic Henry Hedge. New York: Octagon Books, 1943.

2075 WENDELL, Barrett. A Literary History of America. New York: Scribner's, 1901. Emerson, pp. 311-327.

2076 ———— and Chester Noyes Greenough. A History of Literature in America. New York: Scribner's, 1904. Emerson, pp. 254-265.

2077 WERMUTH, Paul C. "Santayana and Emerson." ESQ, 31 (1963), 36-40.

2078 WEST, Harry C. "Hawthorne's Magic Circle: The Artist as Magician." Criticism, 16 (Fall, 1974), 311-325.

2079 WEST, Herbert Faulkner, ed. Mr. Emerson Writes a Letter about Walden. Charlottsville, Va.: Bibliographical Society of the Univ. of Virginia, 1954. Sponsored by Thoreau Society and Friends of Dartmouth Library.

2080 ————, ed. Emerson at Dartmouth: A Reprint of His Oration, "Literary Ethics." Hanover, N. H.: Dartmouth University Press, 1956.

2081 WESTALL, John. "Comments on Nature." The New Jerusalem Magazine, 15 (October, 1841), 48-52. Reprinted in Sealts and Ferguson, eds., Emerson's Nature (1969), pp. 109-11.

2082 WESTBROOK, Perry. John Burroughs. New York: Twayne, 1974. Emerson, pp. 50-63.

2083 WHEELER, Otis B. "Emerson's Political Quandry," in Waldo McNeir and Leo B. Levy, eds., Studies in American Literature. Baton Rouge: Louisiana State University Press, 1960. Pp. 22-32.

2084 ————. "The Emersonian View of American Poetry." Southern Review, 4 (1968), 1077-1080.

2085 WHICHER, George F. This Was A Poet. New York: Scribner's, 1938. Reprinted Ann Arbor: University of Michigan Press, 1957. "Emerson-Emily Dickinson Relationship," pp. 194-197 and passim.

2086 _____. Walden Revisited. Chicago: University of Chicago Press, 1945. Emerson, passim.

2087 _____, ed. The Transcendental Revolt Against Materialism. Boston: D. C. Heath, 1949. Collection of essays and other primary source materials.

2088 _____. Poetry and Civilization. Ithaca, N. Y.: Cornell University Press, 1955. Emerson, passim.

2089 WHICHER, Stephen E. "The Lapse of Uriel: A Study in the Evolution of Ralph Waldo Emerson's Thought." Ph.D. diss., Harvard, 1942.

2090 _____. Freedom and Fate: An Inner Life of Ralph Waldo Emerson. Philadelphia: University of Pennsylvania Press, 1953.

2091 _____. "Emerson's Tragic Sense." The American Scholar, 22 (Summer, 1953), 285-292. Also in Charles Feidelson and Paul Brodtkorb, eds., Interpretations of American Literature. New York: Oxford University Press, 1959. Pp. 153-160.

2092 _____. "A Query on the Sources of Emerson's Early Lectures." ESQ, 13 (1958), 31-32.

2093 _____. "Teaching Emerson." ESQ, 10 (1958), 12-14.

2094 _____. "Emerson's 'The American Scholar.'" Explicator, 20 (April, 1962), item 68.

2095 _____, ed. Selections from Ralph W. Emerson: An Organic Anthology. Boston: Houghton, Mifflin, 1960. (Riverside paperback edition.)

2096 _____. Robert E. Spiller, and Wallace Williams, eds., Early Lectures of Ralph Waldo Emerson. 3 vols. Cambridge, Mass.: Harvard University Press, 1964-1972.

2097 WHIPPLE, Edwin Percy. "Emerson as a Poet." North American Review, 135 (July, 1882), 1-26.

2098 _____. American Literature, with Other Papers. Boston: Ticknor, 1887. "Emerson," pp. 59-68 and reprints "Emerson as a Poet," pp. 259-298.

2099 WHIPPLE, Thomas King. Spokesmen: Modern Writers and American Life. New York: D. Appleton, 1922. Reprinted Berkeley: University of California Press, 1963. See under Robert Frost.

2100 WHITACKER, Thomas R. "The Riddle of Emerson's Sphinx." American Literature, 27 (May, 1955), 179-195.

2101 WHITE, Greenough. Sketch of the Philosophy of American Literature. Boston: Ginn, 1891.

2102 WHITE, James E. "Emerson's 'Hypocritic Days': Actors or Deceivers?" ESQ, 33 (1963), 72-73.

2103 WHITE, K. C. P. "The American Lyceum." Ph.D. diss., Harvard, 1918.

2104 WHITE, Morton Gabriel. "Ralph Waldo Emerson: Overseer of the Oversoul," in Science and Sentiment in America. New York: Oxford University Press, 1972. Pp. 97-119.

2105 WHITE, Robert L. "Emerson's 'Brahma.'" Explicator, 21 (April, 1963), item 63.

2106 WHITE, William. "Two Unpublished Emerson Letters." American Literature, 31 (November, 1959), 334-336.

2107 _____. "Thirty-Three Unpublished Letters of Ralph Waldo Emerson." American Literature, 33 (May, 1961), 159-178.

2108 _____. "Emerson as Editor: A Letter to Benjamin F. Presbury." American Notes & Queries, 12 (1973), 59-61.

2109 WHITEHEAD, Alfred North. Science and the Modern World. New York: Macmillan, 1925.

2110 _____. Adventures of Ideas. New York: Macmillan, 1933.

2111 WHITFORD, Kathryn. "Water, Wind, and Light Imagery in Emerson's Essay 'The Oversoul.'" Wisconsin Studies in Literature, 6 (1969), 100-105.

2112 WHITING, B. J. "Emerson, Chaucer, and Thomas Wharton." American Literature, 17 (1945), 75-78.

2112a WHITMAN, Walt. "Emerson's Books (the Shadows of Them)." Literary World, 11 (May 22, 1880), 177. Reprinted in Whitman's Complete Prose Works (Boston: Small, Maynard, 1898), pp. 314-317. Also in Prose Works, 1892, ed. Floyd Stovall (New York: New York University Press, 1964), vol. II, p. 515.

2113 _____. "By Emerson's Grave." Critic, 2 (May, 1882), 123.

2114 _____. "Estimates of Well-Known Men," from Horace Traubel's Memoranda. Century Illustrated Monthly, 61 (December, 1911), 250-256.

2115 WHITTEMORE, Robert Clifton. Makers of the American Mind. New York: William Morrow, 1964. "Prophet Out of Concord," pp. 167-182.

2116 WHITTIER, John Greenleaf. "Snowbound," in The Complete Poetical Works. Boston: Houghton, Mifflin, 1883. Pp. 209-210. See Whittier's poem (1866) for relation to Emerson's "The Snow Storm."

2117 WICKE, Myron F. "Emerson's Mysticism." Ph.D. diss., Western Reserve University, 1940.

2118 WILDER, Amos N. Modern Poetry and the Christian Tradition. New York: Scribner's, 1952. Emerson, pp. 30, 34-37.

2119 WILKINSON, L. A. "Emerson: Militant Pollyana." The Thinker, 3 (April, 1931), 4, 33-44.

2120 WILLERT, James. "Between the Lines with Ralph Waldo Emerson." Yankee (March, 1971), 79, 160-167.

2121 WILLIAMS, Francis Howard. "Clough and Emerson: The Metaphysical Significance of 'Dipsychus' and 'The World-Soul.'" Poet-Lore, 6 (June-July, 1894), 348-356.

2122 WILLIAMS, John Brindley. "The Impact of Transcendentalism on the Novels of Herman Melville." Ph.D. diss., University of Southern California, 1965. DA, 26 (1965), 1052-1053.

2123 WILLIAMS, M. L. "'Why Nature Loves the Number Five': Emerson Toys with the Occult." Papers of the Michigan Academy of Science, Arts, and Letters, 30 (1944), 639-649.

2124 _____. "They Wrote Home About It." Michigan Alumnus Quarterly Review (Summer, 1945), 337-351.

2125 WILLIAMS, Oscar, and Edwin Honig, eds. Mentor Book of Major American Poets. New York: New American Library, 1962. Emerson, pp. 44-63.

2126 WILLIAMS, Paul O. "The Transcendental Movement in American Poetry." Ph.D. diss., University of Pennsylvania, 1962.

2127 _____. "Meaning in Emerson's 'Una.'" ESQ, 31 (1963), 48.

2128 _____. "An Unnoticed Emerson Lecture." American Notes & Queries, 3 (1964), 5.

2129 _____. "Emerson Guided: Walks with Thoreau and Channing." ESQ, 35 (1964), 66-68. Emerson grew dissatisfied with Thoreau's botanical view of nature.

2130 _____. "Emerson in Alton, Illinois." ESQ, 47 (1967), 98-100.

2131 WILLIAMS, Ray S. "Emerson's Relevance Today." Brigham Young University Studies, 11 (1971), 241-248.

2132 WILLIAMS, Stanley T. "Unpublished Letters of Emerson." Journal of English and Germanic Philology, 26 (October-December, 1927), 475-484.

2133 _____. "Emerson: An Affirmation." Tennessee Studies in Literature, 2 (1957), 41-50.

2134 WILLIAMS, Wallace Edward. "Ralph Waldo Emerson and the Moral Law." Ph.D. diss., University of California at Berkeley, 1963. DA, 24 (1964), 4204-4205.

2135 WILLIAMSON, Bruce Eric. "Unity and Structure in Ralph Waldo Emerson's Essays: First Series." M.A. Thesis, University of Texas at Arlington, 1977.

2136 WILLIAMSON, George. "Emerson, the Oriental." University of California Chronicle, 30 (July, 1928), 271-288.

2137 WILLSON, Lawrence. "The Gods of New England." Pacific Spectator, 9 (Spring, 1955), 141-153. Discusses "The Divinity School Address."

2138 _____. "The Great Reversal." Dalhousie Review, 39 (Spring, 1959), 5-18.

2139 WILSON, Edmund, ed. The Shock of Recognition. Garden City, N.Y.: Doubleday, Doran, 1943. Reprints "Emerson and Whitman: Documents on Their Relations (1855-1888)," pp. 208-228; and John Jay Chapman, "Emerson" (1897), pp. 595-658.

2140 WILSON, John B. "An Analogue of Transcendentalism." Journal of History of Ideas, 27 (1966), 459-461.

2141 _____. "Emerson and the 'Communities.'" ESQ, 43 (1966), 56-62.

2142 _____. "Emerson and the 'Rochester Rappings.'" New England Quarterly, 41 (1968), 248-258.

2143 WILSON, S. Law. The Theology of Modern Literature. Edinburgh: Clark Publishers, 1899. "The Theology of Emerson," pp. 97-128.

2144 WINTERICH, J.T. "Romantic Stories of Books: Emerson's Essays: Second Series." Publisher's Weekly, 118 (July, 1930), 271-275.

2145 WINTERS, Yvor. "Jones Very and Ralph Waldo Emerson: Aspects of New England Mysticism," in Maule's Curse: Seven Studies in Obscurantism. Norfolk, Conn.: New Directions, 1938. Pp. 125-146. Also in In Defense of Reason (Denver: Allan Swallow, 1947), pp. 262-282.

2146 WISE, James N. "Emerson's 'Experience' and Sons and Lovers." Costerus, 6 (1972), 179-221.

2147 WISEMAN, James. "The Meaning of God for Emerson." The Month, 212 (September, 1961), 133-140.

2148 WISH, Harvey. "Emerson's Scholar Reconsidered." Journal of Higher Education, 35 (December, 1964), 475-480.

2149 WITEMEYER, H. A. "'Line' and 'Round' in Emerson's 'Uriel.'" PMLA, 82 (March, 1967), 98-103.

2150 WITHINGTON, Mary S. "Early Letters of Emerson." Century Magazine, 26 (July, 1883), 454-458.

2151 WOLFE, Don M. "A Contrast in Democratic Men: Lincoln and Emerson." Western Humanities Review, 9 (Autumn, 1955). Also in The Image of Man in America. Dallas: Southern Methodist University Press, 1957. "A Contrast in Democratic Temper: Lincoln and Emerson," pp. 92-101.

2152 _____. "Perfection A Priori: Ralph Waldo Emerson," in The Image of Man in America (1957), pp. 70-83.

2153 WOOD, Ann Douglas. "Reconsiderations--Ralph Waldo Emerson." New Republic, January 1 and 8, pp. 27 and 29. Comments on Representative Men.

2154 WOOD, Barry. "The Growth of the Soul: Coleridge s Dialectical Method and the Strategy of Emerson's Nature." PMLA, 91 (May, 1976), 385-397.

2155 WOODBERRY, George E. America in Literature. New York: Harper & Brothers, 1903. The papers in this volume originally appeared in Harper's Magazine and in Harper's Weekly.

2156 _____. Appreciation of Literature. New York: Harper, 1907.

2157 _____. Ralph Waldo Emerson. New York: Macmillan, 1907. Reprinted New York: Haskill House, 1968. (English Men of Letters series.)

2158 WOODBURY, Charles J. Talks with Ralph Waldo Emerson. New York: Baker & Taylor, 1890. Reprinted with new Intro. and ed. by Henry LeRoy Finch. New York: Horizon Press, 1970.

2159 WOODRESS, James, ed. American Literary Scholarship: An Annual Survey, 1963-to date. Durham, N. C.: Duke University Press. See "Emerson, Thoreau, and Transcendentalism" by different authors in each volume.

2160 _____, ed. Ph.D. Dissertations in American Literature, 1891-1966. Durham: Duke University Press, 1968.

2161 _____, ed. Eight American Authors [new ed.]. New York: W. W. Norton, 1971. See also Stovall, Floyd, Eight American Authors, 1956 ed. [item 1905].

2162 WOODRUFF, Stuart C. "Emerson's 'Self-Reliance' and 'Experience': A Comparison." ESQ, 47 (1967), 48-50.

2163 WOODWARD, Robert H. "Emerson's 'Seashore' and Bryant: Poetic Theory in Practice." ESQ, 19 (1960), 21-22.

2164 _____. "Emerson's Giant Sequoia." ESQ, 22 (1961), 44-45.

2165 _____. "Voyage Imagery in 'Terminus' and 'O Captain! My Captain!'" ESQ, 27 (1962), 37.

2166 _____. "Emerson's Cinder Metaphor in 'The American Scholar.'" ESQ, 33 (1963), 17.

2167/8 WOODWELL, R. H. "Whittier on Abolition: A Letter to Emerson." Essex Institute of Historical Collections, 93 (October, 1957), 254-259.

2169 WRIGHT, Conrad. "Emerson, Barzillai Frost, and 'The Divinity School Address.'" Harvard Theological Review, 49 (January, 1956), 19-43.

2170 WRIGHT, Nathalia. "Ralph Waldo Emerson and Horatio Greenough." Harvard Library Bulletin, 12 (Winter, 1958), 91-116.

2171 WYMAN, Mary A. The Lure for Feeling in the Creative Process. New York: Philosophical Library, 1960. "Goethe, Emerson, and Whitehead on God in the World," pp. 43-103. Influence of Emerson and others on Whitehead's Science and the Modern World (1925).

2172 WYNKOOP, William M. Three Children of the Universe: Ralph Waldo Emerson's View of Shakespeare, Bacon, and Milton. The Hague: Mouton, 1966. Based on Ph.D. diss., Columbia University, 1962.

2173 YAHAGI, Hiromichi. "The Position of Ralph Waldo Emerson in the Formation of Americanism." Taisho Daigaku Kenkyukujo, 45 (March, 1960), 85-146. In English.

2174 YODER, Ralph A. "Emerson's Poetry: A Study of Form and Technique." Ph.D. diss., University of Pennsylvania, 1967. DA, 28 (1967), 1453A-1454A.

2175 _____. Emerson's Dialectic." Criticism, 11 (1969), 313-328.

2176 _____. "Toward the 'Titmouse Dimension': The Development of Emerson's Poetic Style." PMLA, 87 (1972), 255-270.

2177 _____. "The Equilibrist Perspective: Toward a Theory of American Romanticism." Studies in Romanticism, 12 (1973), 705-740.

2178 _____. "Transcendental Conservatism and The House of the Seven Gables." Georgia Review, 28 (Spring, 1974), 33-51.

2179 YOHANNAN, J. D. "Emerson's Translation of Persian Poetry from German Sources." American Literature, 14 (January, 1943), 407-420.

2180 _____. "The Influence of Persian Poetry upon Emerson's Work." American Literature, 15 (March, 1943), 25-41.

2181 YOSHIDA, Osamu. "A Study of Emerson: His Early Religious Philosophy as the Basis of His Thought." Research Bulletin of the Hiroshima Institute of Technology, 3 (1969), 233-242. In English.

2182 YOUNG, Charles Lowell. Emerson's Montaigne. New York: Macmillan, 1941.

2183 YOUNG, Daniel. "Emerson's Struggle with the Problem of Evil." M.A. thesis, University of Texas at Arlington, 1977.

2184 YOUNG, Gloria. "The Fountainhead of All Forms: Poetry and the Unconscious in Emerson and Howard Nemerov," in DeMott and Marovitz, eds., Artful Thunder (1975), pp. 241-267.

2185 ZELANY, L. D. "The Educational Philosophy of Emerson." Education, 45 (December, 1924), 232-239.

2186 ZINK, Harriet R. "Emerson's Use of the Bible." University of Nebraska Studies in Language, Literature, and Criticism, 14 (1935), 5-75.

INDEX OF COAUTHORS, EDITORS, TRANSLATORS

Aaron, Daniel 1132
Allen, Francis H. 1968
Allen, Gay Wilson 539, 749
Anderson, Wallace L. 1856

Baker, Joseph E. 1723
Baldwin, Marilyn 1880
Bartlett, George B. 1234
Bartol, Cyrus A. 1234, 2031
Bellows, Henry W. 1234
Bethuram, Dorothy 1893, 1894
Bode, Carl 1971, 1973, 1974
Bradley, Sculley 1997
Briggs, Le Baron Russell 510
Broderick, John C. 2044
Brooks, Charles T. 101
Brown, Roger 853

Cady, Edwin H. 1054
Channing, William Henry 736
Chapman, John Jay 2139
Clarke, Helen Archibald 1594
Clarke, James Freeman 736
Collins, L. C. 563
Condee, Ralph W. 915

Cooke, George Willis 1234
Craig, Hardin 78
Curtis, George W. 1234
Custard, Edith May 622

Dod Albert 69
Duncan, Jeffrey L. 1976

Eaton, William Lorenzo 510
Edward, Herbert W. 1020
Eichstaedt, Alfons 2069
Emerson, Edward Waldo 510
Erdmann, Gustav 2069
Erskine, John 2000

Falk, Robert P. 787
Faust, Clarence 192
Ferguson, Alfred R. 1765
Finch, Henry Le Roy 2158
Fisch, Max Harold 98
Flanagan, John T. 270
Forbes, Edward Waldo 1993
Forbes, Waldo Emerson 732
Fuller, Arthur B. 821, 822, 823

185

Gross, Seymour 1887

Harding, Walter 1973, 1977
Hazard, Caroline 510
Hedge, Frederic H. 1234
Hiatt, David F. 1054
Higginson, Thomas Wentworth 510, 1234
Hill, William B. 1234
Hoaglund, John, trans. 285
Hoar, George Frisbie 510
Hoar, Samuel 510
Hodge, Charles 69
Honig, Edwin 2125
Howe, M. A. DeWolfe 1715
Howe, Will D. 301

James, William 510

Kennedy, William S. 1935

Leisy, Ernest E. 1113
Levy, Leo B. 2083
Lewis, Arthur O. 915
Lewis, R. W. B. 263
Ludwig, Richard M. 1113
Lydenberg, John 2039

McNeir, Waldo 2083
Moore, Merritt H. 1360
More, Paul Elmer 2001
Moses, M. J., trans. 1302
Muller, Max 1234
Munsterberg, Hugo 510

Norton, Charles Eliot 510

O'Connor, William Van 1776

Parsons, Thornton H. 1805
Phillips, George Searle 1768

Rees, Robert A. 286
Roy, Rajay R., trans. 1877
Rusk, Ralph L. 1250
Russell, J. D. 1880

Sanborn, Frank B. 516, 1234
Schiffman, Joseph 1944
Shepard, Odell 1970
Smith, L. P. 1731
Social Circle in Concord 510
Spiller, Robert E. 2096
Stanley, A. P. 1234
Stern, Philip Van Doren 1975
Storey, Moorfield 510
Stovall, Floyd 2112a
Swing, David 1234

Torrey, Bradford 1968
Traubel, Gertrude 1997
Tucker, Martin 1422

Warren, Robert Penn 263
Weiss, John 1524
Whicher, Stephen E. 1165
Whipple, E. P. 1234
Whitman, Walt 1234
Whittier, John G. 1234
Wichelus, Herbert A. 249
Williams, Wallace E. 1852, 2096
Woodress, James 1905

SUBJECT INDEX

"The Adirondacks" 746, 1097, 1098, 1099, 1895
Aeolian Harp (see also Romantic Motifs) 40, 914, 1342
Aesthetics (see also Critical Theory) 143, 192, 212, 273, 278, 290, 1012, 1013, 1014, 1015, 1375, 1531, 1773, 1991
Alcott, Amos B. 64, 65, 66, 67, 256, 388, 436, 452, 484, 497, 998, 1270, 1769, 1784, 1785, 1896
"The American Scholar" (see also Essays; Education) 162, 163, 533, 742, 788, 1105, 1139, 1277, 1337, 1353, 1354, 1355, 1442, 1449, 1700, 1737, 1825, 1827, 1981, 1983, 2094, 2148, 2166
"The Amulet" 1310
Anthologies [college texts] (see also Editions) 83, 115, 191, 238, 239, 263, 270, 785, 786, 787, 851, 990, 1048, 1113, 1289, 1368, 1393, 1397, 1398, 1577, 1618, 1858, 1887, 1893, 1894
"The Apology" 1309
Arnold, Matthew 37, 108, 305, 306, 954, 1404, 1940
Art and Artists [fine arts] 244, 430, 592, 672, 746, 807, 850, 1015, 1088, 1107, 1239, 1295, 1296, 1460, 1531, 1648, 1664, 1773, 1787, 1791, 1991
Asia: India, Japan, Orientalism (see also Persian Poetry ...) 179, 183, 401, 409, 413, 417, 431, 439, 475, 477, 478, 492, 530, 531, 842, 890, 932, 938, 950, 962, 963, 965, 1082, 1083, 1122, 1123, 1126, 1205, 1206, 1305, 1447, 1491, 1492, 1518, 1598, 1608, 1613, 1619, 1620, 1650, 1651, 1732, 1773, 1812, 1877, 1878, 2136

"Bacchus" 203, 427, 1325, 1519
Bibliography and Manuscripts [collected and uncollected] (see also Letters) 176, 196, 220, 224, 287, 318, 345, 346, 428, 429, 458, 478, 490, 591, 687, 756, 780,

876, 887, 1078, 1122, 1181, 1197, 1198, 1199, 1208, 1252, 1331, 1442, 1468, 1572, 1875, 1876, 1905, 1909, 2159, 2160, 2161
Boehme, Jakob   240, 707
"The Bohemian Hymn"   80, 469
"The Boston Hymn"   404, 1908
"Brahma"   121, 514, 811, 898, 938, 1142, 1143, 1213, 1288, 1306, 1311, 1550, 1566, 1672, 1695, 1880, 2105
"Brahmans" [Brahmins]   11, 12
Brook Farm, Fruitlands, Communal Societies   801, 1346, 1445, 1446, 1708, 1769, 1944, 2141
Brownson, Orestes A.   281, 282, 283, 466, 859, 1209, 1698, 1844
Burroughs, John   304, 305, 306, 307, 308, 309, 835, 1264, 2082

California   88, 1435, 2164
Carlyle, Thomas   18, 90, 120, 167, 168, 296, 305, 306, 768, 943, 975, 1007, 1143, 1152, 1172, 1367, 1475, 1549, 1815, 1816, 1819, 1959, 1961, 2021
"Celestial Love"   1314
Channing, Dr. William Ellery   681, 703, 704, 933, 1178
Channing, William Ellery (the younger)   384, 515, 516, 980, 1063, 1284, 1716, 1801, 2129
Channing, William Henry   106, 734, 1928
Chapman, John Jay   276, 518, 722, 1484, 2129
Churches [organized religions] (see also Puritanism; Swedenborgism)   130, 132, 185, 519, 586, 606, 663, 750, 901, 933, 953, 1020, 1050, 1072, 1084, 1085, 1129, 1133, 1473, 1992, 2016
Clough, Arthur Hugh   1250, 2121
Coleridge, Samuel Taylor   148, 323, 335, 626, 1211, 1282, 1959, 1960, 2154
Collections of Criticism, Handbooks, and Guides   39, 126, 217, 471, 490, 582, 828, 966, 1164, 1165, 1214, 1355, 1422, 1456, 1678, 1710, 1805, 1949
"Concord Hymn"   104, 882, 991
Cousin, Victor   69, 1121, 1334
Cranch, Christopher Pearse   607, 1385, 1494, 1755
Critical Theory [Emerson as critic, editor, reviewer] (see also Aesthetics, Art, Essays, Poetry)   39, 51, 54, 110, 150, 159, 212, 302, 322, 329, 520, 537, 539, 543, 592, 656, 684, 690, 728, 739, 783, 784, 818, 861, 1119, 1470, 1485, 1593, 1604, 1605, 1615, 1616, 1702a, 1786, 1792, 1843, 1904, 1925, 1941, 2069, 2071, 2108

"Days" 56, 105, 548, 775, 877, 973, 1082, 1114, 1312, 1322, 1489, 1913, 2010, 2102
Death see Tragedy ...
Democracy (see also Public Affairs and Politics of Emerson) 96, 231, 314, 498, 669, 826, 985, 1179, 1227, 1394, 1438, 1741
The Dial (see also Critical Theory; Fuller, Margaret) 387, 587, 656, 969, 1439a, 1579, 1670, 2057
Dickinson, Emily 30, 467, 633, 634, 635, 641, 654, 843, 1430, 2041, 2085
"The Divinity School Address" (see also Lectures and Addresses) 81, 281, 450, 870, 1154, 1472, 1473, 2003, 2137, 2169

"Each and All" 107, 171, 636, 647, 1390, 1594
Editions [of Emerson; with introductions and/or notes, listed by editor]
    Poems 44, 195
    Essays 549, 632, 706, 716, 866a, 1112, 1265, 1537a 1553, 1562, 1609, 1639, 1640, 1641, 1832, 1990
    Prose and Poetry 111, 480, 581, 857, 1010, 1132, 1341, 1789, 1849, 2025, 2095
    Works 731, 757, 899, 1557
    Letters 730, 825, 900, 1008, 1250, 1475, 1476, 1688, 1816
    Journals 732, 855, 1233, 1560
    Sermons 1276
    Lectures 873, 2096
    Uncollected 182
    Nature 174, 319
    "Napoleon" 638
    English Traits 1110
    Article about editions 1923
Education (see also "The American Scholar") 199, 256, 493, 494, 495, 505, 533, 577, 643, 798, 852, 986, 1105, 1111, 1216, 1301, 1303, 1353, 1367, 1387, 1638, 1701, 1766, 1767, 1982, 2064, 2185
Edwards, Jonathan see Puritanism
Emerson Family (see also Life of Emerson--Biographical Sketches) 48, 330, 351, 352, 355, 365, 373, 374, 385, 392, 414, 423, 696, 725, 737, 738, 740, 754, 900, 944, 947, 1586, 1993, 2005, 2011
Emerson "Today" [reappraisals, relevance, and related topics] 21, 45, 76, 79, 184, 200, 235, 236, 269, 271, 286, 349, 405, 435, 471, 472, 529, 553, 601, 602, 664, 674, 766, 771, 793, 896, 1075, 1109, 1157,

1235, 1279, 1352, 1371, 1378, 1431, 1432, 1433, 1561, 1581, 1632, 1680, 1693, 1797, 1813, 1829, 1863, 1902, 2053, 2124, 2131, 2133, 2138, 2153
Emerson's Influence on Others   see Influences ...
England   27, 558, 560, 594, 716, 744, 874, 875, 1225, 1254, 1335, 1401, 1423, 1613, 1756, 1757, 1758, 1759, 1760, 1761, 1762, 1763, 1821, 1838, 1839, 1840, 1841, 1842
English Traits   82, 594, 987, 1110, 1465, 1466, 1510, 1617, 1830, 1888
Essays (see also individual titles; Critical Theory)
General   146, 192, 211, 291, 292, 294, 300, 509, 523, 550, 557, 574, 598, 608, 637, 755, 764, 936, 1007, 1076, 1136, 1155, 1161, 1162, 1186, 1187, 1188, 1189, 1223, 1242, 1349, 1409, 1420, 1457, 1525, 1530, 1539, 1543, 1554, 1555, 1623, 1631, 1673, 1674, 1676, 1677, 1681, 1848, 2006, 2135, 2144
"Art"   989
"Circles"   1480, 2002
"Compensation"   1203, 1517, 1585
Conduct of Life   2029
"Eloquence"   1945
"Experience"   1770, 2146, 2162
"Friendship"   1292, 1687
"Heroism"   1450
"History"   989, 1879
"Intellect"   1454, 1571
"Love"   941
"Nature" (second)   802
"Oversoul" (see also Philosophy)   2111
"Power"   226
"Prudence"   1736
"Spiritual Laws"   222
"Etienne de la Boêce"   1313

Fiction and Fiction Writers and Emerson [by and about] (see also individual names)   11, 213, 376, 485, 489, 668, 676, 697, 773, 1009, 1046, 1090, 1095, 1128, 1175, 1276, 1596, 1629, 1751, 1860, 1861, 1881, 2033, 2146
Folklore and Language of the Folk   87, 91, 212, 526
French (see also individual names associated with)   13, 17, 114, 145, 1047, 1092, 1207, 1739, 2014
Frost, Robert [by and about]   29, 42, 43, 580, 654, 658, 762, 814, 815, 816, 905, 1177, 1230, 1329, 1547, 1699, 1964, 2040
Fuller, Margaret [by and about] (see also The Dial; Critical

Theory) 169, 243, 499, 525a, 625, 652, 656, 736, 819, 820, 821, 822, 823, 824, 977, 1051, 1399, 1441, 1670, 1671, 1775, 1930, 2019, 2037, 2038, 2058

Gerando, Marie Joseph de 1910
German (see also individual names of German writers) 22
    69, 138, 337, 529, 803, 884, 1100, 1253, 1254, 1469, 1575, 1704, 1804, 1988, 2036, 2048, 2067, 2068, 2070
"Give All to Love" 595
"Gnothi Seauton" 408
Goethe, Johann Wolfgang von 243, 243a, 367, 883, 917, 1013, 1365, 2047, 2049, 2171
"Good-Bye" 1946
"Grace" 255, 720, 1021, 2043
Greenough, Horatio 278, 672, 1370, 2170
Grimm, Herman 2, 1008

"Hamatreya" 247, 1661, 1778, 1779, 2010
Handbooks and Guides see Collections ...
Hawthorne, Nathaniel 153, 155, 488, 501, 555, 558, 605, 694, 1278, 1740, 1862, 1927, 2043, 2078, 2178
Hedge, Frederick Henry 468, 955, 2074
Hegel, Georg W. Friedrich 241, 1413, 1573, 1574, 1833
"Hermione" 1326
History 46, 47, 149, 1212, 1269, 1287, 1647, 1880, 2023
Humor and the Comic 35, 36, 496, 583, 593, 688, 691, 880, 1115, 1248

"Indian Superstition" 413, 417, 431
Influences on and/or by Emerson; Relations to other figures (see also individual names) 210, 251, 347, 524, 525, 546, 741, 758, 762, 882, 939, 951, 958, 962, 964, 965, 1015, 1016, 1047, 1088, 1091, 1093, 1101, 1107, 1115, 1116, 1124, 1137, 1154, 1176, 1182, 1190, 1191, 1201, 1202, 1238, 1257, 1265, 1266, 1290, 1302, 1343, 1344, 1358, 1415, 1424, 1471, 1472, 1478, 1493, 1495, 1497, 1505, 1556, 1570, 1628, 1645, 1666, 1956, 2018, 2066, 2171
"Initial Love ... " 1936
Italy 103, 244, 655, 868, 1343, 1344

James, Henry, Sr. 137, 1094, 2060
James, Henry, Jr. 122, 1095, 1679, 1771, 1855

Subject Index 192

James, William 138, 476, 482, 1096, 1563, 1684
Japanese 183, 409, 439, 1082, 1083, 1122, 1126, 1943, 1990, 1991, 2173, 2184
Journals and Notebooks 152, 193, 231, 259, 308, 309, 381, 593, 721, 732, 739, 855, 856, 897, 980, 1131, 1184, 1233, 1263, 1433, 1559, 1560, 1853

Kennedy, William Sloane [by and about] 967, 1140, 1141, 1142, 1143, 1144, 1145

Lazarus, Emma [by and about] 142, 1195, 1735
Lectures and Addresses, Lyceum (see also individual titles) 20, 59a, 68, 81, 88, 140, 156, 215, 249, 257, 281, 339, 366, 377, 393, 394, 395, 396, 397, 398, 406, 437, 445, 446, 451, 454, 522, 551, 618, 620, 640, 705, 734, 763, 790, 863, 873, 874, 907, 945, 946, 992, 993, 994, 995, 996, 1037, 1041, 1042, 1056, 1070, 1146, 1156, 1170, 1182, 1185, 1192, 1249, 1251, 1277, 1286, 1330, 1356, 1361, 1470, 1481, 1502, 1559, 1583, 1599, 1654, 1665, 1685, 1686, 1694, 1747, 1748, 1754, 1756-1762 (in England), 1802, 1820, 1848, 1883, 1945, 1955, 1978, 1985, 1986, 1989, 2003, 2009, 2046, 2063, 2080, 2092, 2096, 2103, 2128, 2130, 2142
Letters, Collected and Uncollected 3, 7, 26, 327, 340, 363, 379, 403, 616, 623, 646, 713, 730, 735, 739, 768, 808, 825, 927, 948, 976, 978, 1006, 1008, 1017, 1232, 1247, 1250, 1271, 1280, 1285, 1379, 1407, 1436, 1439, 1444, 1475, 1476, 1477, 1612, 1689, 1713, 1803, 1815, 1816, 1836, 1837, 1851, 1867, 1987, 2079, 2106, 2107, 2108, 2132, 2150, 2167
Life of Emerson
   Biographical Sketches [brief articles and tributes] 5, 6, 8, 9, 10, 15, 61, 221, 230, 244a, 275, 277, 279, 301, 309, 391, 502, 510, 511, 517, 518, 527, 541, 565, 569, 589, 621, 670, 685, 727, 806, 807, 836, 920, 935, 979, 1094, 1095, 1096, 1102, 1215, 1234, 1259, 1294, 1416, 1451, 1464, 1506, 1527a, 1538, 1606, 1721, 1731, 1749, 1835, 1885, 1886, 1966
   Book-Length Biographies 60, 66, 67, 267, 313, 575, 585, 833, 1011, 1052a, 1079, 1151, 1236, 1374, 1376, 1383, 1417, 1691, 1696, 1715, 1718, 1768, 1833, 1852, 1980, 2039, 2157, 2158
   Articles on Early Life 34, 154, 312, 682
   The Writer and the Man 189, 310, 316, 563, 683, 689, 893, 1462, 1543

Subject Index

The Farmer 223, 1884
Character Sketches 233, 258, 314, 487, 610, 675, 834, 981, 1053, 1054, 1055, 1108, 1419, 1692, 1763, 1979
Concord, Emerson in 266, 382, 399, 726, 853, 997, 1260, 1262, 1351, 1712, 1719, 1891
Travel [does not include lecture tours] 680, 889, 959, 1401, 1448, 1955, 2009
Miscellaneous Biographical Details 331, 336, 368, 372, 390, 438, 440, 441, 561, 729, 931, 1118, 1153, 1160, 1257, 1285, 1350, 1954, 2113
Lincoln, Abraham 84, 528, 2151
Literature, Histories and Studies of American [in which, see chapter or section on Emerson] 151, 153, 227, 234, 262, 264, 268, 280, 315, 463, 491, 617, 662, 758, 762, 770, 831, 867, 875, 892, 906, 923, 1020, 1049, 1058, 1059, 1103, 1112, 1135, 1163, 1194, 1220, 1241, 1299, 1300, 1339, 1347, 1348, 1369, 1400, 1418, 1431, 1463, 1498, 1515, 1516, 1528, 1529, 1532, 1534, 1541, 1551, 1558, 1644, 1688, 1807, 1811, 1814, 1845, 1846, 1951, 2000, 2001, 2032, 2051, 2075, 2076, 2099, 2101, 2143, 2155, 2156
Lowell, James Russell 237, 1248, 1249

Manuscripts see Bibliography
Melville, Herman 124, 197, 242, 394, 600, 686, 694, 751, 752, 753, 791, 795, 1001, 1130, 1395, 1421, 1488, 1490, 1520, 1521, 1522, 1597, 1662, 1667, 1668, 1697, 1724, 1882, 1927, 1998, 2034, 2050, 2122
Merlin and Merlin Poems 203, 326, 333, 348, 375, 1317
Milton, John 1567, 1568, 1580, 1642, 2172
Ministry and Sermons 26, 288, 322, 330, 343, 358, 369, 415, 416, 419, 420, 421, 422, 432, 433, 576, 708, 709, 1283, 2016, 2035
"Mithridates" 1308
"Monadnoc" 1315
Montaigne, Michel 2020, 2182
Mouse-Trap 48, 356, 1889, 1890
Murat, Prince Achille 92, 1646

Nature (1836) and Discussions of Nature (see also Essays-- General) 14, 28, 141, 174, 175, 213, 223, 228, 299, 319, 321, 334, 412, 443, 461, 686, 714, 776, 800, 926, 934, 937, 957, 972, 1003, 1073, 1183, 1231, 1588, 1611, 1690, 1765, 1809, 1938, 2006, 2007, 2081, 2154

Nietzsche, Friedrich   100, 389, 1372, 1750, 1831

The Occult   2123
"Ode Inscribed to W. H. Channing   106, 1928
Optimism (see also Tragedy ...)   161, 571, 627, 695

"Pan"   97, 556
Parker, Theodore [by and about]   356, 564, 566, 567, 568, 1180, 1359, 1458, 1523, 1524, 1525, 1526, 1720, 1828
Persian Poetry and Translations of Josep von Hammer   1318, 1701a, 2008, 2179, 2180
Philosophy [ideas, thought, religion] (see also individual authors)
   Emerson as Philosopher   16, 23, 90, 125, 136, 139, 179, 190, 206, 298, 552, 585, 604, 614, 615, 624, 627, 639, 679, 692, 693, 708, 709, 717, 724, 765, 796, 842, 849, 872, 879, 914, 955, 984, 1005, 1019, 1071, 1081, 1222, 1237, 1272, 1366, 1403, 1434, 1511, 1569, 1653, 1730, 1794, 1808, 1810, 1850, 2015, 2055, 2059, 2119, 2120
   Philosophy and Religious Ideas   131, 134, 135, 188, 465, 542, 667, 846, 885, 933, 942, 956, 1062, 1066, 1389, 1584, 1682, 1683, 1892, 2056, 2147, 2181, 2186
   American Philosophy [in which, see chapter or section on Emerson]   59, 98, 128, 198, 544, 718, 794, 1113, 1221, 1360, 1391, 1405, 1509, 1513, 1592, 1652, 1744, 1790, 1903, 1995, 2028, 2061, 2062, 2101, 2115, 2152
   Emerson and Other Philosophical-Religious Ideas   613, 619, 645, 665, 702, 743, 813, 912, 939, 953, 1027, 1068, 1158, 1190, 1201, 1202, 1335, 1484, 1590, 1610, 1626, 1643, 1655, 1656, 1780, 1958, 2117
   Discussions of Specific Philosophical Concepts   94, 507, 562, 622, 631, 666, 829, 830, 878, 910, 1026, 1080, 1127, 1188, 1229, 1256, 1268, 1357, 1362, 1377, 1382, 1414, 1535, 1536, 1576, 1582, 1585, 1590, 1733, 1897, 1899, 2022, 2043, 2054, 2089, 2090, 2104, 2134
Photographs   25, 31, 414, 449, 699, 1345
Phrenology   573
Plato   157, 158, 274
Plotinus   260, 925
Plutarch   172
Poe, Edgar Allan   78, 187, 504, 832, 903, 1086, 1258, 1542, 1578, 1611, 1659, 1742

"The Poet, I" 32
Poetry, Emerson's
   Brief Articles, "Emerson as Poet" 1, 2, 23, 229, 282, 304, 307, 352, 513, 779, 797, 858, 891, 955, 1019, 1060, 1149, 1150, 1195, 1200, 1332, 1425, 1426, 1474, 1709, 1711, 1714, 1717, 1868, 1869, 1957, 2017, 2097
   Book-Length Studies 95, 160, 460, 503, 745, 841, 914, 1057, 1140, 1316, 1327, 1622, 1870, 1911, 1935, 2044
   Studies of American Poetry with Chapter or Section on Emerson 70, 73, 116, 148, 207, 208, 473, 497, 535, 540, 571, 628, 659, 782, 837, 844, 915, 940, 982, 1167, 1168, 1193, 1210, 1381, 1384, 1388, 1479, 1496, 1508, 1514, 1547, 1601, 1729, 1772, 1776, 1777, 1806, 1856, 1865, 1871, 1872, 1873, 1937, 1939, 1950, 2024, 2026, 2027, 2042, 2073, 2088, 2098, 2118, 2125, 2126
   Longer Discussions of Poetry 127, 192, 250, 288, 289, 290, 526, 599, 611, 660, 661, 781, 799, 845, 909, 924, 970, 991, 1141, 1145, 1274, 1281, 1319, 1320, 1380, 1437, 1546, 1552, 1621, 1624, 1727, 1738, 1795, 1907, 1912, 1915, 1916, 1918, 1919, 1920, 1921, 1924, 1929, 1931, 1932, 1934, 1942, 2045, 2174, 2175, 2176, 2177, 2183
   Emerson's Poetry and Related Sources (see also Influences ...; Aesthetics; Critical Theory) 57, 85, 303, 307, 332, 338, 383, 1224
   Emerson's Concept of the Poet 86, 715, 792, 888, 1077, 1487, 1742, 1943, 1962, 2084, 2172
   Parnassus [anthology edited by Emerson] 733, 812, 916
Poets, Emerson and Other (see also individual names; Influences ...) 19, 101, 177, 205, 248, 347, 353, 481, 483, 547, 603, 678, 710, 719, 804, 854, 898, 949, 1000, 1074, 1125, 1226, 1275, 1406, 1411, 1461, 1544, 1545, 1602, 1657, 1660, 1742, 1783, 1834, 1857, 1901, 1948, 1959, 2112, 2163, 2172, 2184
Pragmatism (see also Education) 138, 486, 570, 669, 671, 840, 1630
"The Problem" 350, 410, 1323
Prophet, Emerson as 165, 173, 186, 674, 859, 954, 1211, 2115
Pseudo-Sciences: Phrenology 573; The Occult 2123
Psychology, Psychotherapy 75, 245, 532, 968, 1018, 1104, 1625
Public Affairs and Politics of Emerson (see also Democracy; Slavery; War) 4, 33, 38, 63, 89, 93, 96, 129, 170, 231, 232, 265, 311, 314, 407, 498, 538, 572, 584,

596, 597, 642, 649, 663, 669, 673, 759, 760, 761,
769, 772, 774, 777, 778, 789, 794, 810, 826, 839,
847, 848, 878, 922, 952, 958, 971, 985, 1052, 1064,
1065, 1117, 1147, 1179, 1180, 1204, 1217, 1218,
1227, 1228, 1273, 1293, 1298, 1333, 1339, 1340,
1394, 1408, 1438, 1455, 1486, 1507, 1512, 1614,
1627, 1658, 1663, 1664, 1685, 1686, 1706, 1707,
1722, 1723, 1728, 1741, 1764, 1781, 1796, 1798,
1799, 1800, 1802, 1817, 1818, 1822, 1826, 1854,
1884, 1896, 1897, 1953. 2013, 2083, 2141, 2167, 2173

Puritanism [includes Jonathan Edwards] 285, 570, 953, 1134, 1137, 1196, 1246, 1392, 1396, 1527, 1652, 1743

Reading [includes newspapers] (see also individual authors; Influences ...) 320, 324, 341, 342, 354, 365, 371, 376, 378, 424, 444, 455, 650, 651, 928, 1061, 1291, 1501, 1504, 1734, 1786, 1952, 2186

Relations to Others, Emerson's see Influences ...

Renaissance, American (see also Romanticism; Transcendentalism) 38, 39, 50, 53, 442, 446, 447, 448, 456, 582, 908, 966, 1087, 1348, 1459, 1703, 1933

Representative Men 1173, 1740, 2004, 2153

"The Rhodora" 113

Ripley, George 612, 1752

Romantic Motifs 40, 117, 144, 370, 904, 914, 1219, 1342

Romanticism [general discussions of] (see also Renaissance, American; Transcendentalism; Romantic Motifs) 41, 50, 55, 181, 202, 203, 204, 214, 521, 657, 694, 903, 1002, 1069, 1219, 1225, 1243, 1244, 1245, 1328, 1386, 1418, 1600, 1753, 1823, 1926, 1927, 1929, 1967, 2027, 2177

Santayana 272, 1729, 1730, 1731, 2077

Science, Emerson and 77, 147, 307, 462a, 325, 386, 534, 571, 653, 749, 918, 919, 1134, 1231, 1427, 1482, 1483, 1788, 1874, 1922, 1963, 2109, 2110, 2171

"The Seashore" 2163

The Self (see also "Self-Reliance") 99, 112, 129, 166, 218, 246, 295, 508, 694, 864, 881, 1090, 1138, 1429, 1576

"Self-Reliance" 225, 648, 720, 974, 1159, 1533, 1668, 2162

Shakespeare 102, 748, 1564, 2172

"Siphars" 434, 1702, 1965

Slavery 63, 84, 311, 528, 789, 971, 1339, 1340, 1685, 1686, 1817, 1818, 2167

"The Snow-Storm" 886, 1635, 2116
"Song of Nature" 1917
"The Sphinx" 1307, 1321, 1607, 1659, 1667, 1900, 1970, 2052, 2100
Stevens, Wallace 178, 201, 261, 700, 838, 1428
Swedenborg, Emanuel 361, 412, 1022, 1023, 1024, 1025, 1026, 1027, 1028, 1029, 1030, 1031, 1032, 1033, 1034, 1035, 1036, 1038, 1039, 1040, 1041, 1042, 1043, 1044, 1637, 1994
Symbolism 164, 751, 752, 753, 983, 2050

Teaching Emerson (see also Education) 52, 58, 113, 216, 362, 470, 579, 647, 911, 960, 1174, 1267, 1847, 1996, 2012, 2093, 2139
"Terminus" 1338, 1914, 2165
Thoreau, Henry David
    Personal Relations of Emerson and Thoreau 7, 328, 334, 356, 360, 453, 863, 929, 930, 1045, 1063, 1169, 1412, 1453, 1713, 1716, 1725, 2079, 2129
    Biographies of Thoreau 145, 464, 1171, 1364, 1537
    Comparison of the Work of Emerson and Thoreau 144, 173, 284, 350, 354, 444, 445, 451, 455, 479, 512, 827, 895, 902, 999, 1246, 1488, 1500, 1520, 1521, 1590, 1607, 1674, 2006, 2043
    Comparison of the philosophies of Emerson and Thoreau 246, 296, 578, 1297, 1503, 1587, 1589, 1703, 1746, 1898
    Thoreau's Poetry and Other Writings 253, 297, 332, 497, 701, 1774, 1782, 1859, 1906, 1939, 1968, 1969, 1971, 1972, 1973, 1974, 1975, 1976, 1977, 2086
    Emerson and Thoreau and Other Relationships 254, 325, 357, 371, 407, 698, 789, 963, 1004, 1083, 1130, 1424, 1896
"Threnody" 554, 1633
Tragedy, Death, and Evil 109, 184, 347, 506, 545, 554, 560, 677, 1067, 1120, 1148, 1255, 1540, 1705, 2010, 2090, 2091, 2183
Transcendentalism (see also Renaissance...; Romanticism)
    Language and Style of 62, 180, 289, 293, 1805
    Foreign Sources 69, 492, 1207, 1613, 1739, 1938, 2067
    Anthologies of Works by 126, 588, 990, 1393, 1397
    Periodicals (see also The Dial) 817, 1037, 1636
    James Marsh 1336, 1467, 2074
    Frothingham, Octavious B. 500, 817
    Teaching Transcendentalism 359, 362

Transcendentalism in New England 220, 252, 380, 418,
  425, 426, 459, 462, 536, 723, 809, 865, 866, 1089,
  1166, 1440, 1499, 1595, 1634, 1745, 1984, 2126
Emerson and Transcendentalism 578, 590, 894, 1363,
  1373, 1503, 1565
Transcendental Ideas, Religion 194, 205, 245, 559, 629,
  630, 747, 750, 850, 890, 926, 1020, 1113, 1196,
  1212, 1362, 1429, 1947, 2000, 2065, 2087, 2140
Transcendentalism and Its Critics and Advocates (see
  also individual names) 486, 629, 644, 921, 1001,
  1072, 1178, 1395, 1402, 1522, 1526, 1662, 1664,
  1670, 1958, 1996, 2072, 2122, 2178

"Una" 2127
"Uriel" 323, 814, 961, 1324, 2089, 2149

Very, Jones 118, 133, 133a, 364, 860, 1939, 2030, 2031,
  2045

Walden [does not include Thoreau's Walden] 49, 360, 400,
  402, 1452
War (see also Public Affairs and Politics of Emerson) 38,
  63, 93, 349, 663, 1064, 1065, 1117, 1217
Water-Motif (see also Romantic Motifs) 144
Wheeler, Charles Stearns 457, 711, 712
Whitman, Walt 71, 72, 74, 119, 123, 153, 201, 209, 212,
  246, 261, 344, 411, 474, 694, 805, 867, 869, 1106,
  1116, 1117, 1144, 1240, 1247, 1257, 1304, 1410,
  1603, 1637, 1649, 1669, 1675, 1703, 1824, 1942,
  1997, 2112a, 2113, 2114, 2139, 2165

"The Young American" 96, 555, 988, 1854